D1682142

WAREHOUSING PROFITABLY
A MANAGER'S GUIDE

"How to tell what's wrong with your warehouse ... and fix it!"

KEN ACKERMAN

An Update

ACKERMAN PUBLICATIONS
COLUMBUS, OHIO

Copyright © 2000 by K. B. Ackerman company

All rights reserved. No part of this work covered by the copyright hereon may be reproduced in any form by any means — graphic, electronic, or mechanical, including photocopying, recording, taping, or information storage and retrieval systems — without written permission of the publisher.

Cover photograph copyright © by Pete Lacker.

ISBN: 0-9631776-3-X.

Library of Congress: 99-96560

Printed in the United States of America

Typographic design by William F. Blinn, Worthington, Ohio.
Body text is set in Palatino with headings, subheads, and tables in Zurich. Word Perfect was used for preparation of the text, which was then imported into Ventura Publisher for formatting and output.

Ackerman Publications
1328 Dublin Road
Columbus, Ohio 43215-1059
Phone: 1-614-488-3165
Fax: 1-614-488-9243
E-mail: information@warehousing-forum.com
Web site: http://www.warehousing-forum.com/.

Why you should read this book, and why I wrote it ....

Since *Warehousing Profitably* was published, there have been substantial changes in warehousing. This updated version deals with these changes, but it does so in the same format used in the original edition.

Another book on warehousing! Why should you read it? Why did I write it?

My early books about warehousing were designed to be handbooks for managers. They collected everything about the subject and organized it in a fashion that would help people manage warehouses. In my zeal to collect information, I was tempted to include "everything but the kitchen sink."

This book is different. *Warehousing Profitably* is for both the warehouse manager and for that manager's boss. Unlike other books, you'll find a page or two after each chapter with *Questions that Solve Problems*. Each question is followed by a comment rather than an answer. The purpose of this is not to test your ability to read and remember, but rather to help management review warehousing problems.

Warehousing is deceptively simple. Many believe that the function is so basic that any decent manager could run an effective warehouse. When it doesn't run smoothly, nobody can understand why.

Our goal is to illustrate what it takes to profitably manage warehouses. While other books may try to tell you how to build a watch, this one is designed to tell you what time it is. Furthermore, I hope you will find it capable of telling you how to adjust the watch if it isn't keeping accurate time.

About the Author

Ken Ackerman has been active in logistics and warehousing management for his entire career. Before entering the consulting field, he was chief executive of Distribution Centers, Inc., a public warehousing company which is now part of Exel Logistics USA.

In 1980, Ackerman sold the company and joined the management consulting division of Coopers & Lybrand. In 1981, he formed the Ackerman Company, a management advisory service.

He is editor and publisher of *Warehousing Forum*, a monthly subscription newsletter. His previous book, *Warehousing Profitably: A Manager's Guide*, was published in 1994. He also produced an audio tape which contains highlights from this book.

Words of Warehousing, a glossary of the terms used in the field, is the only book of its kind in print today.

Harvard Business Review published an article, "Making Warehousing More Efficient", co-authored with Bernard J. La Londe.

His by-lined article "Just-in-Time, Right for Retail" was published in The New York Times.

A video tape, *Effective Warehousing*, was produced in 1997 by the National Association of Wholesaler-Distributors (NAW). He is the author of numerous other articles dealing with warehousing and management.

Ackerman holds a BA from Princeton and an MBA from Harvard. He is past president of Council of Logistics Management and founder of Warehousing Education and Research Council.

Ken Ackerman has provided management advisory services to companies throughout the United States, Canada, Latin America and Europe. These clients include manufacturers, wholesale distributors, retailers, warehousing firms, and carriers. He has provided advisory support to several large consulting firms.

In addition to providing advisory services, he has conducted training seminars on warehousing. He has served as a speaker at conferences and conventions in North and South America as well as in Europe and Asia. His fluency in Spanish enables him to lecture and consult in that language.

Ken Ackerman received the Distinguished Service and Leadership Award in 1999 from International Warehouse Logistics Association. Earlier, he received the Distinguished Service Award from Council of Logistics Management.

He is an honorary life member of the Ohio Warehousemen's Association and a former director of American Warehouse Association. He was chapter chairman for Young Presidents Organization.

In civic activities, he is past president and founder of the Wellington School, former officer of Columbus Association for the Performing Arts and past president of Opera Columbus.

Acknowledgments

While there are dozens of footnotes throughout this work, we always fear that we have overlooked thanking the many people who have helped us in our writing.

For the past dozen years, Dewey Abram has been our adviser and coach in the preparation of a monthly newsletter, *Warehousing Forum*. His many suggestions have improved our writing, and much of the newsletter material was used in this work.

The book is a successor to several earlier works. A 1972 book titled *Understanding Today's Distribution Center* was co-authored with R.W. Gardner and Lee P. Thomas.

Larry Gadd originally gave us the idea of developing the work for the warehouse manager's boss.

Bill Ransom suggested the name for the book, as well as many significant contributions to our writing.

Cathy Avenido handled the word processing and the nearly hopeless task of keeping the author organized.

The text was edited by Brian Baresh under the direction of Bill Blinn, who provided valuable suggestions on composition as well as production of the material. Holly Day quickly and efficiently compiled the index.

TABLE OF CONTENTS

Part 1: Understanding Today's Warehouse

1 An industry in transition 1
    The ancient history of logistics 2
    The U.S. and the deregulation experiment........... 2
    A critical labor dispute...................... 3
    Globalization 4
    The information revolution 4
    Third-party growth......................... 4
    Cycle time............................... 5

2 Improving warehouse productivity...................... 7
    Reducing the order cycle time................... 7
    Emphasis on quality 10
    Asset productivity......................... 11
    A new workforce 11

3 Supply chain, JIT, and benchmarking................... 15
    Supply chain management, "a rose by any other name ..." . 16
    Just-in-time and its variants 19
        JIT is a product of both fact and myth 19
        JIT vs. congestion — a collision course 21
        Using JIT for service and repairs 21
        The role of warehousing 22
    Benchmarking and the Holy Grail................ 22
        Internal benchmarking...................... 23

4 Adapting to the information age 27
    Technology and forecasting 27
    Information technology and control................ 28
    EDI and the warehouse...................... 28

The impact of electronic commerce 30
　　Evaluating system options 31
　　What to look for in warehouse management software . . . 32

5 Avoiding labor pains **37**
　　Creating a participatory environment 37
　　　　The crucial role of the supervisor 38
　　　　The fine line of delegating properly 39
　　Logistics outsourcing 40
　　Labor disputes 41

6 Reverse logistics management **43**
　　Environmental returns 44
　　Marketing returns 45
　　Organizing for reverse logistics 45
　　　　The role of the warehouse manager 46
　　A retail example 47
　　Should you outsource reverse logistics? 48

Part 2: Warehouse Control

7 Quality and productivity **51**
　　The growth of quality awareness 51
　　　　Quality metrics in the distribution center 52
　　　　TQM within the warehouse 52
　　　　Success factors for TQM 53
　　Quantity vs. quality 54
　　Increasing warehouse productivity 54
　　　　Establish improvement targets 55
　　　　Reduce distances traveled 55
　　　　Increase unit load size 56
　　　　Round trips 57
　　　　Improve cube utilization 57
　　　　Free labor bottlenecks 58
　　　　Reduce item handling 58
　　　　Improve the container 59
　　A different way to look at productivity 59

8 Third-party or do-it-yourself?.............................63
Outsourcing logistics services................64
Core competency and outsourcing.................65
The preparatory steps...................67
How to select a third-party operator............67
Fourteen criteria to consider..................69
1. Multiple warehouse facilities nationwide..........69
2. Inventory management and control.............69
3. Order acceptance and processing..............69
4. Pick-and-pack operations...................70
5. Order fulfilment.......................70
6. Assembly/packaging/value-added activities........71
7. Credit card verification...................71
8. Invoicing, credit, and collection...............72
9. Pre-sort capabilities....................72
10. Returns handling......................73
11. Manifesting.........................73
12. Operational management structure.............73
13. Organizational strategic direction.............74
14. Financial stability.....................74
Evaluation............................75
The contract.........................75
The pricing challenge....................76

9 Planning and scheduling............................83
Corporate strategy and warehousing.............83
Data drives decisions in warehousing............84
Short-interval scheduling..................87
The importance of proper sequence..............90
Planning for equipment use.................93
Shift scheduling......................94
Contingency planning.....................94

10 Understanding warehousing costs.....................97
Measuring storage costs....................98
A unit storage cost calculation................100
The influence of inventory turns...............101
Measuring handling costs...................102

Appendix A 104

11 Asset accountability and utilization 119
Cargo liability vs. warehouse liability 119
Managing inventory. 121
Controlling space utilization 122
    The typical storage space calculation 125
Controlling the lift truck fleet. 126

12 Reducing errors. 129
The cost of an error 129
Preventing warehouse errors 130
    A locator system prevents errors. 130
    Markings as a source of errors 130
    Dyslexia and inventory errors 131
    Picking documents 131
    Use of bar coding 131
Receiving — locking the barn door 132
    To check or not to check? 132
    Physical factors in the warehouse 133
Personnel factors 133
    Identification with work 134
    Pareto analysis and errors 134
    Rewards for the stars 135

13 Measuring performance. 137
The unique factors. 137
Measuring effectiveness. 138
    How efficient is your warehouse? 138
    Quantifying space utilization 140
Improving storage productivity 140
    Calculating a storage payback 141
    Quantifying handling productivity 141
    Justifying handling improvements 142
    Simulation in the warehouse. 143
    Measuring performance by account. 144
Monitoring several warehouse locations 145
A sixty-minute warehouse evaluation 145

Part 3: Warehouse Management

14 Finding the right people 149
Finding people in a scarce labor market 149
Nontraditional employees 150
Retaining good people 151
The interview process 151
Evaluation 154
Reference checks 155
Probation 156
Proficiency tests 156

15 Management productivity 161
Success factors 162
Motivation 163
People development 163
Management's ethical responsibility 163
Generation management in warehousing 164
Maintaining service expectations 166
Improving your managerial skills 167
The importance of communication 168
Running effective meetings 168
Transition from worker to manager 169
Developing future managers 170

16 Training for excellence 173
Managers as teachers 173
Training goals 174
Orientation 174
Mentoring 176
The transition from worker to manager 176
The fine art of delegating 176
Leadership by example 177
Training lift truck operators 178
Training for superior performance 179

17 Motivation, discipline, and continuous improvement ... 181
Motivation and retention programs 181

    Flexible work schedules 182
    New approaches to work. 184
Six ways to motivate warehouse workers 185
Managing performance 186
    Maintaining warehouse discipline. 190
    Discipline by peer review. 190
    Continuous improvement 192

Part 4: Security

18 Controlling the inventory 197
Physical inventories *197*
    Preparing for the physical count. 198
    Anticipating problems 199
Cycle counting 200
    Acceptance of cycle counting. 202

19 Theft and mysterious disappearance. 205
Responsibilities of the warehouse operator 205
Two kinds of losses 206
    Controlling collusion theft 206
    Confirming employee honesty. 206
    The handling of references 207
    Other collusion theft controls 209
Undercover investigations 210
Security audits 211
Physical deterrents. 212
    Restricted access. 212
    Customer pickups and returns. 213
Security procedures 213

20 Protecting your people. 217
Personal appearance and housekeeping. 217
Safety 218
Federally mandated training 219
Ergonomics and safety 220
    Reducing manual handling risks 222
Substance abuse in the warehouse 224

Warehousing ethics — a matter of trust 226

21 Protecting the property 231
Power failure. 231
Casualty losses. 232
Fire 232
    Sprinkler systems 232
    Dry-pipe systems 233
    Wet-pipe systems 233
    Other protection against fire 233
    A new type of sprinkler system 234
Windstorm losses 235
Causes of cargo damage. 235
    Flood and leakage. 236
    Mass theft 236
    Vandalism 237
Surviving an insurance inspection 237
Plant emergency organizations. 239
Reviewing protection procedures 239

Part 5: Handling of Cargo

22 Receiving, put-away, and storage. 243
Physical aspects of receiving 244
    Receiving as a process 245
    Put-away. 246
Stock locator systems 246
    Installing and maintaining a locator system 247
Your warehouse layout 248
    The affinity factor 249
    Load characteristics. 250
    Special operations 250
Planning for changes 250

23 Order selection and cross docking. 253
The influence of velocity 253
Order picking in your warehouse 254
    Varieties of order picking. 255

  The bucket brigade 257
 Cross docking 258
  Success factors in cross docking 259
  Reverse order picking. 261
 Planning for improvements. 262

24 Unitized loads 265
 The standard pallet 265
 Unitizing without pallets 268
  Mandated slipsheets 268
 The search for a better pallet 270
  Plastic pallets grow in acceptance 272
  Understanding pallet costs. 272
  Store-ready pallets for retailers. 272

25 Specialized storage 275
 Temperature-controlled warehousing 276
 Hazardous materials warehousing. 279
  What is a hazardous chemical?. 279
  Regulations and training 280
  Reliable hazardous-materials information 281
 Fulfillment warehousing 282
 Household goods storage 284

26 Warehouse technology 289
 Tools or toys?. 290
 Understanding space economies 293
  How pallet racks improve space utilization 293
  Other storage rack options 293
  Live storage 295
 Other order-picking tools 297
  Carousel systems 297
  Conveyor systems. 299
  Automatic guided-vehicle systems 299
 Choosing a lift truck. 300
  Operator location 301
  Lift attachments 301
  Narrow-aisle vehicles 303

Brand selection 304

Part 6: Information Systems

27 Computers and customer service 307
   Hardware vs. software 307
   Choosing warehousing software 308
      Finding a warehouse management system 308
      Choosing a WMS 309
      A WMS meltdown. 309
      Other WMS pitfalls 311
   Implementing a WMS 312
      Training 314
   Systems and service 315

28 Electronic identification. 317
   Bar codes 317
      A user's view of bar coding 318
      The myth of bar coding expense 319
      What will bar coding do for you? 319
      The radio frequency epidemic 320
      Bar coding and Luddites 320
      Pitfalls of automatic identification 321
      2-D bar codes 322
   To check or not to check? 322

29 Approaching warehouse automation 325
   How technology fits in 326
      The benefits of mechanization 329
      The risks 330
   Mechanization in the 21st century 331

Part 7: Starting a New Warehouse Operation

30 Finding the right location 335
   Developing a requirements definition 336
      Speed limits and warehousing 337
      Access 337

  Attitudes 338
  Utilities 338
  Climate 339
  Flexibility and financing 339
 The selection process 339
  Outside advice 340
 A checklist to locate your next warehouse 342
  Governmental restrictions 342
  Geographic restrictions 342
  Transportation 343
  Utilities 343
  Security considerations 343
  Labor market 344
  Community attitudes 344
  Taxation **344**
  New construction considerations 344

31 Warehousing is real estate 347
  A case example 348
 Getting around accounting standards 349
 Flexibility vs. control 349
  Real estate as a corporate investment 350
  The decline of cookie cutters 350
  Third-party operators as investors 350
 The make-or-buy question 352
  Understanding real estate costs 352
  When should you build? 353
 The rehabilitation alternative 353
  Repairing warehouse roofs 354
  Rejuvenating warehouse floors 354

32 Warehouse construction 357
 Understanding total development costs 358
 Better ideas for construction 358
  Parking lots 359
  Foundations and floors 359
  Docks and drive areas 361
  Structural system and roof 362

    Illumination and heating 363
    Fire protection systems 364
    Walls and interior finish 364
    Exterior finish 364
Layout design 365
    Economies of scale 365
    Wear and tear 365

33 Warehouse start-ups 369
The importance of a smooth start 369
    Building the project team 370
    Charting the process 371
    Ongoing communication 371
    Resources 373
How much can your warehouse hold? 373
    Developing a procedures manual 375
    Building on successful experience 376
Opening the warehouse 376
    A warehouse start-up checklist 376
    Receiving 376
    Shipping 377
    Materials handling operations 378
    Use of space 378
    Sanitation, security, and safety 379

34 Moving a warehouse 383
Establishing a target move date 383
Estimating moving costs 384
    An example 385
How long will it take? 386
    Volume Assumptions: 386
    Time Assumptions: 386
    Calculations 386
    Continue services or suspend operations? 386
Communications 387

Part 8: The Future

35 Warehousing in a world economy **391**
    Meeting customer demands 391
    Re-engineering the warehouse 392
    Postponement 393
    Expanding into developing nations 394
    The future of world logistics technology 395

36 Staying current in the new century **399**
    The facets of change 399
    Electronic commerce 400
    Information sources 400
        Publications and research 401
        Seminars 402
    A developing professionalism 402
    Upgrading the tools 402
    Putting it all together 403

Index **405**

PART 1

Understanding Today's Warehouse

Chapter 1

An industry in transition

Because people consider warehousing to be one of several cogs in a gear wheel now called business logistics or supply chain management, we start by considering where the warehouse fits in. Other cogs in this wheel include transportation, inventory management, and customer service.

Some say that business logistics went through a revolution in the last quarter of the 20th century. If that word is too strong, it is at least fair to say that this field changed as much in the last decade as it had in the previous century. Several megatrends contributed to these significant changes:

- The deregulation of freight transportation in the U.S.
- The replacement of unionized logistics services by union-free operations.
- The globalization of logistics.
- The new uses for information technology.
- The acceptance of just-in-time as a normal function, coupled with the rise of the overnight express business.

In its simplest form, logistics is nothing more than the art of delivering the right goods to the right place at the right time. That military definition, made popular in World War II, is still valid today.

Business logistics can also be defined as the use of inventory to create customer satisfaction. In the United States, we take for granted the ability to buy fresh foods throughout the year, yet in many places around the globe a high percentage of harvested crops is lost to spoilage, thievery, damage, or infestation. Sadly, this usually happens in those places that need food most desperately. The global adoption of efficient logistics practices promises to be an important factor in raising the standard of living in developing nations.

The ancient history of logistics

The function of logistics is one of the oldest commercial activities in recorded history. In the Old Testament, chapter 41 of Genesis describes an Egyptian king troubled by nightmares about fat cows and thin cows, plump ears of corn and withered corn stalks. The king hires a consultant, who explains that the dreams are a prediction of seven years of farm surpluses followed by seven years of famine. The consultant recommends the construction of granaries to store the surpluses and distribute them in the lean years. This was probably both the first and last time in history when any client followed a management consultant's advice to the letter. That consultant, Joseph, became a hero in the land of Egypt, and the episode was recorded as one of the significant events of ancient times.

In the middle ages, the people in the Italian province of Lombardy developed a system of using paper documents as negotiable receipts for merchandise held in storage. Those receipts, originally called Lombards, allowed a merchant to sell bushels of wheat in a warehouse by transferring a piece of paper rather than moving the product. Others discovered that such receipts could also represent silver, and they developed the "silver certificate," the forerunner of paper money.

Although trading in negotiable receipts for commodities has nearly disappeared in the U.S., it is still a common practice in much of Latin America. In that part of the world, bank warehouses offer deposit bonds to guarantee loans against inventory stored in the warehouse.

The U.S. and the deregulation experiment

Certain factors unique to American history have created a distinct pattern in transportation and especially in warehousing. In the last half of the 19th century, the power of railroad companies reached an unacceptable peak. A body of opinion grew that big business is bad business just as big government had been bad government in the 18th century. Just as Americans revolted against the tyranny of George III, the public wanted to put a leash on the railroad barons. That leash was the Interstate Commerce Act, passed in 1887, the first consumerist legislation in the U.S. It created a commission to watch over the railroads and force them to publish prices for all transportation services. The commission had the duty of judging the fairness of those prices and ruling on any applications to change them. The law was designed to allow the small farmer or businessman to pay the same for transportation services as the corporate giants.

Nearly one hundred years later, the U.S. remained one of the few places in the world with government-regulated freight rates. Ironically, it was again consumerist pressure that encouraged the end of freight-rate regulation.

In warehousing, the American Warehouse Association was formed in 1891 to lobby for legislation to prohibit the railroads from offering free storage. After it successfully blocked that practice, the third-party warehousing industry became dominated by small owner-operators.

The Carter administration deregulated the airlines in the late 1970s. In the presidential campaign of 1980, the Teamsters union supported Ronald Reagan, a Republican candidate who had been president of the Screen Actors Guild. They thought he would be sympathetic to transport regulation and unionism. Instead, Reagan intensified the movement to deregulate transportation.

A critical labor dispute

In addition to deregulation, Reagan presided over the most significant labor dispute of the 20th century. In 1981, the Professional Air Traffic Controllers Association (PATCO) called a strike against the federal government. An earlier president, Calvin Coolidge, gained national prominence when he broke the 1919 Boston police strike by saying, "There is no right to strike against the public safety by anybody, anywhere, or at any time." Reagan spoke more softly, but he used military air traffic controllers to break the PATCO strike. If the government had not prevailed, some expected that we would see a strike at the U.S. Postal Service and possibly even in the U.S. Army. After 1981, the largely unionized logistics industry started the transition that has made it today largely union-free.

Globalization

The first recognition of what is now called business logistics or supply chain management came in the term "physical distribution," which was limited to finished products. As it was recognized that the term should encompass more than finished products, the concept of logistics gradually replaced physical distribution. The prime professional society was first called the National Council of Physical Distribution Management, but in 1985 it became the Council of Logistics Management.

There are two aspects to that name change. First, the broader term of logistics allows practitioners to look at movements of things besides finished products.

More important, the word "national" has been deleted, and today the council has a significant percentage of its active members outside the United States.

In logistics today, it is common to see global companies operating all over the world. Typically, they follow large clients from their home countries and serve them elsewhere overseas. It is also typical for multinationals to keep a low profile outside their home country.

The information revolution

One of the significant developments at the end of the 20th century was the advance in ability and the reduction of costs in processing information, one of the few commodities that has gone down rather than up in price. Many routine logistics tasks today depend on communication and computation capabilities that were undreamt of a few decades ago. They include bar code scanning, computer modeling or simulation, satellite tracking, and warehouse management systems.

Third-party growth

The great business sage Peter Drucker in the 1960s referred to logistics as the dark continent of American business. By the 1990s, he talked about the need to "sell the mail room" and concentrate on core businesses. Business leaders have really listened to this later campaign, and the result has been an explosive growth of third-party warehousing and logistics services.

Although a change in management attitudes may have been the biggest stimulus for growth, other factors have played a part as well. During the days of deregulation, large transportation companies feared government regulation should they expand into other logistics activities. During the 1980s, the threat of government interference disappeared. As a result, anybody could freely enter any kind of logistics service business.

In the mid-1970s came the notable business failure of National Distribution Services, a short-lived company that called itself a logistics utility. NDS promised its customers total control of inventory from the end of the production line to final customer delivery. The company lost millions and was out of business after only a year. After its demise, some of its former customers continued to look for a company that would fulfill its dream.

Cycle time

A remarkable development of the last quarter of the 20th century was the ability to reduce order cycle time. Order cycle time is the interval between the moment a customer orders a product and the moment he or she receives it. In the early '70s, a student named Fred Smith from Memphis, Tennessee, delivered a term paper to his economics professor at Yale University describing a new business offering overnight delivery by air. The professor was unimpressed and gave the paper a C. When Smith a few years later opened Federal Express, it was the largest single venture-capital start-up in the history of American commerce. Smith and his relatives contributed more than $8 million to capitalize the new business.

Fred Smith did not just invent a new company, he invented an industry and a new mind-set. With the success of FedEx, Americans presumed that anything could be delivered nearly anywhere on the next day. The result was a competition to reduce order cycle time that continues today.

The revolutionary changes that have characterized business logistics are really just beginning. The progress that may be realized in the 21st century will make 20th-century activities seem small by comparison.

Questions that solve problems

In this and all succeeding chapters, we close with a list of questions and comments.

Unlike those in student texts, these questions are not here to test the reader's comprehension. They are here for the guidance of the senior manager who believes in MBAGQ — *management by asking good questions*. We believe that asking these questions of a warehouse manager will provide useful indicators about the effectiveness of an operation.

You will not necessarily find the answers to these questions in the text. Because there are not always right or wrong responses, we have provided *comments* rather than answers for each of the questions. In many cases, the manner in which the question is answered will provide valuable information about how effectively the warehouse is managed.

Q What activities do we have today outside our home country?
C Once you have established that your company is now in global commerce, it is important to learn how well you are doing.

Q What information system changes have occurred in the past year?
C If the answer is "none," you probably have a big problem!

Q What is our average order cycle time?
C Beware if the answer is "We don't know"!

Chapter 2

Improving warehouse productivity

The business climate at the end of the 20th century created four changes that will continue to influence the warehousing industry. From these changes come four propositions*:
- **Cycle time** is probably the most important ingredient in effective warehousing. Therefore, the best warehouse operations are those designed to reduce order cycle time.
- **Quality** is as important as punctuality, and customers using warehouses now expect performance that approaches perfection.
- Financial officers are not interested in warehousing if it degrades **asset productivity**.
- Warehouse managers must adapt to a **new kind of workforce**, and requirements for both management and labor have changed significantly.

Reducing the order cycle time

Order cycle time is the interval between the moment a consumer orders a product and the moment he or she receives it. Time spent in the warehouse is only one facet of total order cycle time. If an angry customer has not received a product, nobody cares whether the delay was caused by the order department, the credit department, the ware-

---
* From an article by Bernard J. La Londe, Professor Emeritus at The Ohio State University. The article was published in *Warehousing Forum*, Volume 7, Number 9, ©The Ackerman Company, Columbus, Ohio.

house, or the trucker. The only important thing is to deliver the product to the customer, and everyone is blamed until that happens. The most successful logistics operations are those that reduce order cycle time without increasing costs. In the 21st-century economy, order cycle time is probably the single most important differentiation in logistics performance.

A key concept in cycle time reduction is the "3 percent rule." This rule states that only 3 percent of the time needed for a process is central to that process. The remaining 97 percent is spent waiting, repeating tasks, getting lost, or failing to coordinate among people or departments. Cycle time reduction is not just about speed, it is also about the *effective* use of time.

Reducing order cycle time requires at least five key steps:
- Implementing postponement in your warehouse.
- Using scanners and advanced shipping notices to expedite inbound shipment processing.
- Keeping the warehouse open longer with multiple shifts.
- Using scanner technology to reduce checking time and discover picking errors.
- Using hub warehousing to permit a later shipment cut-off time.

Although the first writings about postponement as a marketing strategy appeared in the middle of the 20th century, the concept is surprisingly little known. It is usually considered a marketing strategy. Postponement is the delay of certain final steps in producing a product until the last moment, sometimes even after the product has been sold.

Postponement saves time in addition to simplifying inventory. The computer manufacturer who performs final assembly of the product just before it is shipped maintains an ample supply of half-finished computers and often delivers product faster than competitors who have not adopted the postponement strategy. By attacking both inventory and time, postponement improves service and saves money by reducing inventory investment.

In some warehouses, the cycle time for inbound shipments is as long as five days. The delay occurs because the buyer wants to inspect the product, a quality control department also makes its inspection, and the supervisor must release goods from inbound staging to a storage location. Until the material is recorded in the computer as received, it cannot be shipped. The bureaucratic process may seem ridiculous, but it is a fact in some warehouse operations.

At the opposite extreme, a cross-dock operation allows goods to be shipped hours or even minutes after they are received. But cross docking requires rapid handling of information as well as freight.

Two information tools can improve both conventional inbound shipments and cross docking. An advanced shipping notice (ASN) can verify the accuracy of the receipt. Then scanners compare carton markings with the ASN.

One obvious way to improve service is to open the warehouse earlier and stay open later. A one-shift operation uses only 40 of the 168 available hours in a week. In contrast, a warehouse with four shifts is equipped to handle receiving and shipping at any hour of any day.

A significant time expenditure in many operations is the checking of both inbound and outbound merchandise to be sure that the product is the right count and the right SKU. Manual checking takes time, and when the error is discovered at a checking station, it must be corrected by a trip to the warehouse to replace the wrong product with the right product. Today's scanner technology enables both receiving and shipping to be virtually error-free by comparing bar codes on the boxes with information on an order. If there is a discrepancy, it is flagged with a warning signal on the scanner or on a monitor. The accuracy of scanning technology makes further checking unnecessary.

The last few decades of the 20th century saw the rise of premium air transportation as a proven way to reduce order cycle time. Overnight carriers such as Airborne, FedEx, and UPS use a hub-and-spoke distribution system in which cargo moves to a hub location where it is sorted and sent to its destination. However, if the shipper is at the hub, the cutoff time can be later.

For example, Airborne has developed a cluster of warehouses at its primary hub in Wilmington, Ohio. For inventory at the hub, the shipment cutoff time can be as late as 1 a.m. rather than late afternoon or early evening as in many other cities. That time advantage can be critical for a shipper with a stringent service requirement.

Emphasis on quality

Improving quality in the warehouse is almost as important as reducing cycle time. Bar-code and scanning technology has allowed some warehouse operators to cut their error rate to less than 1 in 10,000. However, this technology has also increased the expectations of warehouse customers, creating a growing intolerance of errors and damage.

In warehousing, quality is measured by the operator's ability to deliver product on time, in good condition, and precisely as ordered — without overages, shortages, or any other discrepancy. As one logistics executive describes it: *"On spec, on time, and on budget."*

Quality management has become a standard requirement in today's warehouse. In the third-party warehouse situation, the best way to define quality is to ask the customers. The operator should ask warehouse users two questions:

- What do you like about dealing with us?
- What don't you like?

Warehouse managers might ask similar questions of the consignees who receive shipments from them. You will find some surprises when you ask these questions. Outside observers may ignore things you think are important and emphasize things you consider trivial. Asking the customers is the best way to define quality.

Careful handling of merchandise in the warehouse prevents damage and maintains a quality image. It is a sad fact that a portion of warehouse damage as well as maintenance cost originates with operator abuse of lift trucks. Some of this abuse is the result of inexperience, and sometimes it is the result of carelessness. A solid-state microprocessor device can be attached to lift trucks to detect abnormal operation.

Many quality initiatives at the end of the 20th century were based on standards established by the International Standards Organization, commonly known as ISO (see Chapter 7). Some users of warehouse services have demanded ISO certification, and training organizations are equipped to provide that certification quickly and without great expense.

Asset productivity

The 21st-century user of warehouse services places increasing emphasis on asset productivity. This drive to improve asset productivity comes from senior management as a growing number of corporations measure their success by calculating return on assets rather than return on sales.

The drive to improve asset productivity is manifested in three areas:

- Reducing assets or otherwise improving capital turnover.
- Re-using materials.
- Recycling instead of discarding waste.

There are two ways to improve asset productivity. One is to improve the operations to the extent that the same asset investment can be used to handle a significantly greater volume — for example, doubling the throughput of your warehouse with no additional space or lift trucks. Another is to transfer an investment in assets to a third party — outsourcing.

Outsourcing of warehousing is a recognized way to improve asset productivity. When warehouse services are purchased from a third-party, the transaction may be structured to allow the user to *borrow* real estate and lift trucks without creating a balance-sheet liability.

Accounting rules require that long-term leases on buildings and equipment be capitalized. However, such requirements can be avoided for short-term commitments made through the use of public warehousing.

Outsourcing of third-party logistics services has been recognized as an economical alternative, one that will grow in popularity as the facts become more widely known. Although the percentage of warehousing handled with third parties in the United States has grown steadily, it does not approach the nearly 50 percent claimed by the British.

A new workforce

Management is dealing today with a new kind of workforce in the warehouse as well as elsewhere in the business world.

Customers are more concerned than ever about quality of labor. As the computer has moved to the warehouse floor, literacy and numeracy become more important than ever. At the same time, most large U.S. cities face the most severe labor shortage in recent history, and there is no sign that that will change.

The challenge for warehouse managers is to find and develop a quality workforce in a time of extreme labor scarcity. Special efforts may be needed to attract the best people. Some jobs in warehousing can be handled by people with physical handicaps. One apparel manufacturer has used deaf-mute workers for order picking. Another operator has substantial success in using workers in their seventies and even older. Absenteeism and turnover are lower with handicapped or older workers. Still others have tapped a new labor market with creative scheduling. One warehouse in a college town developed a short-workday schedule designed to attract students. The same organization has another shift with hours that appeal to working mothers who want to send children to school and be at home when they return. Creative scheduling may attract good people who are unwilling to accept the conventional workweek.

The challenges of coping with reduction of order cycle time, improvement of quality, enhancement of asset productivity, and a new kind of workforce are certainly enough to test the most determined and talented managers. Yet this is the state of the industry as it enters the 21st century.

Questions that solve problems

Q What have we done to reduce order cycle time in this warehouse?
C Itemize the actions taken to shorten order cycle time. Include other logistics functions as well as steps taken in the warehouse. If there has been little or no progress, find out why.

Q How has quality been improved in the warehouse?
C Start with getting your manager to define quality in his or her operation. Then look at how quality is measured as well as what the measurements tell us. If no measurements are in place, develop an action plan to implement some of the ideas in this chapter, starting with those that are easiest to implement and most relevant to your operation.

Q How is asset productivity measured in our warehouse?
C Since asset productivity measurement usually starts at the top, do not expect the warehouse manager to initiate measurements that are not found elsewhere. Where asset productivity is emphasized, check to see whether the warehouse has measurements, and compare the results to those in other departments.

Q Do we have a warehouse labor shortage? If so, what steps have we taken to attract and retain good people?
C You may wish to ask people from human resources as well as warehousing about this one. If you get complaints about employee turnover, see what can be done to implement creative programs to attract and retain people from non-traditional sources. See if there are internal conditions that degrade your ability to retain workers.

Q Is our workforce improving?
C An affirmative answer to this one may be more important than the answers to the previous questions. However, an important follow-up might be: **How do you know?**

Chapter 3

Supply chain, JIT, and benchmarking

In the last few decades of the 20th century, the language of warehousing and logistics management was enriched (or polluted, according to your point of view) by a succession of new concepts, jargon, acronyms, and occasional linguistic abomination. This chapter will report on only those concepts that seemed to make a difference in the life of a warehouse operator.

Figure 3-1
Courtesy of The Progress Group

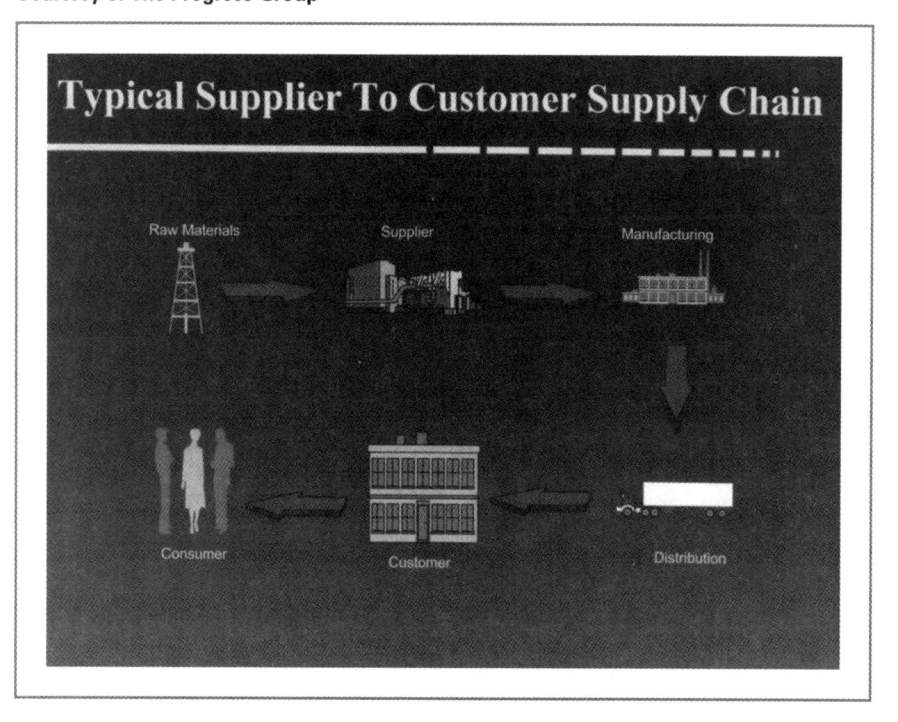

Supply chain management: "A rose by any other name ..."

In the several decades since the formation of National Council of Physical Distribution Management, many terms have been used to describe the process of merging transportation with warehousing, inventory management, and customer service. The original term, *physical distribution,* was limited to finished goods. By 1985, the Council's leaders recognized that *logistics* was a better term because it encompassed raw materials as well as finished products. At that time, the Council changed its name to replace "physical distribution" with "logistics."

Supply chain management is a more recent concept. Is it really different from logistics management, or is it just a different name for the same thing? Where does the warehouse fit in?

Supply chain management has been defined as the integration of business processes from original suppliers to end user. The goal of this process integration is to provide products and services that add value for customers.

Figure 3-1 describes the flow of materials from original source to ultimate consumer. For many companies, the supply chain looks like not so much a chain as an uprooted tree. How many branches and roots of that tree need to be managed?

With all of the new language about supply chain management, at least three ways of doing business are certainly different from past practices:
- Logistics managers have moved from an emphasis on cutting costs to one of adding value.
- Managers have changed from transactional relationships to the creation of long-term partnerships.
- Dealing with suppliers has moved from an adversarial practice to one of trust and cooperation.

The evolution of the process might be described by the titles of the people who control it. In the United States during the century between the creation of the Interstate Commerce Act and the deregulation of freight rates, we had traffic managers. By the middle of the 20th century, the distribution manager emerged. That person had a broader role in managing the flow of finished goods. Next we saw the materials managers, whose function was extended further to include movement of raw materials. By the 1980s, the concept of logistics management became fashionable. Logistics frequently included procurement as well as management of materials. Finally, we have the supply chain manager.

Supply chain management involves more than logistics. The process includes marketing, finance, manufacturing, accounting, and management information systems. In some organizations, the head of the supply chain management team is the chief operating officer of the company.

Where does warehousing fit into this process? The biblical role of the warehouse is well known: the reservoir to prevent disaster. Warehousing is still used for that purpose. The reservoir can be a mechanism to allow level production when demand is cyclical. In contrast, warehousing may balance level demand with seasonal production, such as the packing of vegetables when the crop is harvested. Figure 3-2 shows the traditional flow of material from warehouse to warehouse.

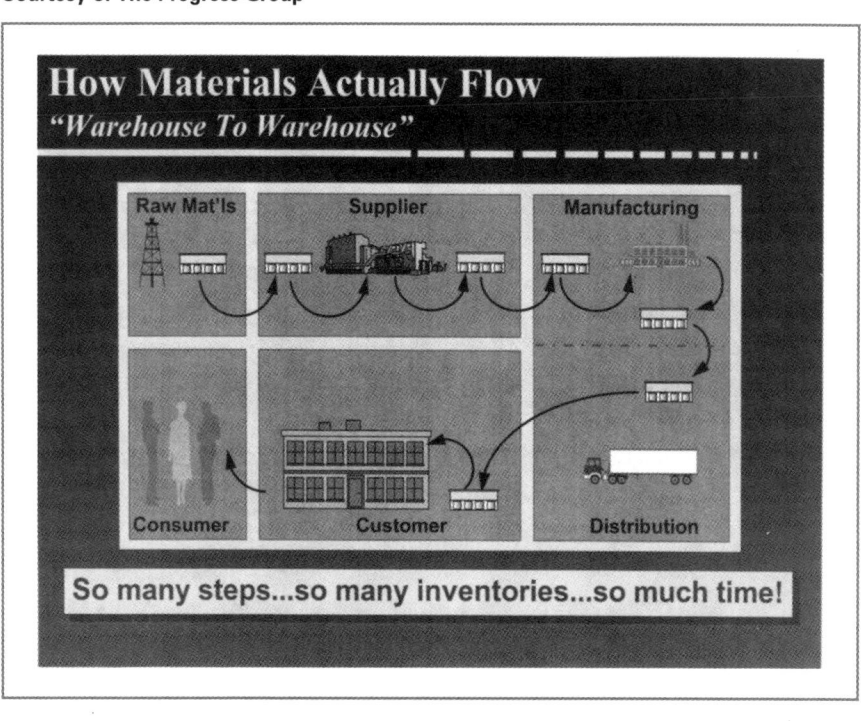

Figure 3-2
Courtesy of The Progress Group

How Materials Actually Flow
"Warehouse To Warehouse"

Raw Mat'ls → Supplier → Manufacturing → Distribution → Customer → Consumer

So many steps...so many inventories...so much time!

Figure 3-3
Courtesy of The Progress Group

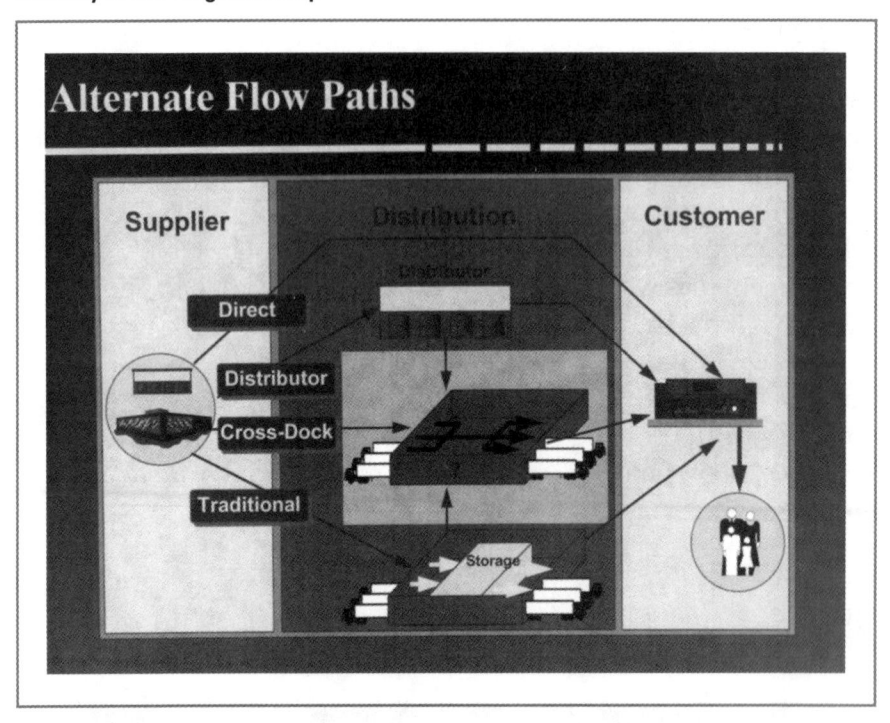

Alternate Flow Paths

[Diagram showing flow paths from Supplier through Distribution to Customer, with options labeled Direct, Distributor, Cross-Dock, and Traditional]

In implementing supply chain management, some users have introduced the concept of vendor-managed inventory. This is a variation of an old corporate shell game, a means of persuading suppliers to hold title to inventory until the moment the customer needs it. At times, a warehouse is part of the vendor-managed inventory supply chain. For example, the retailer may order suppliers to position goods in a third-party warehouse next to the retail store. Goods are withdrawn from the warehouse as late as possible, frequently when they are needed to fill orders that have already been sold. Since title to the merchandise is not transferred until the release from the warehouse, in effect the retailer is able to sell the merchandise before he buys it.

The supply chain concept has offered the alternate flow paths shown in Figure 3-3. The path shown at the top eliminates warehousing as goods move from supplier to customer. The three other options include either warehousing or cross docking as part of the process.

Supply chain management, logistics, and warehousing are closely related. Logistics is the process of filling the gaps, and supply chain management is the process of closing them. A company can achieve excellence in logistics without supply chain management. However, it is not possible to have a great supply chain without also being effective with logistics. At the same time, that effective logistics system requires a competent warehousing function.

Just-in-time and its variants

The intensity with which the just-in-time (JIT) concept engulfed American industry in the last three decades of the 20th century gave it all the trappings of a corporate fad. Seminars were created to sell the concept, and platoons of consultants offered to initiate their clients into a new religion. Few noticed that JIT was another variant of the corporate shell game described earlier, the practice of moving inventory back to the supplier and delaying its delivery until the last possible moment.

JIT is a product of both fact and myth

Several myths about JIT persist:
- The first myth of JIT is that it is a Japanese concept. In fact, JIT is a variant of the postponement strategy developed in the U.S.
- A second myth is that JIT is a production strategy. In fact, it was used in wholesale and retail distribution at least as early as it was in production. Furthermore, its use in merchandising is probably more widespread than it is in manufacturing.
- A third myth is that JIT requires that suppliers be located near the user. In the United States, the use of warehousing and premium transportation systems has allowed JIT to function effectively with a supply chain that stretches over hundreds or even thousands of miles.

Postponement saves money by delaying to the latest possible moment the final stage of production or distribution. To delay shipping a product avoids risking its miscommitment. If the manufacturer can keep the entire stockpile at a factory warehouse at the end of the assembly line, he can avoid the potential waste of committing product to a regional warehouse and later having to cross-ship that merchandise to correct an imbalance of inventory. Postponement has been further refined in the computer industry by the stockpiling of half-finished machines, which are customized and shipped after a sales order has been received. In this situation, postponement reduces inventory because the only stockpiling performed is of half-finished products.

Soft-drink manufacturers began using postponement decades ago by producing concentrated flavor syrup. This concentrate was converted to finished products at soda fountains, which added carbonated water. By postponing the final blending of the product, the manufacturer reduced the cost of transportation and distribution.

Variations of JIT are found in the wholesale and retail industries. Quick response (QR) is a merchandising application of JIT. Like JIT, QR is as much a process as it is a concept. It depends on tools such as bar coding, point-of-sale registers, scanners, and electronic data interchange. Figure 3-4 explains how QR works in a retail environment. Quick response has been described as a customer-driven system that pulls merchandise through the supply chain rather than pushing. When a retail customer buys an item, the clerk scans the bar code at the cash register. Stock information associated with the code initiates a reduction from inventory. When the inventory balance reaches a certain point, a purchase order is

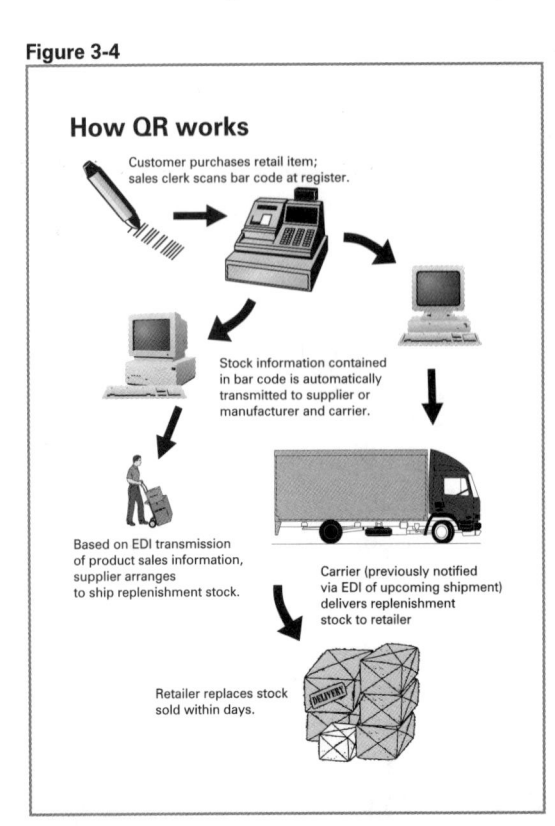

Figure 3-4

How QR works

- Customer purchases retail item; sales clerk scans bar code at register.
- Stock information contained in bar code is automatically transmitted to supplier or manufacturer and carrier.
- Based on EDI transmission of product sales information, supplier arranges to ship replenishment stock.
- Carrier (previously notified via EDI of upcoming shipment) delivers replenishment stock to retailer.
- Retailer replaces stock sold within days.

produced to move replenishment stock to the store. Using QR, the retailer replaces sold stock within days instead of months.

Another variant is called efficient consumer response, popularly known as ECR. Designed primarily for the grocery industry, ECR functions like QR. Both QR and ECR are part of a trend toward the use of time as a source of competitive advantage. Buyers are no longer interested in just quantity and price; the emphasis has shifted to the ability to move products quickly. The successful merchant is the one able to respond the fastest. Warehousing is frequently an integral part of that rapid response.

JIT vs. congestion — a collision course

Highway congestion and JIT are in growing conflict. Traffic analysts have discovered that some freeway trips take longer today than they did 20 years ago. As the number of vehicles and miles continues to grow, highway construction falls behind.

Yet there are several ways to maintain JIT capabilities in spite of traffic congestion.

The most important is to improve the physical and administrative processes of handling receipts at a warehouse. This might include adding more dock doors or installing conveyors in truck beds to allow goods to be rolled from trailer to warehouse in just a few minutes. The physical process must be accompanied by improvements in the information side of the delivery process.

Another option is to extend the hours of warehouse operations and to handle more receipts and shipments during off-peak hours.

Freight consolidation also can reduce congestion by combining more than one order on the same vehicle.

Using JIT for service and repairs

JIT can be used to eliminate parts and service centers. For example, a health-care supplier produces an appliance used in hospitals. If the appliance fails, the company uses a premium air carrier to fly in a new unit and return the one that has malfunctioned. Technicians repair the broken units at a central location rather than in scattered repair depots. In another case, a computer service company maintains detailed records for each piece of equipment. When a computer malfunctions, the service company isolates the problem through telephone consultation. Then the failing component is replaced rather than repaired, again delivering the replacement unit and returning the broken one by air freight.

The role of warehousing

Early writings about JIT suggested that it would eliminate warehousing. In the United States, the concept has actually created more warehouses instead of eliminating them. However, some of those new warehouses are flow-through terminals rather than storage depots. As JIT has increased the speed of inventory turns, a growing percentage of product moves through a distribution center without ever being stored.

Both merchant and manufacturer may use a warehouse as a staging point to increase inventory turnover through placement of dock doors close to the location where they will be used. Rather than receive small quantities direct from the source, a distributor receives a full truckload of product from a variety of sources, all stored in the same warehouse.

Benchmarking and the Holy Grail

Benchmarking in warehousing has been defined as an examination of best practices in other warehouses, ideas that can and should be applied in your own operation. At times, the search for benchmarking seems to resemble the search for the Holy Grail. The Holy Grail is the cup used by Jesus at the Last Supper; beginning with the knights of the Crusades, the Holy Grail became an object of search for everyone who believed that it would make the finder morally and spiritually worthy. Like the Grail, the perfect benchmark promises to solve all warehousing problems by providing a standard against which the operation can be judged.

Benchmarking should happen whenever management is concerned about the need for significant improvement. The stimulus for benchmarking warehousing functions may come from the perception that the warehouse is functioning poorly and is in urgent need of improvement. Benchmarking might also be stimulated by knowledge that others in the industry provide a higher level of customer service than you do.

On the other hand, benchmarking is at times an inappropriate strategy. If your purpose is to learn what competitors are doing, the process may be unethical. There are accepted ways of learning about the activities of competitors, and benchmarking should not be one of them.

The test is reciprocity. If you request a visit to any warehouse for the purpose of benchmarking, are you willing to let the managers of that warehouse go through the same process with your operation? If you cannot answer in the affirmative, then the benchmarking effort should not be made.

Internal benchmarking

Most people assume that benchmarking is a process of looking outside your organization; they think of the outside exclusively as they consider the process. Yet any internal look is easier, faster, and less expensive than traditional benchmarking, and it may provide just as much or more information about improvement opportunities.

There are two ways to use the internal warehouse performance measurements. If your company has a group of facilities, use the measurements to compare the performance of one warehouse with that of the others. However, if you have only a single warehouse, use the data to compare performance over time. For example, how does the performance in December of this year compare with last December's? The internal measurements should highlight the quantitative processes in warehousing, such as space utilization, equipment utilization, and

Figure 3-5

Warehouse comparison

Location	Total cost	Units shipped	Cost per unit	Inventory turns/yr	% of complaints to unit	% of return to unit	Space utilization %
Atlanta							
Chicago							
Columbus							

worker productivity. Figure 3-5 offers a chart used to compare warehousing performance in three cities. If you are tracking the performance of a single warehouse, a similar chart should be used with months or years rather than cities in the left column. Such a chart can show graphically how warehouse performance has changed over time.

For most warehouse operators, the best benchmark may be whichever one is available within your own operation. As in the search for the Holy Grail, you could waste mountains of time and money in a quest for information that actually exists now in your own warehouses.

Questions that solve problems

Q Are we using supply chain management, and if so, how do we define the term?

C If your warehousing managers don't respond with a firm yes or no, they may not be conversant with this business development. An inbred corporate culture may produce managers who are ignorant about supply chain management and other corporate symbols of the present decade.

Q Are we using JIT (or its industry-specific variants) anywhere?

C The warehouse is seldom the instigator, but it must always be involved. Third-party warehouses usually install JIT in response to a customer request.

Q Are our competitors using supply chain management or JIT in a way that puts our organization at a disadvantage?

C An affirmative answer should spur you to be more actively involved in the warehousing and logistics activities in your company.

Q Have we done any benchmarking with our warehouses?

C If the answer is yes, learn what, how, and why. See whether benchmarking in your company means the same thing as the operations defined here.

Chapter 4

Adapting to the information age

The greatest potential source of savings in the 21st-century warehouse is the ability to trade information for space and labor. As we continue our transition from the industrial age to the information age, we discover new ways to use information to save both time and space. While costs of time and space tend to increase each year, the cost of handling and transmitting information continues to decrease in both relative and actual terms. Probably no commodity has had the same downward cycle of costs; thus it is obviously sensible to continue the search for ways to use information technology in the warehouse.

When we can learn something quickly and accurately in the warehouse, sometimes wasteful activity can be avoided. For example, when the receiver knows that 100 cases now being unloaded are needed to fill orders, the product can be moved directly to a shipping dock rather than to the storage location. A computer terminal at the dock or a scanner on the lift truck can update inventory files and display information about goods being received or shipped.

Technology and forecasting

An important use of information systems is to forecast space and labor requirements in the warehouse.

For example, at a warehouse in Brazil a computer translates cubic meters of freight into hours of effort. At the end of each day, the warehouse manager determines the number of cubic meters of freight that are ordered for shipment the next day. That information is translated into man-hours, and then management knows how many people will be needed to handle shipping duties on the following day.

Information technology and control

Use of automatic identification can dramatically reduce errors in both receiving and shipping. When an order picker checks bar codes with a scanner, it becomes nearly impossible for the picker to make a mis-shipment. If the code on the box does not match the code on the pick list, the system alerts the order picker. Warehouses using such systems report an error rate of less than 0.01 percent.

Information systems are also used to minimize travel through the warehouse, to pull merchandise in accordance with pre-arranged selection priorities (FIFO, LIFO, or lot number), and to select items of similar size for a stable outbound shipping unit.

An information system will also track the productivity of individual workers or groups of workers. Each time a worker starts a new job, an identity code for that worker is entered. The computer acts as a time clock, and it allows easy measurement of every job done in the warehouse. Management knows not only that the job was completed and how long it took but also who did the work and how productive that person was. When a pattern of errors or damage occurs, it is possible to determine whether one or a few workers have contributed disproportionately to the discrepancies. Because this productivity information is recorded in real time, management can monitor workflow and detect potential bottlenecks as they begin to occur.

Information technology will also improve communication between the warehouse and the production and marketing departments. It can be used to facilitate communication between warehouses in a chain. Production people can determine the ability of each warehouse to accept new product moving out of the factory. Marketing people can verify the shipment of orders. When information technology links the warehouse to a carrier, you can determine whether the product has been delivered or how far it is from the delivery point. The information system should allow warehouse users to have an accurate and continuing update of the status of every warehousing job.

EDI and the warehouse

Electronic data interchange, popularly known as EDI, has been around for decades. Most warehouse managers have few options about whether they will use EDI, but many have questions about when and how they would use it. As the function of the warehouse has changed from storage depot to distribution center to flow-through facility, owners of merchandise have used available technology to track the status of inventory as it moves through the supply chain. The warehouse operator, like every other link in the chain, must cooperate in providing the visibility that the owner of the inventory demands. EDI is the tool with which this visibility of control is maintained.

Figure 4-1

Protocols for EDI

Receipts
  Enroute receipts — warehouse ship advice (inbound).
  Enroute receipts from principal (inbound).
  Receipt confirmations (outbound).

Orders
  Shipping schedule.
  Confirmation.
  Order load (inbound).
  Order change (outbound).
  Order confirmations (outbound).

Inventory
  Inventory status (outbound).
  Inventory adjustments (outbound).

Master file updates
  Product master file add or update (inbound).
  Product information request (outbound).

Carrier communications
  Electronic load notices and advance load notices.
  Appointment notification.
  Delivery notification.

EDI in the warehouse includes at least 15 standard transactions. Figure 4-1 shows a typical transaction format. The globalization of our economy has provided a stimulus for EDI. When language is a barrier, the standard format for transmitting information is a good way to ease the communication problem.

The impact of electronic commerce*

The broad adoption of EDI has never really happened because of the cost of networks and software, confusion over standards, and the need to have compatible technology. Implementation was flawed at the beginning because it usually involved a unique solution for each pair of trading partners. To use the phone system as an analogy, think of wiring a separate telephone line to each person you plan to talk to. The real value of EDI, as with the phone system, is its ability to allow us to interact with everyone in the system.

The Internet has been heralded as the savior of EDI with its widespread network coverage, open standards, and the ability to run existing applications at remote locations over the network. However, connecting these systems over the Internet does not by itself solve the integration problem. We still can't communicate if I speak only Russian and you speak only English. We need a common language.

To offer a complete solution, an Internet-based system must overcome the Internet's inherent weaknesses while improving on key features of the network approach. Those features include security, reliability, and transaction verification.

A newer phase of the Internet revolution is business to business. Electronic commerce operations are becoming a part of many transactions. Never before has a vendor been able to reach the customers so effectively. EDI is more than the exporting of data; it is actual interaction between systems. For example, as a warehouse inventory level is depleted, a planning system automatically checks supplier inventory levels and places replenishment orders. New languages have been developed to handle the translation problem. To return once again to the telephone analogy, I may be speaking in Russian and you may still understand only English, but now we have a translator who speaks both languages well.

---

* Adapted from an article by Craig T. Hall, Digital Commerce, *Warehousing Forum*, Volume 13, Number 10, ©The Ackerman Company, Columbus, Ohio.

Some logistics service companies are persuading customers to move from traditional EDI to an "EDI on the net" model. The system uses encryption to maintain security of sensitive information.

Here is how the system works at one third-party warehouse:
- Client buys inexpensive software to allow files to be encrypted and sent over the Internet.
- Warehouse provides every client with a public encrypted key that allows each user to transform data so that only the warehouse can read it.
- Once data is encrypted, client sends order to warehouse using any Internet provider.
- Warehouse verifies and uses an encrypted key to code the information.
- Warehouse confirms receipt to customer by email.
- When order is shipped, warehouse confirms shipment to customer. *

Evaluating system options**

Before you investigate the further use of computers, you need to make certain that your operation is functioning well now. If you try to add computer-assisted processing to a disorganized warehouse, the end result will be much less than you could achieve otherwise.

It should take only a few days to review the warehouse operation. Scrutinize every function so you can ensure that you are now using the "best practice" in every state of the operation. Work practices should be standardized and workflow streamlined as much as possible. Storage practices should be re-examined. This review will ensure that your new system is based on using best practices in operating your warehouse. It helps you avoid the trap of changing your business to accommodate the method of operation described in a particular software package.

---

* Adapted from an article by Brian Vigneux, USCO, *Warehousing Forum*, Volume 13, Number 11, ©The Ackerman Company, Columbus, Ohio.
** Adapted from an article by Morton T. Yeomans, *Warehousing Forum*, Volume 10, Number 2, ©The Ackerman Company, Columbus, Ohio.

When you have completed the diagnostic operations review and upgraded current warehouse practices, you will be ready to start the selection process. The goal of this search is to find a system that enables you to operate your warehouse the way you want to, but more efficiently, with higher service levels and lower costs.

Many companies will establish a task force responsible for selecting the system of choice. The team should be made up of at least one person from operations, the financial person, and one or more management information systems or data processing people. To keep this team on track, you should identify and describe current customer-service practices. Those include criteria for product quality, order fill rate, accuracy, and order cycle times.

The statement of requirements is the central reference point for your software search. Writing this statement may take months if the members of the group are working at the effort less than full time. The statement should provide a clear description of the system you hope to install and should specify efficiency levels, accuracy levels, and customer-service standards you need to remain competitive. More detail on this subject is in Chapter 27.

What to look for in warehouse management software*

As you compare competitive software to control the warehouse management system (WMS), it is useful to consider three tasks. The first task is to identify the key differences among packages. The second is to identify common deficiencies in WMS software. The third is to provide guidelines for developing a request for information (RFI).

Here are some crucial features that differ among WMS packages:
- Every system should have a means of measurement.
- The better WMS will use a unit of measure method, and it will analyze and define specific cubic volumes per unit.
- The best systems support carton selection and pick-to-carton functions. The WMS that uses a

---

* Adapted from an article by Philip Obal, Industrial Data & Information, *Warehousing Forum*, Volume 14, Number 1, ©The Ackerman Company, Columbus, Ohio.

pick-to-carton method can save money by eliminating packers and packing.
- ◆ A good WMS uses a bin locator system to tell the receiving worker where to store each inbound pallet.
- ◆ The bin locator system should evaluate physical factors of the facility as well as storage rules established by management.
- ◆ The same system should compare optional travel paths for picking, put-away, and replenishment, and then indicate the best path for filling an order.
- ◆ If you plan truck routes for delivery stops, your WMS should include a route optimization feature.

Several deficiencies are commonly found in WMS packages:
- ◆ Some vendors have not integrated the handling of hazardous materials (hazmat) into their systems. The system should access government rules so that it can identify hazardous products as they are received.
- ◆ Some systems do not store error data. Not all WMS will record errors when an employee picks the wrong product.
- ◆ Some systems have productivity reporting but do not have productivity standards.
- ◆ Few system vendors have a program to identify new slots and automatically assign the re-slotting tasks. Re-slotting is necessary in an active warehouse and should be part of your WMS.
- ◆ Many systems omit the load-planning feature; this feature is desirable if you frequently build pallet loads or container loads.

When the request for information (RFI) is prepared, list each factor and then determine whether each item is essential, desirable, or applicable. The vendor should show evidence that the company is financially sound and has a healthy revenue-to-employee ratio. The vendor should also provide specific references to clients with similar operations.

When responses to the RFI are received, develop a matrix with a numerical score based on determination of essential and desirable factors. With three to five finalist vendors identified, ask for these items:

an organization chart, a financial statement, and a quotation of prices for making alterations.

Review the RFI in detail with the vendor. Because you are investing in a product for the long term, focus on quality first and then on price.

Questions that solve problems

Q Does the information system now used in our warehouse provide all of the control capabilities described in this chapter?
C This question should be the subject of a discussion with your people. Recognize that you may not need all of the "bells and whistles" an information system can give you. On the other hand, be open-minded about the possibilities of changing in the future. Examine carefully the motivations and opinions of those in the organization who try to tell you it can't be done. Perhaps the best answer for the doubters is to find another warehousing organization already doing the job that supposedly cannot be done.

Q What are we forecasting in the warehouse today, and how well do our forecasts work?
C Don't be shocked if you find little or no forecasting. If nobody knows how to do it, there are ways to learn — both within the academic world and through management seminars.

Q What tasks are being done in the warehouse today that could be modified or eliminated through the use of available information technology?
C Although related to the first question, this one might help your people zero in on specific modifications that are appropriate to bring your warehouse up to the state of the art in information technology.

Q How does our error rate compare with that of our competition?
C A primary function of the information system is to increase accuracy.

Q Is our order cycle time superior to that of our competitors?
C Better information technology will reduce cycle time.

Chapter 5

Avoiding labor pains

Whether warehouse workers are unionized or not, every manager hopes to develop an atmosphere that prevents the union from being a disruptive factor.

Before 1980, a great majority of logistics activities, including warehousing, were organized by one international union or another. Frequently that union was the one that had organized manufacturing or retailing in the same company. For third-party warehouses or others associated with transportation, the typical organizing group was the International Brotherhood of Teamsters.

Two events in the 1980s and '90s caused a significant change in this situation. The first was the deregulation of all modes of transportation, first at the federal and later at the state level. One after-effect of deregulation was substantial growth of nonunion freight carriers and the failure of many unionized trucking companies. The second event was a strike called by the Professional Air Traffic Controllers Organization (PATCO). Because the strike was illegally called against the federal government, President Reagan could and did use military controllers to break it. Furthermore, public opinion favored the government rather than the well-paid striking controllers. Today, a growing number of hourly workers in the United States are not unionized, and most warehouse managers work hard to keep them that way.

Creating a participatory environment

In practice, you do not need to be union-free to submerge union influence. What you need is an atmosphere that builds loyalty to the company rather than involvement with the union. There are some unionized warehouses where grievances are virtually unknown. Union officials are consulted only for the renewal of the contract, and union business is seldom discussed in everyday operations.

Some nonunion warehouse operators have maintained an environment that does not invite unionization. One retailer provides a dignified and relatively luxurious setting for every worker. Each employee, from president to trainee, comes to work through the same front door and lobby. Every employee uses the same beautiful dining room.

One nonunion manufacturing plant requires everyone to wear a white shop coat on the production floor. When company officers come to the plant from the office, they put on the white uniform, which hides both the pinstripes of the corporate executive and the blue collar of the factory worker. The result is a removal of the "we–they" symbols of business dress.

Many managers believe compensation is the prime motivator for hourly workers. Yet repeated surveys show that money is relatively low among the priorities of American workers, including warehouse people. They are more interested in prestige, security, respect, and a feeling of belonging. Those desires can be frustrated by ineffective supervisors. Although low pay may seem to be the cause, the true motivation to unionize is usually not financial. Workers who support a union are usually reacting to the reality or perception of unfair treatment in the workplace.

The crucial role of the supervisor

For most employees, the warehouse supervisor is the company. The supervisor often has more impact on morale and perceptions of the company than any other single factor. Therefore, careful selection and development of supervisors is absolutely vital.

Today's warehouse supervisor needs more than power and discipline to get the job done. The day has long passed when the prime role of the supervisor or foreman was to assign work and expedite its completion. The supervisor must exercise leadership, and that is done by communicating and setting examples.

Why does every good warehouse manager or supervisor pick up trash on the floor? By picking up things that never should have been there in the first place, the leader demonstrates that he or she is willing to do a task that the hourly people have apparently neglected. Setting an example teaches everyone that housekeeping has top priority in a good warehouse.

The difference between a good and bad supervisor is not what that person knows but what he or she is willing to learn. Your supervisors should be learners and teachers, and once again their learning ability should set an example for those who report to them.

The effective supervisor holds frequent dialogues with people on the warehousing team. If that supervisor does not encourage an open exchange of ideas, you can bet that communication within the work crew will also be lacking.

Today's warehouse supervisor must have five crucial attributes:
- Excellent communication skills.
- Openness to change.
- Problem-solving skills.
- Customer orientation.
- Teamwork skills.

In the 21st-century warehouse there is no place for the traditional autocratic supervisor. On the other hand, the sensitive leader who displays all of the above attributes should be a successful warehouse supervisor.

The fine line of delegating properly

Getting things done through other people requires delegation. Delegation, like most human activities, is effective only when done in the proper proportion. A common problem for warehouse supervisors and others newly promoted to management is under-delegating. Some retain their old duties because they enjoy them. Others hang onto them because they can't believe anyone else will do them properly. The effective supervisor understands that long-run success depends on his or her ability to develop skills through delegation of tasks to workers.

Delegation takes patience and forbearance. Those who lack those qualities will assign the job and interfere with its performance by "straw bossing" and overcontrolling.

However, delegation includes responsibilities. A supervisor who delegates and never looks back is not effective. If the worker never receives correction, he or she never has a chance to grow and profit from errors. The effective supervisor thus must monitor subordinates, provide feedback to workers on performance, and ask for their feedback as well. Proper delegation is like walking a tightrope: it requires constant balance and correction.

Logistics outsourcing*

The end of the 20th century saw an epidemic of outsourcing of logistics services, including warehousing. There are a variety of motives for outsourcing warehousing services formerly handled in-house.

Some managers consider logistics outsourcing for reasons completely unrelated to their current workforce. In fact, they consider it important for the provider of outsourcing services to hire the existing workforce. At the other extreme, some companies' primary motivation for outsourcing is to eliminate a problem workforce. That problem may be high labor costs, poor productivity, or both.

In one situation, a company's labor costs became uncompetitive over a period of years because the company granted wage increases each year, whether there were productivity improvements or not. Outsourcing may not be a solution to that problem.

If your company seeks a third-party logistics firm to take over a group of warehouse employees and expects to pay a low price that will force the provider to reduce wages, then you are asking for trouble. The provider will be faced with the task of maintaining good employee morale in the face of changes that workers cannot be expected to like.

Morale will be an even bigger problem if the provider takes over its customer's employees and then imposes both pay reductions and operational changes that require more effort from the workers. If outsourcing may lead to both substantial labor cost reductions and substantial operational changes, then think twice about asking the third-party provider to keep your current warehouse employees.

Anyone who considers outsourcing will find three problem areas: productivity, labor costs, and labor relations. If you are not satisfied with current productivity, why do you believe that outsourcing will

---

* Adapted from an article by J. Michael Kota, Ryder Integrated Logistics, *Warehousing Forum*, Volume 12, Number 8, ©The Ackerman Company, Columbus, Ohio.

improve it? If you expect the third-party provider to retain your current workforce, how can you achieve a reduction in labor costs? If you plan to cut wages, what will happen to morale of the workers?

In essence, the third-party warehouse is selling two commodities: space and time. The human side involves the sale of time. Both contractor and customer must decide whether the fee charged for that time is low enough to be competitive and still high enough to allow the contractor to attract, motivate, and retain competent warehouse workers.

Labor disputes

Although it is safe to predict that strikes will be less common in the new century than they were in the old one, every warehouse manager must develop alternatives for dealing with a work stoppage. There are two kinds of strikes: those at your own organization, and those at a supplier or customer that affect your warehouse.

When a manufacturer is preparing for a strike, inventories in third-party warehouses are sometimes used as a strike hedge. To prevent picketing of the third-party warehouse, it is essential to begin the warehousing operation before the strike starts, disbursing the product so that it represents a small fraction of the total capacity of each warehousing supplier. Properly applied, the strike hedge inventory can be a bargaining tool in contract negotiations.

Strikes directed at other companies can be as disruptive as disturbances within your own organization. A first step in planning for this contingency is to determine which suppliers are essential to your operations. That depends on whether they are sole sources or supply a critical percentage of volume. The risk of a supplier's strike can be reduced by developing an inventory hedge with advanced stockpiling. A strike against your customer can also disrupt warehousing operations. Consider such special accommodations as direct store delivery to bypass a strike at a retailer's distribution center.

Transportation strikes require particular planning skill. Nonunion transportation companies may be used, although such companies will naturally serve their regular customers first. Probably the most important planning rule is to avoid excessive dependence on any one transportation supplier.

Questions that solve problems

Q Is our warehouse now union-free?
C You should frequently question your people about what they are doing to maintain this status if it exists.

Q What steps do we take for proper training and orientation of our supervisors?
C If your company does not have training and performance review for supervisors, your union-free status could be in jeopardy.

Q What procedures are in place to resolve complaints made by hourly workers?
C Don't consider just the responses of your managers and supervisors. Ask the hourly employees in the warehouse as well.

Q If the warehouse is unionized, ask your people about grievance records and frequency of visits by union organizers.
C Your goal is to learn whether your management has been successful in submerging the union.

Q What steps have we taken to plan for the contingencies of strikes against outside firms as well as against our own company?
C Look for a reasonable number of detailed options to counteract strikes against suppliers, strikes against customers, or strikes against the transportation companies serving your warehouse.

Q How well do our supervisors and managers delegate?
C When you ask this question, be sure to evaluate the delegation ability of the person you are interviewing, as well as your own success as a delegator.

Q If we use third-party services, what are our motives for outsourcing? If we are a third-party warehouse operator, what are the outsourcing motives of our largest customers?
C If the prime motivation of the user is to find cheap labor, consider the probability that the operation will deteriorate when the labor market tightens.

Chapter 6

Reverse logistics management

The traditional management of logistics systems, including warehouses, has traced the movement of materials from sources of supply to points of consumption. We usually assume that the flow moves from source to consumer. Until the past few years, concerns about flow of materials in reverse were unheard of.[*]

Reverse logistics is the process of handling product returns, recycling, reuse, waste disposal, or any other logistics process in which the normal flow of materials is reversed. Reverse logistics is similar to inbound logistics in that it was overlooked in the early research and writing about physical distribution and logistics management. Yet paying attention to reverse logistics can create significant reductions in corporate costs.

Most managers have not done a process map of reverse logistics, so they find it difficult to fully recognize or control reverse logistics flows. When reverse logistics processes are controlled, they are almost always managed within a single company and seldom across supply chains. Financial people have generally overlooked the opportunity to properly value those assets recovered through reverse logistics. In most companies, warehousing and logistics managers are reacting to initiatives from other groups or departments rather than being the initiators of a reverse logistics program.[**]

---

[*] Herb Shear of Genco Distribution System in Pittsburgh provided helpful review and comment on this chapter.
[**] Adapted from an article in *Warehousing Forum*, Volume 14, Number 3, ©The Ackerman Company, Columbus, Ohio.

There are six common reasons why merchandise is returned and enters a reverse logistics flow. Three of them are related to environmental factors, and the other three might be broadly classed as marketing returns.

Environmental returns

The first and most important environmental return is the need to recall products in which a defect or contamination has been discovered. Some manufacturers make test recalls in order to verify the capabilities of warehousing and trucking suppliers to correctly handle the process. The need for speed and precision in a recall is obvious, particularly when the defect could threaten the lives of consumers. In this situation, the prime stimulus is consumer safety.

The second motivator for environmental returns is concern about degradation of the environment. In many urban areas, there is grave concern about the depletion of landfill sites and the subsequent rising cost of solid-waste disposal. The proven way to reduce the volume of waste is to recycle and reuse certain packaging materials. Precision is less important in this kind of return, since consumer safety is not involved. However, the concerns of environmentalists have created almost as much public pressure for return and reuse of packaging as for the recall of defective goods.

The third environmental motive for returns is conservation of assets. Long before we had today's environmental concerns, the beverage industry developed refillable bottles. The glass containers were expensive — in fact, at one time soft drink containers had a higher value than the fluid inside. Although the consumer could not be forced to return the bottle, there was a financial incentive to do so.

In the middle of the 20th century, the railroads began to use boxcars containing reusable dunnage. However, the successful use of damage-free (D. F.) rail cars depends on the cooperation of every user in returning the permanent dunnage to the boxcar after it has been unloaded.

The auto industry was a pioneer in the use of reusable packages, such as racks to hold engines and metal bins or cages to hold the variety of small component parts. Automakers developed a system to ensure that each of these reusable containers was returned. As the cost of warehouse pallets increased, many users developed pallet exchange programs to avoid donating pallets to the customer.

Marketing returns

Nearly every retailer has an obligation to take back defective merchandise or even merchandise that has not satisfied the customer. In some cases, defective merchandise can be repaired or reconditioned without a return to the production plant. In every case, the product is typically accepted for return by the retail store and moved to another location.

Many manufacturers have a stock-balancing feature in their sales to retailers. They agree to take back merchandise if the retailer has bought more than he could sell, and many manufacturers are extremely liberal in executing a stock-balancing program. They want to be certain that the retailer does not suffer because of poor sales projections from the manufacturer's marketing department. In other cases, a manufacturer will perform a stock lift. In persuading a retailer to drop a competing brand and take on his own, a marketing manager will agree to remove and dispose of all of the competitor's merchandise.

Many manufacturers have a regular program to recall obsolescent or discontinued inventory. Sometimes a certain line of merchandise contains circulars that include a special offer. When the offer has expired, the merchandise cannot be sold in its current form. This discontinued inventory must be moved back from the retailer so consumers don't claim a special offer that has expired.

Organizing for reverse logistics

Reverse logistics management requires cooperation from several groups, including production, marketing, finance, information systems, and human resources. Logistics people may be the facilitators, but they cannot act alone.

A few companies with large enough volumes have developed redistribution centers where recycling, remanufacturing, refurbishing, and other reverse logistics operations are carried out.

Substantial volumes frequently make the difference between success and failure in a reverse logistics program. There is therefore a role for a third-party warehouse to combine the needs of several users into a single reverse logistics program.

The role of the warehouse manager

Warehouse operators specializing in reverse logistics must look carefully at storage layout as well as materials-handling equipment and tools for salvage and scrap disposal. For example, such a warehouse may have a pulverizer inside the building to destroy materials that cannot be recycled. Because reverse logistics creates unusual challenges in materials handling, the same equipment that might be ideal for a conventional distribution center may be totally inappropriate for reverse logistics management.

Evaluation of space requirements is also a very different process. If recycling is involved, there may be compactors to reduce the amount of space needed for storage. On the other hand, space will be required to house recycling equipment. The design of the warehouse will also be influenced by the process flow of reverse logistics.

When reverse logistics management is combined with finished-goods movement in a warehouse, you may find that a layout that works well for other distribution operations is inappropriate for reverse logistics management. In those cases, reverse logistics may require a "warehouse within a warehouse" with distinct flow patterns, layout, and materials-handling equipment. When recycling takes place within the warehouse, the potential for mixing materials must be minimized, and the process should be designed to keep all materials dry and contaminant-free. The warehouse operator needs to understand the potential for cross-contamination or chemical reactions when recycling takes place.

In addition to dealing with recyclables and hazardous materials, warehouse operators have two other opportunities to improve reverse logistics management. First, they should use inventory control methods that reduce waste through proper stock rotation. Second, when stock is outdated, the warehouse manager should find a way to return it for regeneration or to dispose of it safely.

Design failures can be very costly. In one case, a manufacturer established a refurbishing center that used toxic chemicals. Because the materials were not properly discarded, the entire site was contaminated. New owners spent $1.5 million cleaning the site, but the Environmental Protection Agency still would not allow a new warehouse to be built on the land.

A retail example

A third-party reverse logistics specialist, Genco Distribution System, developed a return process for a national chain of stores.

The process starts when a consumer takes a defective purchase back to the retail store. The store ships pallet loads of return goods to a national return center. These pallets are unitized and sealed with a security stretch wrap that will show evidence of pilferage. The store also attaches a bar-coded "license plate" to identify each unitized load. As these loads are received at the return center, they move down a conveyor lane where workers examine each item, scan the license tag, and attach a sort label that provides additional information. Goods are then separated into three types. Type 1 is merchandise that fits in plastic tote bins. Type 2 is boxes up to forty pounds that are too large for the totes. Type 3 is product over forty pounds, which requires a "team lift."

Products then move to a "home slot" or staging area until a full pallet load has been accumulated. Items improperly packaged are repacked at the return center.

Returns are then graded into three categories. Red-tag items are those that should be destroyed. Green-tag items are those that should have been salvaged at the store. Remaining items are those that require further research before disposition.

Once a full pallet of returnable merchandise is accumulated, it is placed in a storage rack to wait for a "vendor cut," which is permission to ship the product back to the resource. Pallets awaiting vendor cut have an identification tag coded to show the age of the product. Returns to the vendors are in full pallets, again sealed with a security stretch wrap. The carrier signs only for the total number of pallets, with the presumption that the sealed pallet has an accurate count. To control accuracy, an audit team rechecks a random sample of the orders that move each day. The inventory in this reverse logistics warehouse turns more than 50 times a year. In addition to a significant amount of pallet rack, gravity flow rack and conveyors are used for certain parts of the sorting process. An on-site representative of the retailer is available to handle communication with the stores.

Should you outsource reverse logistics?

In considering the make-or-buy decision, you will consider questions involving employees, product, transportation, warehousing, and miscellaneous factors.

The first consideration regarding employees is to study how many hours a week are spent on return handling and supporting paperwork. These are converted into a cost for all efforts involved in the returned-goods process.

In considering products, the first appraisal is the value of returned-goods inventory. If that value does not reach an economy of scale, the reverse logistics process may not be worthwhile. Look at the percentage of units and monetary value of returned goods that are destroyed, liquidated, given to charity, remanufactured, reworked, returned to vendor, or returned to stock. What percentage of returned goods are damaged or defective? What percentage are returned because of marketing errors such as overstocks or remainders from promotions? What percentage of returned goods can be returned to stock? What percent involve warranty defects?

Other questions concerning outsourcing will depend on transportation. What is the typical size of a returned-goods shipment? After goods have moved through the center, how will they be shipped back to the original source? How frequently will returned goods be shipped to the reclamation center?

Warehousing and inventory control specifications will be governed by the answers to these questions:

- What is the total volume moving through a reclamation center each week, month, or year?
- How many reclamation centers will be used to process returned goods?
- What portion of each reclamation center will be devoted to processing returned goods?
- How much warehousing time will be devoted to returned goods (for example, total warehouse hours divided by number of units processed)?
- How many inventory turns per year can be expected in each returned-goods category?
- Is there a computerized control over the returned-goods process?

- Are returned goods labeled or bar coded? If so, where does the coding occur?
- What is the cost per unit to process returned goods?
- How many vendors provide returned-goods authorizations, and what are the conditions of those authorizations?

Reverse logistics, like all other logistics decisions, is governed by the proverb "You can only manage what you can measure." Answering those questions helps develop a measurement for the logistics process. At the same time, intangible factors will also influence the outsourcing decision. Those include the amount of experience or expertise available in your organization, the requirements of customers, the internal corporate culture, and the capabilities of external third-party bidders.

The first efforts at describing reverse logistics tended to emphasize environmental concerns, but a growing number of reverse logistics programs are designed to reduce corporate costs. As in any other logistics program, warehousing eventually plays an important role.

Questions that solve problems

As you discuss reverse logistics with your managers, the questions should focus on those changes in your company that could require you to handle increased reverse logistics where they never were handled before. Here are some points for discussion:

Q Do our people have proper training and rehearsal in the handling of product recalls?
C Recalls are not an issue in all businesses, but if they are important with your products, your survival may depend on effective training and rehearsing of the recall process. This practice insures that the recall process will be handled correctly when and if it should happen.

Q How much could our company save each year by developing refillable containers, reusable packages, pallet exchange programs, or other similar initiatives dedicated to conservation of assets?
C The cost study for conservation of assets will probably involve a team effort on the part of logistics and financial people. Depending on the nature of your business, a conservation program may or may not be a worthwhile investment.

Q What is the annual value of material that is destroyed today but could be salvaged or resold?
C Answering this one will also involve a team effort from several departments. The purpose is to determine the potential savings involved in a reverse logistics program dedicated to repackaging, reconditioning, returns to source, resale, or other reclamation processes designed to reduce the cost of accepting returned merchandise.

Q Should we outsource reverse logistics or do it ourselves?
C Attitudes towards outsourcing will have a strong influence on the success of an outsource program. While measuring attitudes, it is also important to measure the comparative costs of doing it yourself as opposed to hiring a specialist.

PART 2

Warehouse Control

Chapter 7

Quality and productivity

Quality and productivity are closely related. There is a growing belief that emphasis on quality will automatically raise productivity. This is based on the knowledge that it is usually more economical to do the job right the first time than to pay the cost of doing it over again.

It is best to define both concepts before describing them. Quality is precisely conforming to requirements. Productivity is the relationship between effort and output.

The growth of quality awareness

Emphasis on quality did not emerge until the last half of the 20th century. During and after World War II, quantity was more important than quality as our factories and warehouses raced to meet the demands of war and postwar consumption. In the last few decades of the century, there was a new emphasis on quality in manufacturing. Statistical quality control and the manufacturing theories of Deming and Juran were enthusiastically adopted by Japanese manufacturers. The rest of the world moved quickly to meet a new competitive challenge.

Yet total quality management (TQM) is still resisted by people who don't understand the need to change, feel threatened by change, or perhaps have a general fear of the unknown. A pervasive quality initiative has been ISO 9000 and its variants. As the ISO programs were adopted by major manufacturers, many demanded that all suppliers, including warehouses, pass the tests for ISO certification.

Quality metrics in the distribution center

The most important measurements of warehouse quality are the perceptions of the customers and others who work with the warehouse. Six quality metrics are based on customer perceptions:
- Customer complaints.
- On-time delivery.
- Timely receiving.
- Prompt and accurate documentation.
- Effective handling of special requests.
- Compliance with loading, marking, and tagging rules.

Perhaps the easiest activity to measure is frequency and nature of errors (see Chapter 12). One company bases its entire quality program on reduction of errors. As errors are identified, the ratio between mistakes and error-free activity is noted, as well as the probable cause of the error. For example, an error may be caused by poorly marked containers. In this case, quality improvement must involve the supplier that shipped product to the warehouse.

Inventory control is part of the quality process. Improper segregation of product on receipt can contribute to difficulties with inventory control. Carrier damage is clearly a quality problem, and a first step is to separate damage caused in the warehouse from damage caused by the carrier or the shipper.

TQM within the warehouse

Some quality measures are primarily internal, but these are just as important as the quality metrics outlined earlier:
- Housekeeping.
- Accidents and injuries.
- Employee turnover.
- Equipment downtime.
- Reduction of warehouse damage.
- Compliance with government regulations.

Housekeeping has always been considered the primary barometer of management effectiveness in the warehouse. Whether your housekeeping is subject to inspection by customers, your boss, the customer's truck driver, or a casual visitor, first impressions are not soon forgotten.

A sometimes overlooked aspect of warehouse housekeeping is the personal appearance of the people who work there. This includes hourly employees as well as supervisors and managers. Some warehouses use uniforms to create a neat personal appearance for every worker. Sloppy personal appearance is a sign of low self-esteem, which is usually accompanied by lack of concern for quality. That is why we react positively to people who have a neat and clean personal appearance.

Measurement of injuries and accident-free days is relatively simple, and it is an effective way to communicate to your people that safety is a high priority in your company.

Unusual turnover of employees is a sign of difficulty in any business, and unfortunately it is a common problem in warehousing. Although some turnover is normal, losing more than 15 percent of your employees annually is a probable indicator of problems with compensation, supervision, quality of work life, or some combination of those.

Equipment downtime is a simple and noncontoversial measurement. All machinery breaks down occasionally, but poor maintenance or employee abuse may cause downtime to reach abnormal levels. Measurement of breakdown time will show whether the warehouse operation is above or below expected norms.

When measuring product damage, consider both the damage caused by warehouse errors and that caused by carriers. It is important to ensure that no one in your warehouse is allowed to falsely blame damage on carriers or shippers when it was actually caused within your warehouse.

At a time when government regulations are an increasing burden on warehouses and many other businesses, your ability to remain free of citations from OSHA (Occupational Safety and Health Administration) and FDA (Federal Drug Administration) is an important measure of quality.

Success factors for TQM

Quality experts have developed specific philosophies and approaches to quality management. They include a number of common principles:

- **Strive for continuous improvement.** Your warehouse operation should work to improve system performance

each year.
- **Understand the full cost of low quality.** When the cost of not doing it right the first time is fully understood, your people will display an increased interest in maintaining and improving warehouse quality.
- **Focus on causes, not symptoms.** Do not try to achieve quality by inspecting after the fact. Instead, change the system that causes the errors.
- **Monitor system performance.** Use statistical tools to monitor the performance of every warehouse control system.*

Quantity vs. quality

Warehousing people, by the nature of their jobs, deal in quantity-based activity. They calculate pounds per man hour and other quantitative measures to show how much they are doing.

It is important to avoid confusing quantity with quality. A highly productive warehouse operation that has high error rates, poor housekeeping, and poor service could deteriorate to a point where the quantity of output is less significant than the poor quality.

In the warehouse, as in manufacturing, quality is the result of eliminating defects. Warehouse product quality is measured by the loyalty of customers and workers.

Increasing warehouse productivity**

Only your imagination will limit the ways you can improve productivity in your warehouse. Of the eight productivity improvements considered here, five are crucial:
- Establish improvement targets.
- Reduce travel distance.
- Reduce the average size of each load handled.
- Develop round-trip opportunities (task interleaving).

---

* Adapted from an article by William C. Copacino, Andersen Consulting, *Warehousing Forum*, Volume 6, Number 10, ©The Ackerman Company, Columbus, Ohio.
** Adapted from Making Warehousing More Efficient, by the author and Bernard J. La Londe of The Ohio State University, *Harvard Business Review*, March-April 1980.

♦ Improve cube utilization.

Establish improvement targets

Just as athletes perform better in competition, warehouse workers are more productive when they are confronted with performance targets. Because warehousing involves random operations, developing work standards is more difficult than assembly-line production. Yet the use of productivity goals based on predetermined engineered standards is feasible in some warehouse operations.*

Although day-to-day workload is often difficult to predict, reasonable estimates can be established. Estimates of product to be moved can be developed from sources such as activity records, current inbound or outbound appointment schedules, recaps of future orders to be filled, marketing forecasts, and supervisory experience. By expressing workload in units to be handled, you can convert to hours to be scheduled. But first you need to establish benchmarks. How long an activity takes can be determined from supervisory estimates, historical records, or highly sophisticated engineered time standards. Benchmarks can be created manually or with packaged software.

Reduce distances traveled

In many order-picking operations, the largest cost element is travel from the beginning of the pick path to the end. Thus, reducing this travel may be the most effective way to improve productivity.

One of the best tools for reducing travel distances is Pareto's law, or the 80/20 rule. Pareto's law, adapted for warehouses, states that 80 percent of the customer demand is satisfied with only 20 percent of the stock-keeping units. If management will identify this 20 percent of items and revise the layout to place them close to the shipping and receiving doors, the effect on distance traveled will be dramatic. Yet in most warehouse operations, goods are stored by product family. In a grocery product operation, for example, you may have all canned goods in one zone, all paper items in another, housewares in another,

---

* Adapted from an article by John A. Bohm, Consulting Services Company, *Warehousing Forum*, Volume 10, Number 11, ©The Ackerman Company, Columbus, Ohio.

and so on. Sometimes storage characteristics of the product require such separation, but often they do not. Where family groupings seem necessary, the Pareto analysis should still be performed within that family. For example, the SKUs of housewares stored in the grocery warehouse can be analyzed to isolate the fast-moving items.

Pareto analysis starts with an ABC report, which is available in virtually every information system. This report takes every SKU in the inventory and lists it by activity volume. It may be expressed in several ways:

- Pounds or tons of product shipped.
- Number of units shipped.
- Number of times each SKUs was selected (hits).

Each option has value to different departments of a business, but the one most valuable in the warehouse is tracking of velocity by hits. In the warehouse, the key effort factor is the number of times an order picker must visit any location to fill an order. Therefore, if you have a choice, prefer that option.

Are your order pick lists designed for warehouse efficiency? A document that lists items in the order they are found in an order pick line allows the stock picker to start at the top of the sheet and the head of the aisle and move down the aisle and down the document at the same time.

Inbound handling offers additional opportunities for reducing distances traveled. In many warehouses, the responsibility for finding an inbound location rests with the lift truck operators. In the absence of instructions, they may put an inbound load into the first available slot. The result is the needless proliferation of stock locations for the same item.

Consider the relationship of storage locations and dock doors. Do the same with respect to warehouse aisles. Unlike our highway network, the warehouse "roadway system" of aisles can be changed without substantial cost. Layout of aisles should be fine-tuned regularly with a goal of reducing travel distance.

Increase unit load size

As you examine your warehouse operation, ask whether the average size of units handled could be increased. The warehouse that supplies convenience stores may open cases of canned products and ship individual cans because the customer cannot justify ordering full-case quantity. At the other extreme, a 40-foot marine container may be unloaded at the harbor and stored and subsequently reshipped as a unit load. Increasing unit load size may require changes in marketing policy. Some grocery product distributors offer their customers an incentive to buy in pallet-load quantities, offering a discount when the customer orders an exact pallet load. Similar discounts may be offered as an incentive to buy a full case rather than a partial case, or a pallet tier or layer rather than an odd number of cases.

Round trips

In highway transportation, truck operators refer to a backhaul. Every trucker is sensitive to the economies of carrying a payload in both directions. Yet in the warehouse, most lift trucks travel empty half the time. A lift truck operator takes a loaded pallet from the receiving dock to storage and returns to the receiving dock without a payload. If he could haul a loaded pallet in both directions, he would achieve a significant operational savings.

Unfortunately, implementing this idea is far more difficult than talking about it. The implementation is a process called task interleaving, and some warehouse management systems promise to show the way to do this. It is rare to find computer-directed task interleaving functioning in a warehouse operation. However, the process may also be achieved through planning by supervisors rather than relying on a computer system. That planning must be accompanied by radio communication to instruct the lift truck operator to retrieve the return load. Also, shipping and receiving docks will require larger staging areas to accumulate a bank of work needed to support round-trip movements.

Improve cube utilization

The cheapest space in any warehouse is that closest to the ceiling. If you built a warehouse with a 22-foot clear height, you might develop a cost figure of $20 per square foot, or 91 cents per cubic foot ($20 divided by 22). However, if you raise the clearance from 22 feet to 24 feet, the total cost of the building increases only slightly, to about $20.30 per square foot. This means that the cost per cubic foot drops from 91 cents to 85 cents.

As cube utilization improves, travel distance in the building is reduced. Yet there is always a trade-off in using overhead space. Elevating the product takes time. Storage plans are influenced by speed of turnover. It is important not to overemphasize space utilization. Years ago, a warehouse manager surveyed an overcrowded building and observed: "One thing about aisles is they cost a little less each year. Aisles don't bargain for pay increases or increased benefits. If we save a few aisles and add many people, we'll never be ahead of the game."

Although improving cube utilization may seem to be a cheap way to get more product into your building, the key to improving overall warehouse productivity is to find the best compromise between storage utilization and handling efficiency.

> The next three areas may be less important, but they will improve warehouse productivity.

Free labor bottlenecks

Because bottlenecks and managers are always at the top, managers have the prime responsibility for correcting labor bottlenecks.

A typical bottleneck might occur in unloading a floor-loaded trailer. Two laborers may be assigned to the trailer to palletize cases for a lift truck driver, who removes loaded pallets. When laborers work faster than the operator, they wait until he returns to remove a load. Changing the crew size will clear the bottleneck. One approach is the one-man, one-machine technique, which gives each worker a lift truck so that no worker is waiting for someone else. Whenever you tour a warehouse operation, look for workers who are waiting and find out what is causing the bottleneck.

Reduce item handling

In a typical warehouse, products are handled and rehandled more often than necessary. Each movement of product is an opportunity to damage it. Each lifting further fatigues the package.

As you review your warehouse operation, ask why it is necessary to stage each inbound load on the dock before moving to a storage bay. Ask the same thing about staging of outbound loads. In reducing the number of item handlings, pay particular attention to temporary storage locations and explore ways to eliminate them.

Improve the container

From the warehouse operator's point of view, the perfect package is made of cast iron and can be stacked fifty feet high with no artificial support. Warehouses built in the last half of the 20th century usually have ceiling heights that exceed the free-stacking capabilities of the products stored in them. Packaging engineers are asked to design containers that are light and cheap — just strong enough to get the item to the consumer. There is an obvious trade-off. If more money is spent on packaging, stacking capabilities in the warehouse are improved and the product is less likely to be damaged in storage and distribution. If the container cannot be improved, there are artificial warehousing "packages" such as self-stacking pallets and pallet rack.

A different way to look at productivity

In the North American culture, productivity may be confused with the Puritan work ethic. This legacy is part of the Anglo-Saxon culture. The patron saint of the Puritan ethic was Benjamin Franklin, whose almanac was one of the most popular books of his day. It borrowed heavily from the Puritan culture of New England. Whether "early to bed and early to rise" was actually invented by Franklin is debated, but no one argues the lasting popularity of this and other proverbs.

But the Puritan work ethic has its pitfalls, and one is a tendency to confuse activity with accomplishment. The activity trap catches those who become exceedingly busy without increasing their productivity. In our pursuit of productivity, we may overlook the people who work closest to us. This is a sort of class chauvinism — people like us are OK, but those other people must be watched.

Often the most important reason to measure productivity in a warehouse is to ensure that you have properly charged for services rendered. If you learn the actual time taken to do each job and then develop a proper charge for the task, you have used productivity measurement in a useful way for your company If you discover that the fee developed is not competitive, then — and only then — you should conclude that warehouse productivity is too low. When your people understand that the prime reason for measuring productivity is to verify that fees for warehouse services are high enough to earn a profit, they will cooperate with management in maintaining the measurements.

One third-party warehouse developed a cost committee made up of supervisors and hourly workers. When a prospective customer requested a price quotation, the specifications in the RFP were referred to the cost committee. The committee was asked to estimate the number of hours needed to handle each task. Those estimates became the basis of a rate proposal.

Productivity standards allow us to communicate our expectations. A supervisor who knows how long it will take to complete a task can give a worker a stack of orders and say, "I'll see you here at four o'clock," knowing that both he and the worker understand that the time estimate is reasonable. Of course there will be good days when the worker finishes early, and bad days when the task takes longer than estimated. But on average, the performance time will nearly equal the estimated time.

As you look at productivity, keep your eye on the bottom line. The goal of any warehouse is to produce steady profits with a stable workforce. That result is based on customers who are happy with both the product and the warehouse service that supports it.

Questions that solve problems

As you audit quality and productivity performance at your warehouse, these questions should be asked of your warehouse manager.

Q What measurements do we use today to indicate the quality of customer service in our warehouse?
C Compare your manager's answers to the quality metrics shown here. If they are not measuring anything, you have a significant opportunity to improve quality awareness.

Q What measures to we have for quality items as reviewed in the bullet points on page 52?
C If none of those factors are measured either, the opportunity is even more significant.

Q What productivity measures are in place today?
C Compare the productivity measures given by your managers with the eight productivity improvements on pages 54 to 60 of this chapter.

Q What steps have we taken to increase warehouse productivity during the past year?
C This chapter describes eight ways to improve warehouse productivity. Have your people used any of them? Have they used others that you never thought of? Answers to this question will indicate both creativity and competency of warehouse managers.

Q If our productivity is better (or worse) today than it was last year, why did this happen?
C The answer to this question will tell a lot about your management's attitude toward continuous improvement.

Chapter 8

Third-party or do-it-yourself?

Before you consider starting up or re-engineering any warehouse operation, consider whether you should run that warehouse with your own people or hire a third party to manage it for you.

Before considering this question, it is essential to define some terms. Within the third-party warehousing industry there are several subdivisions. Public warehouses offer outsourced services on a thirty-day standard contract, which offers great flexibility for users. A growing portion of warehouse outsourcing is contract warehouse service, which includes an agreement of somewhat longer term. Many of the companies offering these services are specialists. Functional specialists include those handling temperature-controlled storage, fulfillment, bulk warehousing, or hazardous materials. Others may be industry specialists with extensive experience in handling products or serving companies similar to yours. Some providers operate in just one city; others have multicity or even multinational operations. Some are small, family-managed enterprises; others are large corporations traded on the stock exchange.

Outsourcing warehousing is a make-or-buy decision, driven by the same factors as similar decisions in manufacturing or marketing. In 1997, a University of Tennessee study team ran a survey to find out why people use third-party logistics providers. The most important factors were the following:
- Reducing costs.
- Enhancing customer service.
- Globalization.

Those who would neither use nor consider a third-party provider stated these reasons:

- Concern that control would be lost.
- Belief that a third-party would increase costs.
- Belief that we have more expertise than they do.

Older research indicates that the outsourcing decision is often driven by these factors:

- Philosophy of management.
- Cost and availability of capital.
- Labor cost and availability.
- Need for flexibility.

Outsourcing logistics services*

Although outsourcing of logistics services has gained a renewed emphasis in recent years, it is not a new concept. Throughout the 1950s and '60s, outsourcing of transportation and warehousing was common. However, the relationships were transactional and short-term in nature. Longer-term contracts were the exception rather than the rule. During the 1970s, manufacturers placed heavy emphasis on cost reductions and improved productivity. In the 1980s, the services offered by outside companies expanded rapidly. Value-added services included packaging, blending, systems support, and inventory management. In addition, common carriers were newly freed from federal regulation and able to enter into innovative long-term relationships with customers. True logistics partnerships began to surface.

The 1980s also saw a phenomenal number of mergers and acquisitions, particularly in the food industry. The logistical result of these combinations was a collection of more warehouses than any one company ever wanted. At Quaker Oats the number of warehouses increased from 13 to more than 200 in three years, and others had similar experiences. A consolidation was necessary, and what better time to re-analyze the system and put distribution centers where they really ought to be?

---

* Adapted from an article by Clifford F. Lynch, C. F. Lynch & Associates, *Warehousing Forum*, Volume 10, Number 1, ©The Ackerman Company, Columbus, Ohio.

The reasons for outsourcing vary by industry, but developments in the retailing and grocery industries provide good examples.

Just-in-time techniques have been used for many years, but they came late to the grocery industry with a program called *efficient consumer response* (ECR). The ECR technique results in smaller and more frequent shipments. Rather than handle them from their own facilities, grocery manufacturers turned to contract logistics companies that could combine many small shipments into truckloads, thus reducing freight and handling costs.

Outsourcing is also stimulated by the changing retail landscape for consumer goods. Buying one of anything is almost impossible in a club or box store. Manufacturers are asked to put twelve or twenty-four packages in a case, seal it, palletize it, and move it to the shipping area. The difficulty arises when Wal-Mart wants three tubes of toothpaste shrink-wrapped together, Kmart wants two tubes, and Target wants a toothbrush thrown in. Much of this labor-intensive customization is contracted to third-parties.

The subtle difference here is that no longer are we simply *managing* inventories, we are changing them. These changes can be made more economically by a nimble supplier free of the superstructure and overhead of the large manufacturer.

Core competency and outsourcing

In the last half of the 20th century, the percentage of warehousing performed by third-parties increased significantly. In fact, outsourcing of all kinds became a corporate trend at the end of the century. Peter Drucker and other corporate gurus started talking about outsourcing decades ago, but the momentum did not really begin to build until the 1990s. Corporate strategists convinced managers that profit and growth can be increased by concentrating on the "core competency" and outsourcing those tasks that a subcontractor might do more efficiently.

In warehousing, outsourcing the service allows capital to be released from investments in real estate or material-handling equipment. It also eliminates the exposure of employees who might be more attracted to unions than other workers in the corporation. As a growing number of companies begin handling overseas operations, it becomes attractive to find a third-party to handle the difficult job of warehousing in a distant land. In a time when labor is in short supply, it becomes more desirable to hire a specialist who is skilled at attracting, training, and motivating warehouse workers.

Loss of control is a frequently expressed fear. However, intelligent use of outsourced warehousing should actually improve management control. Today's warehouse management systems may provide better knowledge of warehouse activity with a third-party than you can achieve with the systems that exist today in your own organization.

Management philosophy is frequently the predominant factor in a make-or-buy decision. If your managers believe that their advancement is based on growth in the number of employees or assets under their control, it is natural for those managers to resist outsourcing of warehousing. In contrast, if your company rewards managers for reducing personnel and assets under their control, downsizing through the outsourcing of warehousing is likely to be a popular decision.

Financial strategy can also have a large influence on the make-or-buy question. When a corporation concentrates on improving its return on assets, managers should be rewarded for reducing inventories and minimizing the quantity of fixed assets. One way to do that is to eliminate ownership of warehouse real estate. By using a third-party, you can gain the use of such real estate without having to capitalize a lease to comply with public accounting standards.

At times third-party warehousing can be a vehicle to obtain inventory financing. In Latin America, some third-party warehousing companies are branches of banks. They routinely offer negotiable warehouse receipts and financing of inventory. There is some indication that this type of financing, sometimes called field warehousing, will be more common as global logistics operations increase.

For some users of third-party warehousing, the dominant decision factor is a need for flexibility. If you knew that you would always need to store 10,000 pallets and would always have enough activity to keep 12 workers busy, a private warehouse operation might be very economical. The problem is that few users have such stable requirements, and that instability will sometimes make the use of a third-party provider attractive.

The preparatory steps*

Before you reach a final decision on outsourcing, take a look inside your operation to be sure that your company's logistics goals are defined and understood. For example, is your company trying to be the service leader or a price leader? If your growth has been through the ability to charge the lowest cost, you need a different kind of warehouse supplier than if your goal is to provide the highest level of customer service.

Will you develop new products in the future that are different from the present line, and how will new products affect volume, seasonality, or warehousing requirements? Will the distribution channels be the same as they are today, or will you be opening new channels in the foreseeable future? For example, if you sell through retailers today, is there a chance that you will be selling through Internet commerce tomorrow?

The type of third-party warehouse you select will depend on the answers to questions raised above. Certain warehouse providers are specialists in serving particular distribution channels, and others have made their mark because of superior service or rock-bottom costs. Knowing your own objectives will prevent you from wasting time with a potential supplier that does not fit your pattern.

How to select a third-party operator**

A first step is to gather the information needed to develop a request for proposal (RFP). If the details contained in that RFP are not correct, the prices quoted cannot be accurate. This means that either the successful bidder will lose money performing the job and demand a rate adjustment or you will pay more than you should to get the job done. Here are some questions that must be answered as the RFP is developed:

- ♦ What are weights and cubes of each item?
- ♦ What are risks of spoilage, breakage, or theft?

---

* Adapted from an article by Mark E. Richards, Associated Warehouses, *Warehousing Forum*, Volume 7, Number 3, ©The Ackerman Company, Columbus, Ohio.
** Adapted from an article by Thomas L. Freese, Freese & Associates, *Warehousing Forum*, Volume 11, Number 6, ©The Ackerman Company, Columbus, Ohio.

- What is the safe stacking height?
- How is a product received?
- What are anticipated volumes for shipping and receiving?
- What are our seasonal peaks and valleys?
- How will orders be transmitted to the warehouse?
- How many lines per average order?
- How many units per line?
- What is the average order size?
- What percentage is full truckload?
- Who will manage the transportation function?
- Who pays the freight bills?
- What specialized services will be needed, such as repackaging, labeling, wrapping, counting, or documentation?

Figure 8-1 provides an overview of the selection process.

Once the data has been developed and an accurate RFP has been prepared, you are now ready to assemble a list of potential suppliers. A number of directories and trade associations list such suppliers. In many cases these sources are incomplete. Directories may list only those who pay for listing, and trade associations will naturally list only their own members. Some buyers seek the assistance of people familiar with the third-party marketplace; they could be people within your company or other pro-

Figure 8-1

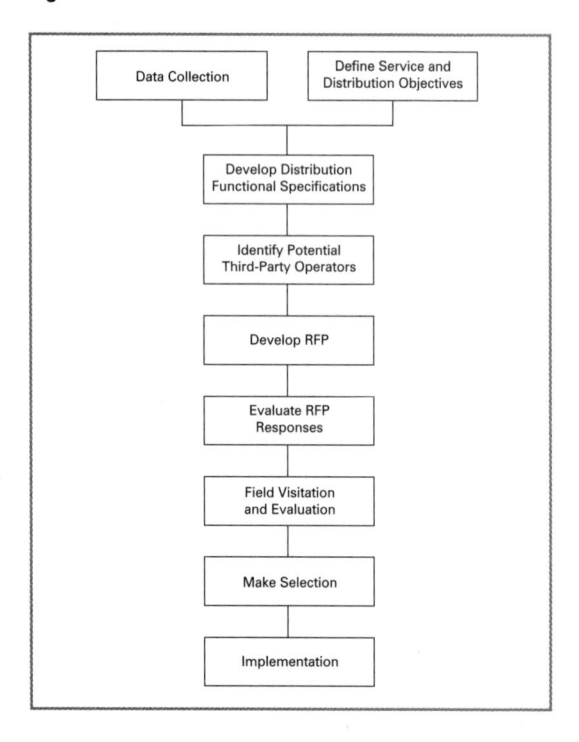

```
    Data Collection          Define Service and
                             Distribution Objectives
              │                     │
              └──────────┬──────────┘
                         ▼
              Develop Distribution
              Functional Specifications
                         │
                         ▼
              Identify Potential
              Third-Party Operators
                         │
                         ▼
                  Develop RFP
                         │
                         ▼
                 Evaluate RFP
                  Responses
                         │
                         ▼
                Field Visitation
                 and Evaluation
                         │
                         ▼
                 Make Selection
                         │
                         ▼
                 Implementation
```

fessionals you are involved with through other associations. Some may engage a logistics consultant who has expertise in this area.

Fourteen criteria to consider

Here is a list of 14 criteria that should be considered in evaluating potential suppliers.

1. Multiple warehouse facilities nationwide

If national coverage is of importance for your organization, ideally a third-party warehouse operator would have strong national coverage with regional locations available corresponding with your organization's markets. Such a third-party would have a strong network of capabilities to service all points within 24-, 48-, and 72-hour responses.

Rating and Description
1. Strong national coverage with regional locations.
2. Good national coverage with some gaps.
3. Limited national coverage.
4. Does not provide national coverage.
5. Does not currently have multiple facilities.

2. Inventory management and control

In providing a complete offering it is often necessary to manage inventories. In order to do so the third-party should possess inventory management and control capabilities to include stock rotation, re-order management, procurement, and forecasting capabilities.

Rating and Description
1. State-of-the-art inventory management systems in place.
2. Fundamental inventory management applications in place.
3. Basic structure exists.
4. Minimal capabilities.
5. Inadequate inventory management.

3. Order acceptance and processing

The ideal third-party operator has a state-of-the-art order acceptance and processing or "front end" system in place.

Rating and Description
1. A state-of-the-art order acceptance system with satisfied reference users.

2. An order acceptance system operating with some improvement opportunities.
3. A partial order acceptance and processing system.
4. Currently examining purchase and/or start-up of an order acceptance system.
5. No order acceptance system in place.

4. Pick-and-pack operations

Your organization may require a pick-and-pack fulfillment service.
Rating and Description
1. State-of-the-art.
2. Individual pick-pack operations currently in operation.
3. Partial pick, pick-pack operations.
4. Experience with pick-pack/currently none in operation.
5. No pick-pack operations exist.

5. Order fulfilment

In addition to each pick or pick-pack operations the existence of current capabilities in individual order fulfillment are crucial to the success of such a third-party. Such individual order fulfillment would include the operations of order capture, processing, picking, packing, shipping, tracking, and order acknowledgment activities.

Rating and Description
1. State-of-the-art capabilities are in place and operating to handle individual order fulfillment to include systems, order capture, acknowledgment, manifest tracking, etc.
2. Existing order fulfillment activities are in place and operating for a number of potential reference accounts.
3. Management is experienced in the order fulfillment activities and, although not currently operating order fulfillment activities in all its regional locations, has the management depth to do so.
4. Limited order fulfillment capabilities and/or management experience.
5. No existing order fulfillment capabilities and/or management experience.

6. Assembly/packaging/value-added activities

In addition to the normal four steps of order capture, inventory management, fulfillment, and transportation generally associated with the outsourcing of logistics, there is a growing need for value added services to be provided at the point of distribution. These activities would include such things as packaging, kitting, sortation, burn-in, testing, repair, modifications and bench work activities.

Rating and Description
1. Existing operations are underway to provide numerous value added activities for a number of different customers to include many of the above noted value added services.
2. Value added activities are being performed in a number of locations for a number of different customers.
3. Limited value added activities currently are in place.
4. Management understands and is capable of providing value added activities although none are currently being conducted.
5. No evidence exists of value added activities and/or management capabilities to set up such activities.

7. Credit card verification

As a subset of the order capture activities your organization may require credit card verification. If your organization requires full fulfillment activities such credit card verification may be essential.

Rating and Description
1. Current state-of-the-art computer tie-in capabilities exist as a part of the order acceptance and processing systems to handle all credit card verifications.
2. A credit card verification system exists and is presently operating.
3. Limited credit card verification is available through a manual or semi-automated process.
4. Credit card verifications could be accommodated through individual contact with credit card companies to verify credit.
5. No credit card verification exists, nor is the third-party capable of accommodating same.

8. Invoicing, credit, and collection

In addition to credit card verification, it is often necessary with sales on a business to business basis to have the capability of a credit and collection activity to include invoicing of individual shipments.

Rating and Description
1. A state-of-the-art system exists as part of the order acceptance and processing system to handle credit and collection activities, credit verifications, credit limits, and conduct invoicing on individual shipments.
2. Systems capability exists to conduct credit and collection activities and individual shipment invoicing.
3. The basic elements exist to provide a system that will handle credit and collection activities and individual shipment invoicing.
4. No existing systems are in place to conduct credit and collection activities and invoicing, but management is confident of their capabilities to handle same.
5. No existing systems exist for credit and collection and invoicing, nor has the third-party indicated any willingness or desire to enter into this area.

9. Pre-sort capabilities

In order to best accommodate your organization's transportation and delivery requirements a presorting activity may be necessary for a third-party operator to prepare shipments to be passed off with the maximum discounts available.

Rating and Description
1. A full presort capability exists to accommodate your organization's parcels and afford potential customers the lowest possible discount rates for such presorting.
2. Limited presort capabilities presently exist.
3. Presort capabilities are understood and could be accommodated.
4. The third-party operator is willing to accommodate presorting of parcels.
5. No existing presorting is in place, nor is there any willingness on the part of the third-party to institute same.

10. Returns handling

As a practical matter if your business requires returns handling the third-party must have such capabilities. Capabilities to accommodate the returns from potential customers, catalog, business to business and other forms of distribution is often extremely important for a third-party operation to be successful.

Rating and Description
1. Existing systems are in place to accommodate returns handling and processing of partial shipment and the recoup and recovery of inventories.
2. Limited systems are currently in place to handle returns of parcels and the recoup and recovery of inventories.
3. Manual returns handling capabilities exist.
4. Minimal experience exists with return handling.
5. No returns handling capability exists.

11. Manifesting

In order to accommodate many organizations, it is necessary to have an automated manifest system in place with capabilities to confirm individual order shipment and tracing.

Rating and Description
1. State-of-the-art shipment manifest systems are in place and are an integral part of an order entry/processing system.
2. Individual shipment manifest systems are in place and currently being utilized.
3. Individual manifest shipment capabilities exist.
4. The third-party is examining or studying the placement of individual shipment manifest systems.
5. No manifest systems exist nor are they under study.

12. Operational management structure

In order for a third-party operator to provide an offer of logistics capabilities, it is necessary that they have the management depth and operational structure to provide rapid deployment and consistency of operational practices across operations.

Rating and Description
1. Has in place an operational management structure that provides uniform operations on a nationwide basis and supports

individual roll outs through centralized staff support activities with a strong field management organization.
2. Has strong central staff support to accommodate individual field roll outs.
3. Has operational organization with strong operational experience in fulfillment activities that could support operational needs.
4. Has strong operational management experience.
5. Questionable operational, organizational capabilities.

13. Organizational strategic direction

In order for a partnership between your organization and a potential third-party operator to be successful, both parties must have as a part of their strategic mission the specific objective of servicing the type of business your organization handles. Many third-party logistics organizations are strategically aligned to provide full truck load or full pallet shipments to retail or wholesale activities and/or support of small parcel fulfillment activities. If your organization's type of business is not a part of their strategic direction such a fit may not exist.

Rating and Description
1. Third-party operator strategically seeks out your type of activities and shipments.
2. Your type of activities and shipments are an integral part of the strategic plans of a third-party operator.
3. Your type of activities, while not the central strategic objective of the third-party operator, are a part of their overall strategic growth plan.
4. Your type of activities and shipments are a minor portion of the strategic plan of the third-party operator.
5. Your type of activities and small parcel shipments are not a part of the strategic direction of a third-party operator.

14. Financial stability

No user of third-party services wants a provider who is financially unstable. You need to ensure that the provider will be a trustworthy custodian of your inventory and that there will be a reasonable probability of continuity in the business. Furthermore, your supplier's financial failure could also tarnish your market image.

Rating and Description
1. Clear financial stability has been well demonstrated and would represent no concern in such a third-party.
2. Strong financial position, although while not yet clearly demonstrated, there is no reason to believe that such financial strength does not exist.
3. Good financial stability is a concern due to length of time in business, recent acquisitions, heavy debt load and/or other extenuating circumstances.
4. Uncertain financial stability and/or questionable ability to support such a partnership.
5. Unacceptable level of financial risk.

Evaluation

Once you have received the responses from the RFP, an initial evaluation can be made using the criteria listed in Figure 8-2.

Ultimately, the final decision in selecting a supplier should be based on a level of comfort with that company and its management. That comfort level is usually achieved by visiting the companies that are finalists in the contest and getting acquainted with senior management as well as the operating people. Unless you are perfectly comfortable with the level of commitment displayed by that potential supplier, it is wise to keep looking.

The contract

For any relationship beyond the traditional thirty-day public-warehouse agreement, a formal contract is customary. Eventually, the individuals who made the agreement move on through promotion, transfer, or retirement, and those who follow may have a completely different set of expectations than the agreement intended. A typical warehouse agreement might address these points:
- Scope of work.
- Responsibilities.
- Extra services.
- Damages.
- Risk management.
- Remedies.
- Agreement modification.

Figure 8-2

Evaluation criteria	Third-parties being considered		
	A	B	C
Service and Customer Satisfaction	1	1	1
Experience with Similar Business	1	2	1
Flexibility and Future Opportunities	2	3	3
Total Operating Costs	1	3	2
Ability to Improve Service to Distributors	3	2	4
Location, Physical Facilities, and Operating Procedures	2	2	3

- Compensation.
- Rate adjustments.
- Service expectations.
- Termination.

Of all those points, the most important is the last. Every agreement must end sometime, and an orderly termination process must be formulated. The agreement should be flexible enough to accommodate normal changes in prices and procedures.

The pricing challenge*

The RFP sets the parameters from which the price is prepared. Obviously, if the RFP is wrong, the bid will be wrong as well. There are

---

* Adapted from an article by A. Sam Krause, *Warehousing Forum*, Volume 11, Number 1, ©The Ackerman Company, Columbus, Ohio.

six ways in which the pricing process can go wrong:

1. Crucial information about manufacturing and marketing forecasts was not included.
2. The operation is a start-up with no history of start-up costs.
3. The outsourcing of warehousing is being handled in secret.
4. The purchasing department designed an RFP with the emphasis on simplicity.
5. The RFP contains growth forecasts that are not realistic.
6. Start-up problems were not considered.

There are answers for each of the six pricing problems:

1. When the buyer does not have enough information to create an accurate profile, the fairest way to start the operation is establish pricing on a trial basis. The warehouse operator stipulates certain assumptions and provides temporary prices based on these assumptions. Buyer and seller agree that they will adjust the prices as they adjust the assumptions. The contract provides for review and adjustment each ninety days for at least the first year. Adjustments can go either way, with prices raised or lowered depending on various conditions.

2. When the operation is a start-up, the approach just described is the fairest way to develop pricing. However, buyer and seller should agree to handle the extra costs involved in the start-up, possibly on a time-and-material basis or with a flat fee.

3. When the move must be done in secret, the buyer should reduce the risk through very careful choice of suppliers. By considering only third-parties that have extensive background with the same commodity, the buyer narrows the risk of pricing or service problems.

4. When the purchasing department demands simplicity, the vendor should provide an extensive summary of assumptions on which the prices were developed. Those are followed with this statement: *The assumptions listed above were the basis for calculating the prices shown in this proposal. Should these assumptions prove to be inaccurate, the above prices are subject to adjustment, which will be related to the degree of change in warehousing specifications.* A quote prepared in this manner satisfies the purchasing department's desire for simplicity and still protects the warehouse operator from the possibility that the RFP is not accurate.

5. When the RFP is based on growth projections, the operator should develop multilevel rates. One price is developed for start-up levels, with stipulated discounts as volumes move higher. Sometimes

Figure 8-3

Quarterly account review

Parameters	Contract	January	February	March	Qtr. average	Variance
No. SKUs						
Avg. inventory						
Inv. turn						
Stack height						
INBOUND PER RECEIPT						
# SKUs						
# pallets						
# cases						
% pallet						
% slipsheet						
% floorload						
% clamp						
OUTBOUND TRANSACTIONS						
% TL						
% LTL						
% UPS/RPS						
ORDER PARAMETERS						
% pallet pic						
% case pic						
% piece pic						
OUTBOUND PARAMETERS						
% palletized						
% slipsheet						
% strap wrap						
% floor load						
% clamp						
Inv. reqmts.						
Cycle cnt. req.						
Order/ship cycle hours						
SYSTEM REQUIREMENTS						
EDI						
ASNs						

pricing is adjusted based on the level of inventory turns, with a predetermined adjustment when turns are slower or faster than projected.

6. Start-up costs are a significant factor in every new warehouse operation. When such costs are not isolated, the operator will suffer a financial loss in the start-up and then seek to recover that loss with an unreasonably high rate adjustment. Since start-up costs are a one-time expense, they should be quoted as a separate and non-repetitive fee.

Figure 8-3 provides the format for the quarterly account review described above. The pricing challenge exists in every new warehouse relationship. When it is not properly met, the results can be ugly for both buyer and seller. When both make plans to deal with change and adjust pricing appropriately, the challenge of maintaining an enduring partnership can be met.

Questions that solve problems

The questions below assume that the reader is an actual or potential *user* rather than an operator of third-party facilities. If you are a third-party operator, you should also study these questions because they are the ones your customer is likely to ask.

Q Do you see any reason why we should run the warehouse ourselves?
C Carefully analyze the answers — if they are illogical or emotional, the respondent may be reacting from a desire to maintain or expand a personal empire.

Q What good reasons are there why a third-party operator cannot handle this job?
C Again, the nature of the answer will reveal whether the opinion is fact-based or emotional.

Q What term is needed for the contract to govern this operation?
C Answering this forces your people to look at the risks involved in a long- or short-term agreement.

Q What services do we need that we could not get from a third-party logistics organization?
C Those who do not understand outsourcing may describe services that are available but not fully understood.

Q Did we select the finalists because of price or quality?
C Be sure you get details to support the answer.

Q Are we absolutely certain that we accurately described the operation when we wrote the RFP?
C Ask this only after you have initiated a review of the RFP and formed your own opinion about its accuracy and completeness.

Q What steps did we take to check on the quality of the potential supplier?
C This is a due-diligence question, and the quality of the answer must be carefully measured.

Q After a third-party operation is started, what steps will we take to review quality and costs with the warehouse supplier?
C Since the outsourcing process is a continuous effort, it is essential to understand the review process, which is designed to monitor both quality and cost.

Chapter 9

Planning and scheduling*

A plan is a detailed scheme worked out beforehand to accomplish a project. A plan becomes a schedule when certainty is such that specific times can be added. Plans may be divided into three categories: strategic, managerial, and operational.

Strategic or long-range plans require the setting of overall objectives, allocation of research to fulfill those objectives, and policymaking. Strategic planning requires the answering of questions such as, *What part will warehousing play in the future of our company?* Strategic plans are usually restricted to establishing guidelines rather than making everyday decisions.

Managerial planning includes procedures to achieve the organization's strategic objectives. In warehousing, managerial plans often involve coordination with other divisions. Inadequate managerial planning could result in bickering or conflicts between departments.

Operational planning includes the everyday management of warehousing tasks, and this is the level where plans are most likely to become schedules. Operational plans might include disaster and emergency plans, product recall procedures, equipment maintenance programs, training schedules, and vacation schedules.

Corporate strategy and warehousing

Healthy companies plan to grow, and the question of how to grow is crucial to any corporate strategy. Warehousing organizations deal

---

* Adapted from an article by Leon "Bud" Cohan, management consultant, Gahanna, Ohio.

with four primary assets: people, real estate, equipment, and transportation services. The way those assets are managed is likely to be influenced by corporate strategy. Your corporate mission statement should provide some strategic indications. Here are some typical ones:
- ◆ We aim to be the largest company in our industry.
- ◆ Our objective is to have the highest quality rather than the greatest size.
- ◆ We plan to be the lowest-cost provider in our industry.

If your company plans to be the largest in its industry, your warehousing operation should be geared toward constant expansion. If your company plans to emphasize quality, you should look for ways to both measure and improve the quality of work done in warehouses. When you aim to be the low-cost provider, your prime emphasis in warehousing is cost reduction. In each case, the mission and objectives of your company will influence the way warehousing is done.

A good example is the make-or-buy decision described in Chapter 8. The questions of whether and how to outsource should be strongly influenced by your company's strategy.

Data drives decisions in warehousing*

How does product flow from demand determination to procurement to manufacturing and eventually to warehousing and shipping?

Making sense of data within a warehousing function is a process. Use the Deming *plan, do, check, act* process to make a complex story understandable. Figure 9-1 illustrates how the Deming process might work in a warehouse (see Chapter 17 for more about Deming). There is a fine line between "paralysis by analysis" and decision making by intuition without the data. Data gathering should focus on the customer and the warehousing process. What is the customer doing now, and what will it take to delight that customer tomorrow? The warehousing process includes any activity involving equipment, space, systems, handling methods, volumes, and quality.

---

* Adapted from an article by John A. Tetz, *Warehousing Forum*, Volume 11, Number 11, ©The Ackerman Company, Columbus, Ohio.

Figure 9-1

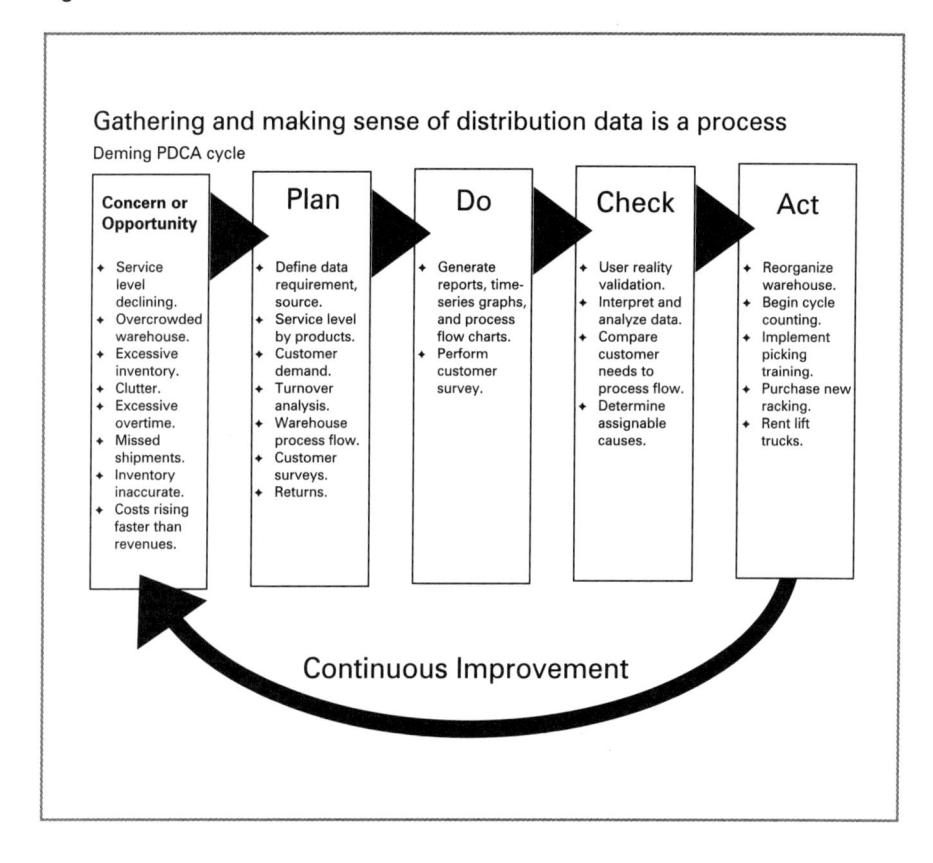

Gathering and making sense of distribution data is a process
Deming PDCA cycle

Concern or Opportunity
- Service level declining.
- Overcrowded warehouse.
- Excessive inventory.
- Clutter.
- Excessive overtime.
- Missed shipments.
- Inventory inaccurate.
- Costs rising faster than revenues.

Plan
- Define data requirement, source.
- Service level by products.
- Customer demand.
- Turnover analysis.
- Warehouse process flow.
- Customer surveys.
- Returns.

Do
- Generate reports, time-series graphs, and process flow charts.
- Perform customer survey.

Check
- User reality validation.
- Interpret and analyze data.
- Compare customer needs to process flow.
- Determine assignable causes.

Act
- Reorganize warehouse.
- Begin cycle counting.
- Implement picking training.
- Purchase new racking.
- Rent lift trucks.

Continuous Improvement

Let's examine three analytical tools that are readily applied to warehousing:

- **Pareto analysis**: The Pareto, or ABC, analysis (see Figure 9-2) sorts all SKUs shipped in descending order. This analysis can be used to refine a storage layout or allocate labor.
- **Turnover analysis**: This analysis (shown in Figure 9-3) indicates the number of days of supply on hand for each SKU, calculated at the current rate of usage. Inventory balances are ranked by expected usage and sorted in descending order of days of supply. Turnover analysis will identify out-of-stock, low stock, and excess inventory of any SKUs and thus highlight inventory

Figure 9-2

Example of ABC distribution analysis
Abbreviated format

SKU or Item #	Order of demand/ usage (declining)	Line items	Demand $	Picks	Weight shipped	Cube shipped	Inventory
			\multicolumn{4}{c	}{CUMULATIVE PERCENTAGES}	
2004	58289	1	20	10	56	53	21
6041	10692	6	65	33	86	81	48
4004	4981	13	90	55	94	93	62
5321	2861	37	92	88	96	99	84
4031	1824	55	94	96	97	99	85
4384	1008	60	96	98	99	99	86
5636	775	70	98	99	99	99	87
5721	342	85	100	100	100	100	88
7051	1	91	100	100	100	100	93
8017	0	100	100	100	100	100	100

management problems.
- **Demand analysis**: Demand analysis (shown in Figure 9-4) shows the SKUs shipped by day, weight, cube, cartons, pallets, or product line. Finding ways to smooth daily demand can result in significant savings. Demand analysis helps you to understand what is really triggering activity.

Perhaps the most important step in a data-driven improvement process is reality checking. Does a warehouse walk-through confirm that there are really excess inventories? Does perceived activity by warehouse supervisors agree with reported pick frequency? Often cursory comparisons will identify errors.

Figure 9-3

Distribution analysis

Abbreviated form: 10 of 1300 items

Item code	Cumulative % items	Annual $ sales/usage descending	Cumulative % usage	Inventory units	Inventory $ value	Cumulative % inventory
2004	(Note 1) 1	58,289	19.9	0	0	9.8
6041	10	10,692	65.0	0	0	44.4
4004	(Note 2) 20	4,981	80.8	19	830	55.6
5321	30	2,861	88.8	0	0	65.6
4013	40	1,824	93.7	45	1,026	72.5
4348	50	1,008	96.6	13	222	77.8
5632	56	775	97.7	8	304	79.3
5721	70	342	100.0	46	2,097	87.3
7051	91	1	100.0	12	3	95.3
8017	100	0	100.0	102	2,703	100.0
	TOTALS	6,057,922	1		1,262,300	

Average turnover rate: 4.8 times.

Note 1: Item #13 of 1300
Note 2: Item #260 of 1300

Short-interval scheduling*

The concept of short-interval scheduling is simple: identify the work to be done within short time periods and assign resources. When workload changes, change the assignments. Implementation, however, is more complex.

Effectively assigning labor to a changing warehouse workload requires a discipline both flexible and highly responsive. This involves

---

* Adapted from an article by John A. Bohm, Consulting Services Company, *Warehousing Forum*, Volume 10, Number 11, ©The Ackerman Company, Columbus, Ohio.

Figure 9-4

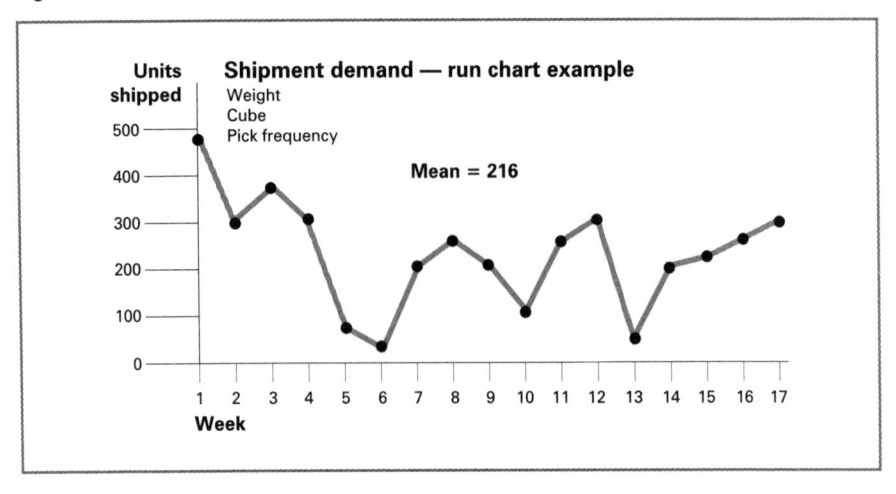

Shipment demand — run chart example

Units shipped: Weight, Cube, Pick frequency

Mean = 216

(Chart showing units shipped by week 1–17)

four tasks:

- Documenting warehouse workload in measurable units.
- Establishing benchmarks to convert the workload to labor hours.
- Expressing workload as labor hours and employees.
- Assigning labor resources to manage workload.

Simply saying that the workload is unloading inbound trailers, taking orders, and loading outbound trailers does not provide the information needed for accurate personnel decisions. You need greater detail, such as: How many trailers are expected to be unloaded? How many pallets or cases will be handled? How many orders will be filled? How many SKUs are involved? The answers are loaded into a computer file that is continually updated as jobs are completed and new work is added. The sample file is shown in Figure 9-5.

When you express warehouse workload in units to be handled, you can convert those units to schedule hours — once you've established benchmarks. Benchmarks can be created manually or with packaged software; which you use should depend on how much time and money can be spent in developing standards and on how effectively the standards will work in your warehouse. The sample standards database is illustrated in Figure 9-6. The database is updated as requirements change, new functions are added, and old functions are

Planning and scheduling

Figure 95

FORECAST WORKLOAD FILE			
ACCT/DEPT	FUNCTION	PROD UNIT	QUANT
000120 HARSUN	0010 INBTRK	PALLET	400
000210 RAVEN	0010 INBTRK	SLIPSHEET	320
000050 STAMM	0020 STOCKING	CARTON	2000
000050 STAMM	0040 OUTBTRK	CARTON	248

deleted.

Employee requirements can be determined by dividing the calculated labor hours by the number of hours per employee (that is, shift

Figure 9-6

LABOR STANDARDS MASTER FILE				
ACCT/DEPT	FUNCTION	UNIT	HRS/UNIT	UNITS/HR
00050 STAMM	01 INBCHK	CARTON	0.00083	1205
00050 STAMM	10 INBTRK	CARTON	0.00564	177
00120 HARSUN	15 CHCKNG	CARTON	0.00083	1205
00120 HARSUN	20 STCKNG	PALLET	0.00295	339
00210 RAVEN	30 PICKING	PALLET	0.00438	228

hours expected to be available for work); consider your people's current performance levels to calculate the realistic number of employees required. For example, assume that each warehouse employee represents a theoretical capacity for work of eight hours per shift and that it has been determined that inbound workload totals 56 standard hours of work per shift. At 100 percent performance, seven employees are required to handle the inbound activities (56 hours divided by eight hours per employee). However, when the current average performance level is only 80 percent, two additional people (or a total of nine) are needed to accomplish the same amount of work. Figure 9-7 shows a similar calculation. Management skill comes into play when limited labor resources must be allocated. Tightly controlled warehouse operations will have periods when there is more work to be done than there are workers to do it. *If you always have enough people to do the work, you are probably overstaffed.* The challenge in assigning labor resources is deciding which activities take precedence. Higher-priority jobs are done first. You may assign several employees to a single task to shorten the elapsed time. However, since team assignments are less efficient, be prepared for a productivity decline. Which approach is appropriate may depend on the availability of the dock doors, space, equipment, and employees. A computer can make evaluations fast and easy so decision-making can be timely. However, the computer is only a tool. Success depends on how well that tool is used.

Figure 9-7

LABOR PLANNING DATA LISTING

ACCT/DEPT	FUNCTION	UNIT	PRD QTY	WRK HRS	PERF FCTR	PLAN HRS	SHFT HR/E	EQUIV EMPS
00120 HARSUN	0010 INBTRK	PALLET	400	1.4	0.80	1.75	8.00	0.22
00210 RAVEN	0010 INBTRK	SLPSHT	320	1.4	0.80	1.75	8.00	0.22
00050 STAMM	0020 STCKNG	CARTON	2000	5.3	0.80	6.63	8.00	0.83
00210 RAVEN	0020 STCKNG	PALLET	320	1.6	0.80	2.00	8.00	0.25
00050 STAMM	0030 PICKNG	CARTON	248	2.2	0.80	2.75	8.00	0.34
00050 STAMM	0040 OUTTRK	CARTON	248	0.9	0.80	1.13	8.00	0.14
00120 HARSUN	0030 PICKNG	PALLET	24	0.1	0.80	0.13	8.00	0.02
00120 HARSUN	0040 OUTTRK	PALLET	120	0.1	0.80	0.13	8.00	0.02
00050 STAMM	0010 INBTRK	CARTON	2000	11.3	0.80	14.3	8.00	1.77
*** TOTAL ***				24.3		30.40		3.81

The importance of proper sequence

When evaluating performance in any warehouse, one aspect sometimes overlooked is the sequence in which tasks are performed. Any diagnostic examination should ask five questions:
♦ Who does this job?

- Where is the job done?
- How is the test performed?
- When is it performed?
- Why is it done that way?

The last two questions are emphasized in any sequence analysis. Seven work steps are performed in the typical warehouse:

- Receiving.
- Put-away.
- Re-warehousing.
- Order picking.
- Shipping.
- Customer returns.
- Value-added services.

In the traditional warehouse, product is unloaded in a receiving dock staging area, where it stays until inspection is completed. Then it is moved to a storage area. If inspection is delayed, the receiving dock remains cluttered with material that cannot be shipped and has not been stored. But what if the procedures change?

Consider this variation: Every inbound shipment has an advance shipping notice (ASN). Any vehicle arriving with merchandise not identified with an ASN is not unloaded. A storage planner analyzes each ASN before the load arrives and assigns a location for the merchandise. The receiver scans the bar codes of each unitized load as it is removed from the vehicle. Each pallet then moves directly from the inbound truck to a preassigned storage area, where the scanner creates a receiving manifest that is compared with the ASN when the put-away is complete. When there is a discrepancy, the delivering driver and receiver walk to the storage area together to verify the discrepancy. When there is no discrepancy, the bill is signed and the delivering truck is released.

What is the proper sequence for re-warehousing? Some believe that no product should ever be rehandled within the warehouse. Yet planned relocation of stock will save space and time. A space planner will find two short rows of the same SKU. Combining the two into one longer row will create a free slot for storage of new merchandise. Rewarehousing is also accomplished on an opportunity basis. The need to rewarehouse may be identified, but the actual movement is made at a time when it can be used to balance the workload. Careful consideration of the time sequence for rewarehousing can create significant savings in materials handling costs.

Should orders be pulled and staged as soon as they are received? Or should they be selected just in time to load directly to outbound trucks? In some cases, it is best to pick a portion of the order in advance and handle another part on a just-in-time basis. One example would be an order that combines material moving from the warehouse dock with other items received in a cross-dock operation.

If shipping and receiving operations both use the same dock area, it may be desirable to separate the functions by sequence. For example, in one warehouse all receiving is done before noon, and the docks are used for shipping operations from noon until the end of the day.

The handling of merchandise returned by customers is a difficult part of warehouse operations, and the sequence of activities should be carefully considered. When returned goods are received, they must be graded into one of five categories:

- Salable and returned to stock.
- In need of repackaging.
- Damaged but capable of being refurbished at the warehouse.
- Significant damage, returned to source for repair.
- Total loss, must be destroyed.

When volume is heavy, it may be necessary to stage the entire returned shipment and handle this classification later. Repackaging or refurbishing may be fill-in projects to improve labor utilization. The sequence in which customer returns are handled can greatly affect the efficiency of this labor-intensive process.

Value-added services include kitting, stretch wrapping, and final labeling of merchandise. In some operations, kitting is done in advance, with a bank of new kits built as soon as component materials are available. In other warehouses, the kitting is performed on a just-in-time basis, with each new kit shipped almost as soon as it has been assembled.

In looking at each of the operations just described, it is necessary to ask why as well as when. An answer that "We have always done it that way" is an invitation to consider a change. Changing the sequence of tasks can significantly improve warehouse operations.

Planning for equipment use

In most warehouse tasks, as well as many office tasks, the number of hours needed to finish a job will depend on the equipment or tools available to the worker. The planner begins by considering the kinds of equipment available.

For example, lift trucks are available with a wide array of attachments besides the conventional forks. A warehouse operation designed for carton-clamp handling will require significantly different planning for space and people than one designed to receive loose-piled cases that will be palletized at the receiving dock. Use of slipsheet handling devices requires still different planning. The best time to do this planning is before the warehouse is opened.

At the planning stage, the warehouse manager should select the equipment that can best be used in the operation, taking into account lifting capacities and storage heights as well as any environmental considerations that would restrict the design of the lift trucks. For example, trucks with internal combustion engines may not be acceptable in freezers or other confined areas.

Six basic pieces of information should be gathered during the process of worker and equipment planning:

- The average order size provides a good indication of the amount of time needed to ship each order.
- Physical characteristics of the merchandise also may define the amount of effort needed to handle it.
- The ratio of receiving units to shipping units and the question of whether goods are received in bulk or as individual units will greatly affect the effort involved.
- Seasonal variations and their intensity must be measured.
- Shipping and receiving requirements should be defined, including the times of day when goods will be received and shipped.
- Picking requirements must be defined. A strict first-in, first-out system is more costly both in labor and space.

Once the planner has collected this data, a useful definition of manpower and equipment needs can be reliably projected.

Shift scheduling

Most of our ideas about shift schedules are monuments to a departing industrial era. As manufacturing became more efficient and people more prosperous, the work week gradually shortened from six long days to five eight-hour days. Yet for thousands of years, the 5/8 schedule was not at all common. Even today, the farmer has a work schedule governed by seasons and weather. Other occupations, such as fire departments and airline crews, may have longer shifts. With today's emphasis on improvement of asset productivity, a forty-hour schedule in warehouses is rapidly disappearing. When capital is not available for more facilities and equipment, the most economical way to extend the life of a warehouse is to use it for more hours each day. When you lack the time or the money to acquire additional assets, a multishift operation may be the only way to increase warehouse output.

One popular option is the 4/10 workweek. This schedule is popular with hourly workers because everybody has a three-day weekend.

Many managers worry that unconventional work schedules will be unpopular. Yet there is ample evidence that many hourly workers welcome a job that doesn't call for five eight-hour days.

Contingency planning

Contingency planning is preparing in advance for emergencies not considered in the regular planning process.*

The best approach is to ask the question *What if?* For example, what if our main suppliers are on strike? What if we are unable to get enough fuel to run our truck fleets? What if an earthquake or a tornado destroys our biggest distribution center? What if we cannot find enough secretaries, order pickers, or industrial engineers to staff our distribution facilities? What if we have to recall a major product?

A contingency plan should have certain characteristics. First of all, an adverse occurrence should be less likely than events covered by the regular planning process. Second, the contingency plan must provide

---

* Based on an article by Bernard J. Hale, *Warehousing & Physical Distribution Productivity Report*, Volume, 14, Number 3, ©Alexander Communication, Inc., New York, NY.

the means for a prompt response to a critical event that could cause serious damage.

Contingency plans should be specific. For instance, an organization may develop a contingency plan to be implemented if sales drop below a certain level: *If sales drop 10 percent below plan, our net income will decline by $5 million. To reduce this loss it will be necessary to defer the expansion of our distribution center, reduce the number of employees by 50, and cut variable production costs.*

Wherever possible, the expected results of the actions taken should be calculated in financial terms or in other meaningful measures, such as market share, capacity, and available labor.

Questions that solve problems

The presence or absence of planning and scheduling is not always obvious. These questions will identify the degree to which your warehouse managers have considered this subject.

Q How does the long-range plan for warehousing fit into similar planning for the rest of the corporation?
C If your warehouse managers cannot answer this question, it may not be their fault. If warehousing is not part of the corporate strategic plan, you are missing the opportunity to involve this vital function in the larger planning process.

Q Is short-interval scheduling used in our warehouse?
C If the answer is no, review of the concepts described on pages 87–90 may be helpful, or you may seek outside professionals to help develop this scheduling program.

Q When was the last time that sequence of jobs was analyzed and realigned?
C If your people have never considered the question of proper sequence, it is certainly time to start.

Q When was the last time that shift schedules were reconsidered?
C Again, failure to change could indicate that we have failed to plan.

Q What steps do we take to meet peak demand?
C Look for creativity in the answers to this one, including better scheduling and the use of temporary workers or part-time people.

Chapter 10

Understanding warehousing costs

For many warehouse operators the development of a unit cost — the total cost to move a carton, pallet or bag of product through a warehouse — can be a mystery. The traditional public warehouses (third-party operators) depend on an understanding of unit costs for survival, as their fees are their source of revenue and profit. Many contract warehouses ignore unit costs and base their charges on the amount of time, space or materials consumed. Relatively few private warehouse operators can identify their unit costs. The process of accounting for these units of measure may vary widely, even within the same company, because estimates are based on historical information or experience and are only as accurate as the estimator. This process is no longer good enough, as many competitors in the private sectors completely understand cost accounting and the use of pre-engineered time standards.

Because the prime units of cost measured in most warehouse operations are *storage* (the amount of space occupied by a carton or pallet) and *handling* (the amount of time it takes to move merchandise), the cost for those two categories need to be accounted for. Most warehouse operators allocate costs associated with goods at rest to the storage category and those associated with goods in motion to handling.

As outsourcing of warehouse operations to third-party operators becomes more of a strategic decision, knowing your own unit cost is a requirement for analyzing competitive bids. Many managers quickly discover that the elements are rather simple but the conversion process is not.

A third category of warehouse costs is administration and customer service. This cost center is not detailed in this chapter because new information tools available today have created substantial variation in both methods and costs. The expenses of communicating with the customers and documenting the storage and handling functions can be substantial, and they must be considered in any calculation of total warehousing costs.

Measuring storage costs*

Since storage is the expenditure of space, a first step in determining unit storage costs is to understand the process of space utilization. The total cost of occupying and maintaining a building can be readily determined by adding up all of the *goods at rest* costs. These include either rent or depreciation, heat, light, security, building maintenance, and any administrative cost that would be incurred whether materials were being moved or not.

Part of the process is to develop a standard ratio between gross available space and actual storage utilization. Every warehouse has a capacity, measured in cubic feet or the metric equivalent. From the theoretical capacity, you can deduce a practical capacity by subtracting space dedicated to aisles, staging, and support. Since practical capacity can fluctuate, the truest way to measure capacity is to compare actual space to theoretical capacity.

Assume that you have a warehouse containing 100,000 square feet with a 20-foot practical pile height, or 2 million cubic feet. You store pallets of the standard 48-by-40-inch specification. Each therefore occupies 13.33 square feet, which is rounded to 14 square feet to allow for overhang. These pallets can be stacked three high.

By dividing 100,000 square feet by 14 square feet per pallet, you find that more than 7,000 pallets could be placed on the floor; at three high the capacity is 21,428 pallets. Obviously that theoretical capacity can never be reached, but it can be used to measure your efficiency as a ratio of actual usage to theoretical capacity. If, for example, there were 10,000 pallets in your warehouse on the first day of June, your storage efficiency would be 47 percent (10,000 ÷ 21,428 = 47 percent).

---

* From an article by Roger Carlson, Carlson Consulting, *Warehousing Forum*, Volume 12, Number 5, ©The Ackerman Company, Columbus, Ohio.

By continually recording such ratios, you can track storage performance and determine whether storage productivity is improving or deteriorating.

But what if you have different kinds of storage, some on pallets, some in bins, and some in pallet racks? Divide the warehouse into departments, and then create a storage measurement for each.

Storage efficiency is further influenced by the *honeycomb factor*. Any busy warehouse loses space because partial pallets are stored or because a row is partially depleted and cannot be filled. Just as a half-drunk water glass has half of its available space empty, a pallet or row that is partially filled has unusable empty space. Figure 10-1 shows honeycombing. A continuing comparison between gross storage capacity and net calculated capacity helps you determine how well management has controlled the available space.

Figure 10-1

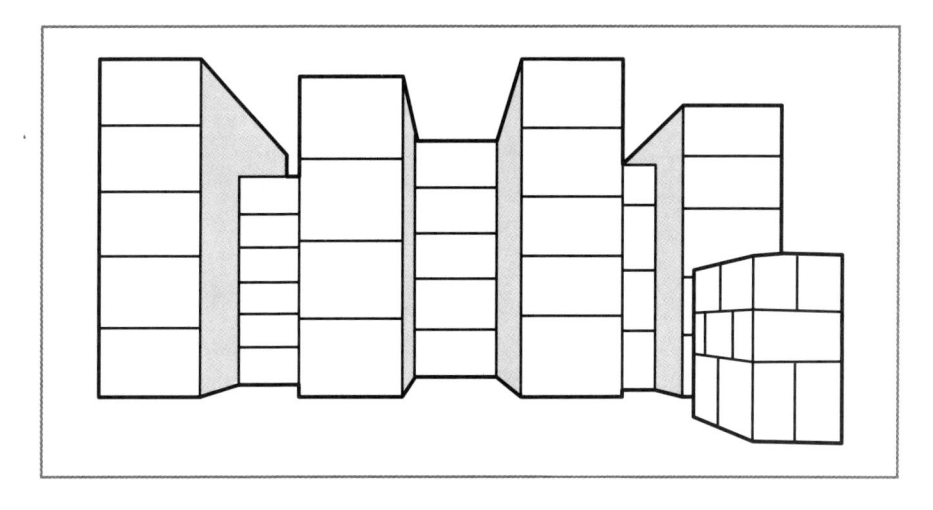

A unit storage cost calculation*

Assume that the inventory contains 115 SKUs and that 50 of them are fast movers. The product is stored on pallets, with 100 cases on each. The average inventory is 3,000 pallets, and the monthly throughput is 2,000 units. The allowance for honeycombing is 20 percent, and an additional 20 percent is added to allow for common-use areas and docks. The product is stacked three pallets high, so 1,000 pallet spaces are needed for the 3,000-pallet inventory. However, with the honeycomb allowance, the 1,000 spaces are adjusted to 1,250. The 50 fast-moving SKUs are stored in the deep-row slots shown in Figure 10-2.

The remaining 65 SKUs that move more slowly are in the short-row area at the left of the same figure. We assume that the 80/20 rule applies and therefore that 1,000 of the 1,250 planned storage spots will be occupied by fast movers. The remaining 250 short-row spots

Figure 10-2

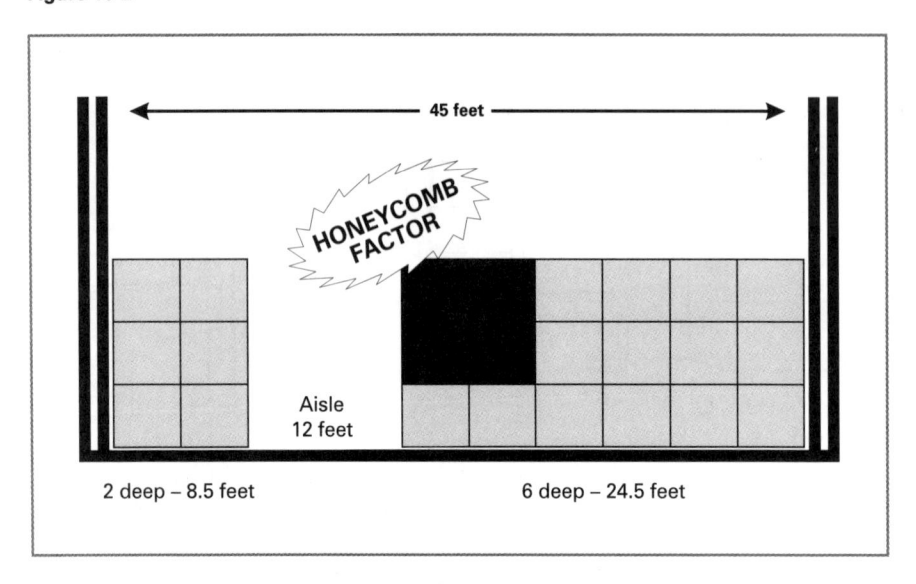

(Diagram showing a warehouse layout: 45 feet wide total, with a 12-foot aisle, 2 deep rows – 8.5 feet on the left, and 6 deep rows – 24.5 feet on the right, with a "HONEYCOMB FACTOR" indicator.)

---

* Figure 10-2 from an article by Hal Searl, Searl Education Services, Columbus, Ohio. Sub-chapter adapted from an article by Robert E. Ness, Ohio Distribution Warehouse, *Warehousing Forum*, Volume 2, Number 5 ©The Ackerman Company.

are occupied by slow movers. The 1,000 deep-row spots are divided by the 50 fast-moving SKUs to produce 20 spots per SKU. The same calculation for slow movers produces 3.8 spots per SKU (250 ÷ 65). The 45-foot storage area shown in the figure is reduced by a 12-foot aisle to 33 feet of actual storage. Since each pallet is four feet long, there is room for eight pallet rows per bay as shown in the drawing. There are 167 pallet facings needed to accommodate the 1,000 deep-row spots for fast-moving SKUs (1,000 ÷ 6 pallets deep). Slow-moving SKUs require 125 short row facings (250 ÷ 2 pallets deep). Each fast-mover (deep-row) facing requires 120 square feet (6 pallets x 4 feet deep x 4 feet wide + 4x12-foot aisle ÷ 2). The aisle space is divided by 2 because storage is available on each side of the aisle. Each slow-mover (short-row) facing requires 56 square feet (2 pallets x 4 feet deep x 4 feet wide + 4 x 12-foot aisle ÷ 2). Therefore, the deep-row storage area requires 20, 040 square feet (120 x 167). The short-row storage area requires 7,000 square feet (56 x 125). The total storage area of 27,040 square feet is adjusted for the 20 percent loss for docks and staging areas (27,040 ÷ 80%) for a total of 33,800 square feet. Assuming that the warehouse operator requires revenue of $0.195 per square foot per month, a rate calculation looks like this:

1. 33,800 square feet x $0.195 = $6,591 per month.
2. Beginning inventory = 300, 000 cases.
3. Product received = 100, 000 cases.
4. Total billing units = 400, 000 cases.
5. $6,591/400,000 cases = $0.0165 per case per month.

The influence of inventory turns

Storage cost for goods at rest is calculated as a unit cost per time period, usually a month. However, with a fast-turning inventory the same spot in a warehouse may be occupied by more than one unit of storage in a given month. Because of this, the number of turns will influence storage costs. An inventory that turns quickly is less costly to store than one that turns slowly.

Here is a method of calculating speed of inventory turn:

1. Determine throughput, which is units received plus units shipped, divided by two.

2. Determine the average inventory, which is beginning inventory plus ending inventory, divided by two.

3. Determine the speed of product turn, the relationship of throughput to average inventory.

Measuring handling costs*

A per-unit handling rate is a calculation of the amount of time devoted to handling each unit, multiplied by labor cost. Determining the time involved is the more difficult part of this process. It normally requires the use of a benchmark or standard. Two approaches can be used in arriving at a standard time:
- Historical data generated from experience.
- Pre-engineered handling standards.

In choosing between the alternatives, a key question is: how long *does* it take to do the job compared with how long it *should* take? There could be a significant difference.

When handling expectations are based on historical data or experience, the numbers are only as good as the person who made the estimates. The foundation is not firm, and it could be difficult to justify or defend the results.

Pre-engineered standards are units of time to measure how much time each function of handling should take. A flow sheet is laid out and each function broken down into a movement, and units of time are assigned to each. Added together, they give the total amount of time to get the job done. Four typical functions are readily measured:
- Unloading, which includes receiving and staging.
- Checking and removal to storage.
- Order picking and transfer to staging.
- Checking and loading on a delivery vehicle.

Within each of these functions, we include travel time, walking, stooping, writing, and reading. Figure 10-3 shows a handling-rate worksheet. The numbers inserted are based on standard times for each of the functions. Appendix A at the end of this chapter shows some typical warehouse time standards. Figure 10-4 is one section of Methods Time Management, which illustrates the job of shipping by

---

* From an article by Roger Carlson, Carlson Consulting, *Warehousing Forum*, Volume 12, Number 4, ©The Ackerman Company, Columbus, Ohio.

Understanding warehousing costs

Figure 10-3
"Tables" referenced here are at the end of this chapter.

Methods Time Management

JOB: Shipping Truck **EQUIPMENT:** Sitdown Forklift

	Minutes
A. **PREPARATION** (per document)	2.822

This includes time to open and close warehouse doors, pick up and position dock plate. Travel to dock plate storage is based on a distance of 50 feet.

B. **READ ITEM DESCRIPTION** (per line item) .185
This includes time to read item description and check off item on document

If necessary, add the following on a per line item basis:
- Read and write item description and calculate quantity per pallet and total cases: .843
- Read date code: .037
- Write date code: .152

C. **TRAVEL TIME** (per pallet)   See Tables
The following tables for forklift and pull-pak are based on one or two pallets per round trip

FORKLIFT / Travel to Truck and Return to Staging*

	40'	60'	80'	100'	120'	140'	160'	180'	200'
1 pallet/trip	.655	.711	.766	.821	.876	.932	.987	1.042	1.097
2 pallets/trip	.327	.355	.383	.411	.438	.466	.493	.521	.549

***TRAVEL TIME INCLUDES:**

	Forklift	Pull-Pak
Pick-up product in staging	.156	.195
Accelerate and stop to truck	.054	.054
Aside product at truck	.210	.348
Accelerate and stop to staging	.054	.054

If applicable, add the following on a per case basis:

Percent of total cases actually handled

	10%	20%	30%	40%	50%	60%	70%	80%	90%	100%
Small	.009	.018	.026	.036	.045	.054	.063	.071	.081	.090
Medium	.012	.023	.035	.046	.058	.069	.081	.092	.104	.115
Large	.014	.025	.038	.051	.063	.076	.087	.100	.113	.125
Bag	.015	.030	.045	.060	.075	.089	.104	.118	.133	.148

Figure 10-4

Handling Rate Worksheet

Building: 15   Prospect/Account: _____   Prepared by: ABC
Date: 3/15   Based on 80% Standard   C/S 4 Documents per Hour

----INBOUND----   ----OUTBOUND----

VARIABLES _Cwt x Plt _ Cs Trans Mode T Hdlg. Mode FLT   _Cwt x Plt. _Cs. Trans. Mode T Hdlg. Mode FLT

	Receive stv +	Check stv +	Stock stv =	Total stv x	Average Receipt =	Total Mins	Order Fill stv +	Check stv +	Ship stv =	Total stv x	Average Order =	Total Mins
Per Document	3.393	1.139	.810	5.442	1	5.442	1.056	1.139	2.822	5.017	1	5.017
Per Line Item	.185	.222	.842	1.249	20	24.980	.353	.222	.185	.76	12	9.12
Per Pallet	.449	.189	.672	1.31	18	23.58	.653	.189	.355	1.197	18	21.55
Per Case												

	54.0	...GRAND TOTAL 36.69
	÷ 60	...Convert Minutes to Hours .... ÷ 60
	.9	...Inbound or Outbound Time in Hours ..... = .59
	.8	...Past Direct Work Performance .... ÷ .8
	1.125	...Probable Time to Complete Task .... = .74
	$28.51	...Labor Cost per Hour .... X $28.51
	32.07	...Cost to Perform Task .... = 21.20

Page 103

truck with a sit-down forklift. Figure 10-3 shows that it takes 54 minutes to receive and stock. The time to ship is 36.69 minutes. Using a fully loaded hourly cost of $28.51, the total cost for inbound is $32.07 and outbound is $21.20.

When the worksheet in Figure 10-3 is completed, it should be checked for reasonableness and accuracy. The results should be reviewed with warehouse workers for feedback. Most workers like to achieve goals, and if they believe the expectations are reasonable they will support the program. If the expectations are not realistic, they should be adjusted.

Although the times calculated and the characteristics selected will be different in each warehouse, the approach to developing unit costing should be the same. When you have a thorough understanding of unit costs in your own operation, you can buy third-party warehouse services knowing that the cost from a third-party contractor should be similar to yours. Furthermore, development of unit costing allows you to budget warehousing costs more precisely than ever.

Appendix A

The pages following **Questions that Solve Problems** illustrate warehousing time standards.*

---

[*] This material was compiled by Roger Carlson, Carlson Consulting, Minnetonka, MN.

Questions that solve problems

You need ask only a few questions to learn whether your warehouse people have a reasonable understanding of costs.

Q Do we know a cost per unit for moving our products through the warehouse?
C If the answer is no, your people need a tutorial on developing warehousing costs.

Q What are our costs per unit?
C These costs might be compared with quotes from third-party warehouse operators.

Q Describe how we developed our per-unit costs.
C Compare the answers to this question with the methods described in this chapter. Don't assume that there is only one valid procedure. There is room for innovation in the development and control of unit warehousing costs. At the same time, be sure that you are satisfied with the reasonableness and precision of the costing method that is used in your operation.

Q How do our unit costs compare with those in the same time period last year?
C When you get the answer, be sure you also get an explanation of why things changed.

Q How do unit costs at X warehouse compare with those at Y warehouse?
C If the differences are significant, be sure to find out why.

WAREHOUSE TIME STANDARDS
(As Defined By Methods-Time-Management)

The following standard time values have been produced from MTM time allowances for a "typical" warehouse operation and can be applied to the following:

- Estimating labor hour requirements
- Measurement of productivity/performance
- Evaluating alternative operations
- Scheduling jobs
- Simulation
- Rate making
- Comparison to established industry standards

Warehousing Throughput Standards

Application	Equipment	Hourly Throughput
Putaway	Counterbalanced lift truck	10-18 pallets/hour
Replenishment	Narrow aisle reach truck	10-15 pallets/hour
	Very narrow aisle man-up turret truck	11-25 pallets/hour
Order picking	Powered pallet jack	30-80 lines/hour
	Man-up orderpicker truck	40-85 lines/hour
	Manual pick cart	25-55 lines/hour
	Broken case pick-to-tote	100-250 lines/hour
	Full case pick-to-belt	250-500 cases/hour
	Carousels (2 modules)	30-120 lines/hour
	Automated broken case order selection	up to 900 orders/hour
	Mini-load system	100-800 cases/hour

Note: Throughput standards may differ significantly depending on the type of working environment, the facility layout, the type of product being handled, and order and inventory profiles.

Travel Speeds	FLT Standard
Empty	444 fpm
Loaded	380 fpm
Vertical, Loaded	50.4 fpm
Vertical, Empty	64.0 fpm

Understanding warehousing costs

STANDARD TIME VALUES
JOB: Receive Rail   **EQUIPMENT:** Sitdown Forklift or Pull-Pak

Minutes

A. **Preparation** (Per document)   4.408
   This includes time to get document, open warehouse door, open
   rail car door, get dock plate. Travel to dock plate storage is
   based on a distance of 50 feet.

   If necessary, add the following on a per document basis:
   - Close car door: 1.413
   - Move bulkhead door (per movement):   .978
   - Remove D.F. bracing (per brace):   5.305
   - Remove excess dunnage to trash: 10.242

B. **Read Item Description** (per line item)   .185
   This includes time to read item description and check off
   item on document

   If necessary, add the following on a per line item basis:
   Read and write item description and calculate quantity
   per pallet and total cases: .842
   Read date code: .037
   Write date code: .115

C. **Travel Time:** (per-pallet)   See Tables
   The following tables for forklift and pull-pak are based on one or
   two pallets per round trip.

Forklift
Travel from Rail Car to Staging and Return Rail Car*

	40'	60'	80'	100'	120'	140'	160'	180'	200'
1 pallet/trip	1.106	1.162	1.217	1.272	1.327	1.382	1.438	1.493	1.548
2 pallets/trip	.553	.581	.608	.634	.664	.691	.719	.746	.774

Pull-Pak or Clamp
Travel from Rail Car to Staging and Return to Rail Car*

	40'	60'	80'	100'	120'	140'	160'	180'	200'
1 pallet/trip	1.249	1.304	1.359	1.415	1.470	1.525	1.580	1.635	1.691
2 pallets/trip	.624	.652	.680	.707	.735	.762	.790	.818	.845

*ADD TO TRAVEL TIME, IF APPROPRIATE

	FORKLIFT	**PULL-PAK**
Pick-up product in rail car	.489	.592
Accelerate and stop to staging	.054	.054
Aside product at staging	.269	.290
Accelerate and stop to rail car	.054	.054
	.866	**.990**

STANDARD TIME VALUES
JOB: Receive Rail   **EQUIPMENT:** Sitdown Forklift or Pull-Pak

If applicable, add the following on a per pallet basis:

	Minutes
Attach gummer label:	.050
Write lot number on sticker:	.153
Tape top tier of product:	.297
Tie top tier of product with twine:	.380
Get pallet and bring into rail car:	.426

D. **Handling** (Per case) Actually Handled

If applicable, add the following on a per case basis:

Percent of Total Cases Actually Handled

	10%	20%	30%	40%	50%	60%	70%	80%	90%	100%
Small	.011	.022	.032	.044	.055	.066	.077	.087	.099	.109
Medium	.014	.026	.040	.054	.068	.081	.094	.108	.121	.135
Large	.015	.030	.045	.060	.075	.089	.104	.118	.133	.148
Bag	.016	.031	.047	.063	.079	.094	.110	.127	.148	.165

NOTE:
Small: More than one per hand
Medium: One per hand or two or more per two hands
Large: One per two hands

Use the following table to determine the appropriate weight allowance factor and add to the corresponding case size:

Weight Allowance

	6-10#	13-30#	31-50#	51-70#	71-90#	91-110#
Small	.002	.010	.024	n/a	n/a	n/a
Medium	.002	.010	.024	n/a	n/a	n/a
Large	n/a	.007	.021	.035	.048	.062
Large Bag	n/a	.009	.026	.043	.061	.078

STANDARD TIME VALUES
JOB: Receive Truck   **EQUIPMENT:** Sitdown Forklift or Pull-Pak

Minutes

A. **Preparation** (Per document)   3.493
   This includes time to get document, open and close warehouse
   door, get dock plate. Travel to dock plate storage is based
   on a distance of 50 feet.

B. **Read Item Description** (per line item)   .185
   This includes time to read item description and check off item
   on document

   If necessary, add the following on a per line item basis:
       Read and write item description and calculate quantity
       per pallet and total cases: .843
       Read date code: .037
       Write date code: .152

C. **Travel Time:** (per-pallet)   See
   Tables
   The following tables for forklift and pull-pak are based on one or
   two pallets per round trip.

Forklift
Travel From Truck to Staging and Return to Truck*

	40'	60'	80'	100'	120'	140'	160'
1 pallet/trip	.842	.897	.952	1.007	1.063	1.118	1.173
2 pallets/trip	.421	.449	.476	.504	.531	.559	.587

Pull-Pak or Clamp
Travel From Truck to Staging and Return to Truck*

	40'	60'	80'	100'	120'	140'	160'
1 pallet/trip	1.007	1.063	1.118	1.173	1.228	1.283	1.339
2 pallets/trip	.504	.531	.559	.587	.614	.642	.669

*ADD TO TRAVEL TIME, IF APPROPRIATE

	FORKLIFT	**PULL-PAK**
Pick-up product in truck	.348	.471
Accelerate and stop to staging	.054	.054
Aside product at staging	.180	.201
Accelerate and stop to truck	.054	.054
	.636	**.780**

STANDARD TIME VALUES
JOB: Receive Truck   **EQUIPMENT:** Sitdown Forklift or Pull-Pak

If applicable, add the following on a per pallet basis:

	Minutes
Attach gummer label:	.050
Write lot number on sticker:	.153
Tape top tier of product:	.297
Tie top tier of product with twine:	.380
Get pallet and bring into rail car:	.426

D. **Handling** (Per case) Actually Handled

Percent of Total Cases Actually Handled

	10%	20%	30%	40%	50%	60%	70%	80%	90%	100%
Small	.011	.022	.032	.044	.055	.066	.077	.087	.099	.109
Medium	.014	.026	.040	.054	.068	.081	.094	.108	.121	.135
Large	.015	.030	.045	.060	.075	.089	.104	.118	.133	.148
Large Bag	.016	.031	.047	.063	.079	.094	.110	.127	.148	.165

NOTE:
Small: More than one per hand
Medium: One per hand or two or more per two hands
Large: One per two hands

Use the following table to determine the appropriate weight allowance factor and add to the corresponding case size:

Weight Allowance

	6-10#	13-30#	31-50#	51-70#	71-90#	91-110#
Small	.002	.010	.024	n/a	n/a	n/a
Medium	.002	.010	.024	n/a	n/a	n/a
Large	n/a	.007	.021	.035	.048	.062
Large Bag	n/a	.009	.026	.043	.061	.078

STANDARD TIME VALUES
JOB: Checking   **EQUIPMENT:** Clipboard

Minutes

A. **Preparation** (Per document)   1.139
   This includes time to read document information,
   initial and date document. Walk to staging is based on
   a distance of 100 feet.

B. **Per Line Item** (if applicable):   .222
   This includes time to read item description, read date code
   and check off item on documents.

   If necessary add the following:

       Write date code: .151

C. **Travel Time** (per pallet)   .189
   This includes time to determine pallet pattern and multiply one
   tier times the total number of tiers. Walking distance between
   pallets is based on 10 feet.

D. **Per Case** (See Table)
   This includes time to locate, identify and count one case.

Percent of Total Cases Actually Handled
(Multiplied by the number of total cases)

10%	20%	30%	40%	50%	60%	70%	80%	90%	100%
.002	.004	.006	.008	.010	.012	.014	.016	.018	.020

Stencil, per case: .020

STANDARD TIME VALUES
JOB: Stocking   **EQUIPMENT:** Sitdown Forklift or Clamp

		Minutes
A.	**Preparation** (Per document) This includes time to get document from supervisor and write information on document. Travel to document drop is based on a distance of 100 feet.	.810

B.	**Per Line Item** (if applicable)
	If necessary, add the following on a per line item basis:
	  Read and write item description and calculate quantity
	  per pallet and total cases:
	  Read date code:
	  Write date code:
		.842
		.037
		.151

C.	**Travel Time:** (per-pallet) The following tables for forklift and clamp are based on one or two pallets per round trip.	See Tables

Forklift
Travel From Staging to Storage and Return to Staging*

	100'	200'	300'	400'	500'	600'	700'
1 pallet/trip	1.067	1.343	1.619	1.895	2.171	2.447	2.723
2 pallets/trip	.534	.672	.810	.948	1.086	1.224	1.362
3 pallets/trip	.356	.448	.540	.632	.724	.816	.908
4 pallets/trip	.267	.336	.405	.474	.543	.612	.681

Clamp
Travel From Staging to Storage and Return to Staging*

	100'	200'	300'	400'	500'	600'	700'
1 pallet/trip	1.125	1.401	1.677	1.953	2.229	2.505	2.781
2 pallets/trip	.562	.700	.838	.976	1.114	1.252	1.390
3 pallets/trip	.375	.467	.559	.651	.743	.835	.927
4 pallets/trip	.281	.350	.419	.488	.557	.626	.695

*ADD TO TRAVEL TIME, IF APPROPRIATE

	FORKLIFT	**CLAMP**
Pick-up product in staging	.278	.310
Accelerate and stop to staging	.054	.054
Aside product at storage	.302	.320
Accelerate and stop to staging	.054	.054
	.688	**.738**

D. **Vertical Lift Time**
   Loaded: 50.4 fpm
   Empty: 64.0 fpm
   Computation: height lifted divided by lift time standard equals min. to lift

STANDARD TIME VALUES
JOB: Order Filling   **EQUIPMENT:** Sitdown Forklift, Pull-Pak or Clamp

		Minutes
A.	**Obtain Order** (Per document)	1.056
	This includes time to get document from supervisor, read document information. Travel distance from staging to order drop basket is based on a distance of 100 feet.	
	If applicable, add the following on a per document basis:	
	Write information on document	.336
	Write information on pallet	.153
	Prepare stencil	.117
B.	**Read and Check** (per line item)	.353
	This includes time to read item description and check off item on document, travel between line items is based on 25 feet.	
	If applicable, add the following on a per time item basis:	
	Write date code	.150
	Get and aside stencil bulb	.036
	Mount and dismount	.334

STANDARD TIME VALUES
JOB: Order Filling   **EQUIPMENT:** Sitdown Forklift, Pull-Pak or Clamp

C. **Travel Time** (Per Pallet)
The following tables for forklift, pull-pak and clamp are based on one or more pallets per round trip.

Forklift
Travel From Staging to Storage and Return to Staging*

#Pallets Per Trip	100'	150'	200'	250'	300'	350'	400'	450'	500'	550'	600'
1	1.029	1.167	1.305	1.443	1.581	1.719	1.857	1.995	2.133	2.271	2.409
2	.515	.584	.653	.723	.791	.860	.929	.998	1.067	1.136	1.200
3	.343	.389	.435	.481	.527	.573	.619	.665	.711	.757	.800
4	.257	.292	.326	.361	.395	.430	.464	.499	.533	.568	.600

Pull-Pak
Travel From Staging to Storage and Return to Staging*

#Pallets Per Trip	100'	150'	200'	250'	300'	350'	400'	450'	500'	550'	600'	650'	700'
1	1.098	1.236	1.374	1.512	1.650	1.788	1.926	2.064	2.202	2.340	2.478	2.616	2.754
2	.549	.618	.687	.756	.825	.894	.963	1.032	1.101	1.170	1.239	1.308	1.377
3	.366	.412	.458	.504	.550	.596	.642	.688	.734	.780	.826	.872	.918
4	.275	.309	.344	.378	.413	.447	.482	.516	.551	.585	.620	.645	.689

Clamp
Travel From Staging to Storage and Return to Staging*

#Pallets Per Trip	100'	150'	200'	250'	300'	350'	400'	450'	500'	550'	600'	650'	700'
1	1.086	1.224	1.362	1.500	1.638	1.776	1.914	2.052	2.190	2.328	2.475	2.604	2.742
2	.543	.612	.681	.750	.819	.888	.957	1.026	1.095	1.164	1.238	1.302	1.371
3	.362	.408	.454	.500	.546	.592	.638	.684	.730	.776	.825	.868	.914
4	.273	.306	.341	.375	.342	.444	.479	.513	.548	.582	.619	.651	.686

*ADD TO TRAVEL TIME, IF APPROPRIATE

	FORKLIFT	PULL-PAK	CLAMP
Pick-up product in bulk storage	.278	.317	.314
Accelerate and stop to staging	.054	.054	.054
Aside product at staging	.269	.290	.281
Accelerate and stop to rail car	.054	.054	.054
	.655	.715	.703
	.688	.738	

D. **Vertical Lift Time**
Loaded: 50.4 fpm
Empty: 64.0 fpm
Computation: height lifted divided by lift time standard equals min. to lift

STANDARD TIME VALUES
JOB: Order Filling   **EQUIPMENT:** Sitdown Forklift, Pull-Pak or Clamp

Percent of Total Cases Actually Handled

	10%	20%	30%	40%	50%	60%	70%	80%	90%	100%
Small	.009	.018	.026	.036	.045	.054	.063	.071	.081	.090
Medium	.012	.023	.035	.046	.058	.069	.081	.092	.104	.115
Large	.014	.025	.038	.051	.063	.076	.087	.100	.113	.125
Bag	.015	.030	.045	.060	.075	.089	.104	.118	.133	.148

STANDARD TIME VALUES
JOB: Checking   **EQUIPMENT:** Clipboard

		Minutes
A.	**Preparation** (Per document) This includes time to read document and item information, initial and date document. Walk to staging is based on a distance of 100 feet.	1.139
B.	**Per Line Item** (If applicable) This includes time to read item description, read date code and check off item on documents.	.222
	If necessary add the following: Write date code:	.151
C.	**Travel Time** (per pallet) This includes time to determine pallet pattern and multiply one tier times the total number of tiers. Walking distance between pallets is based on 10 feet.	.189
D.	**Per Case** This includes time to locate, identify and count one case.	See Table

Percent of Total Cases Actually Handled
(Multiplied by the number of total cases)

10%	20%	30%	40%	50%	60%	70%	80%	90%	100%
.002	.004	.006	.008	.010	.012	.014	.016	.018	.020

Stencil, per case: .020

STANDARD TIME VALUES
JOB: Shipping Truck   **EQUIPMENT:** Sitdown Forklift or Pull-Pak

                                                                                        Minutes

A. **Preparation** (Per document)   2.822
This includes time to open and close warehouse doors, pick up
and position dock plate. Travel to dock plate storage is based
on a distance of 50 feet.

B. **Read Item Description** (Per line item)   .185
This includes time to read item description and check off item
on document.

If necessary, add the following on a per line item basis:

    Read and write item description and calculate quantity
    Per pallet and total cases: .843
    Read date code: .037
    Write date code: .152

C. **Travel Time:** (Per-pallet)   See Tables
The following tables for forklift and pull-pak are based on one or
two pallets per round trip.

Forklift
Travel From Staging to Truck and Return to Staging*

	40'	60'	80'	100'	120'	140'	160'	180'	200'
1 pallet/trip	.655	.711	.766	.821	.876	.932	.987	1.042	1.097
2 pallets/trip	.327	.355	.383	.411	.438	.466	.493	.521	.549

Pull-Pak or Clamp
Travel From Staging to Truck and Return to Staging*

	40'	60'	80'	100'	120'	140'	160'	180'	200'
1 pallet/trip	.859	.914	.969	1.025	1.080	1.135	1.190	1.245	1.301
2 pallets/trip	.430	.457	.485	.512	.540	.568	.595	.623	.650

*ADD TO TRAVEL TIME, IF APPROPRIATE

	FORKLIFT	**PULL-PAK**
Pick-up product in staging	.156	.195
Accelerate and stop to truck	.054	.054
Aside product at truck	.210	.348
Accelerate and stop to staging	.054	.054
	.474	**.651**

STANDARD TIME VALUES
JOB: Shipping Truck   **EQUIPMENT:** Sitdown Forklift or Pull-Pak

If applicable, add the following on a per case basis:

<u>**Percent of Total Cases Actually Handled**</u>

	10%	20%	30%	40%	50%	60%	70%	80%	90%	100%
Small	.009	.018	.026	.036	.045	.054	.063	.071	.081	.090
Medium	.012	.023	.035	.046	.058	.069	.081	.092	.104	.115
Large	.014	.025	.038	.051	.063	.076	.087	.100	.113	.125
Bag	.015	.030	.045	.060	.075	.089	.104	.118	.133	.148

Chapter 11

Asset accountability and utilization

As merchandise moves through the supply chain from resource to customer, one party is accountable for it at any given moment. When losses occur, accountability becomes an issue. For that reason, the responsibility of each party handling the goods must be clearly defined.

With the movement of goods through the supply chain, title is typically transferred many times. Sale terms are used to define when title passes from seller to buyer. For example, the term *FOB destination* means that the seller has title to the property while in transit to the customer.

Cargo liability vs. warehouse liability*

There is a significant difference in the standard of care for liability purposes between that of a warehouse operator and a carrier, particularly when goods in their custody are found to be damaged or lost. In today's integrated logistics industry, it is important to distinguish when liability transfers from carrier to warehouse or vice versa.

The prime source document regarding standard of care for the warehouse operator is the Uniform Commercial Code (UCC). The warehouse operator's liability for goods is limited to *reasonable care* as defined in section 7-204 of the UCC:

---

* Adapted from an article by William W. Clark, Warehouse Insurance Management Company and David S. Sidor, Squire, Sanders & Dempsey, *Warehousing Forum*, Volume 13, Number 12, ©The Ackerman Company, Columbus, Ohio.

A warehouseman is liable for damages or loss or injury to the goods caused by his failure to exercise such care in regard to them as a reasonably careful man would exercise under like circumstances, but unless otherwise agreed he is not liable for damages that could not have been avoided by the exercise of such care.

The UCC is outdated when it is applied to the diverse various activities that today's third-party logistics operator provides to customers. This is especially evident in the long-term arrangements referred to as lease/contract operations. Transportation deregulation laws allow flexibility in provisions for loss and damage, but they recognize that carriers exercise full custody of the goods and typically select the vehicle and route to be used. As a result of this high degree of control, carriers face a stricter liability than warehouse operators for goods that are lost or damaged in their custody. But there are carrier exemptions, which include the following:

- Shippers load and count.
- "Acts of God," including weather.
- Authority of law.
- Riots, strikes, and war.
- The fault of the shipper, such as improperly packaging the goods.

The carrier does not have to be found negligent to be held liable for loss or damage. However, the situation changes if the goods are under control of a third-party warehouse operator. The basis for this different treatment lies in English common law as expressed above in the UCC.

But precisely when does liability shift from the carrier to the warehouse operator? Generally, when the goods cease being in transit, they are considered warehoused. It may be necessary for the carrier to hold goods before they are received by the warehouse operator, without physically unloading them into the warehouse. When this happens, the carrier becomes a warehouse operator subject to UCC 7-204. This issue becomes less clear when the carrier "drops" a loaded trailer at the warehouse. The transition can be confirmed by the issuance of a warehouse receipt, at which time the goods cease to be the responsibility of the carrier and enter the control of the warehouse operator. Conversely, when the bill of lading is signed by the carrier, goods immediately move into the carrier's control.

Both the standard of care and the valuation for lost or damaged goods may vary, depending on whether the carrier or warehouse is at fault. However, the different standards may create a conflict when the same third-party logistics company acts as both carrier and warehouse. Since it may not be clear where the loss or damage occurred, it is important for the contracts to properly deal with these differences.

Because the warehouse and cargo liability insurance are intended to protect both the operator and the carrier, the shipper should not rely on either to fully protect its interests. Shippers should maintain their own insurance coverage.

The warehouse operator should include in any agreement with the shipper three provisions that take advantage of the UCC: First, liability should be limited as expressed by UCC 7-204; Second, a limitation on loss should be established in the event that the warehouse is found liable; third, the operator should state that claims must be presented within a specific time.

As the primary business of warehousing has changed from one of storage to cross docking and contract warehousing, all parties have found the need to change terms and conditions that were written decades ago. New rules are needed to guide the logistics business as it is handled in the 21st century. Those responsible for risk management need to cover the risks faced by today's diversified providers of logistics services.

Managing inventory*

In most warehouses, the most valuable asset is the inventory. Some warehouse managers have little control over inventory management functions. Furthermore, they feel that they can never be involved in inventory planning. However, the best managers do their best to change that notion.

Pareto was a Swiss Italian sociologist in the early 20th century. Although there is no evidence that he ever had anything to do with warehousing, the law he developed has everything to do with inven-

---

* Adapted from an article by Morton T. Yeomans, *Warehousing Forum*, Volume 13, Number 7, ©The Ackerman Company, Columbus, Ohio.

tory management and operations effectiveness. Pareto's law, also known as the 80/20 rule, started with the observation that 80 percent of the wealth in Italy was in the hands of 20 percent of the people, and it was extended to observe that 80 percent of the sales were in 20 percent of the items for sale. In information technology, Pareto's law becomes the ABC report, with the A items as the fastest movers and C as the slowest.

One tool for applying Pareto's law is the product velocity profile. This is a mathematical exhibit of the inventory activity. Nearly every information technology department can produce an ABC report. However, this report can be formatted in four ways:
- Dollar value of product shipped.
- Pound or tons of product shipped.
- Number of units shipped.
- Number of times each SKU was selected (hits).

Tracking of velocity by hits is the most meaningful manner of presenting a product velocity profile, since the key effort factor in the warehouse is the number of times the order picker visits any location to fill an order. Figure 11-1 shows product velocity data, and Figure 11-2 converts those numbers into a graph.

Analyzing product velocity can improve layout and space planning. When the velocity of each item is determined on a continuing basis, the layout should be adjusted for seasonal and periodic changes in volume.

By developing and maintaining product velocity profiles, you can lower your labor costs and use more space in your warehouse.

Controlling space utilization

Many warehouse managers are unable to accurately measure the capacity of their warehouse, and therefore they cannot calculate the percentage of capacity currently held in storage. In those cases, they typically determine that the warehouse is full when a visual inspection shows no space left. In extreme cases, the first awareness of the problem is when lift truck operators report that there is no place to store today's inbound load.

An overstuffed building is a warehouse operator's worst nightmare; trying to put too much material in storage has a disastrous effect on the warehouse operation. In extreme cases, material is stored in

Asset accountability and utilization

Figure 11-1

Product velocity profile data
XYZ COMPANY
Total units shipped: 3,541,853

No. of SKUs	% of total SKUs	Units Shipped	% of total Shipments
1	0.0%	103,918	2.9%
12	1.0%	804,017	22.7%
23	2.0%	1,237,807	34.9%
57	5.0%	2,178,239	61.5%
113	10.0%	2,963,149	83.7%
281	25.0%	3,427,663	96.8%
562	50.0%	3,528,181	99.6%
843	75.0%	3,541,180	99.9%
1,123	100.0%	3,541,853	100.0%

Figure 11-2

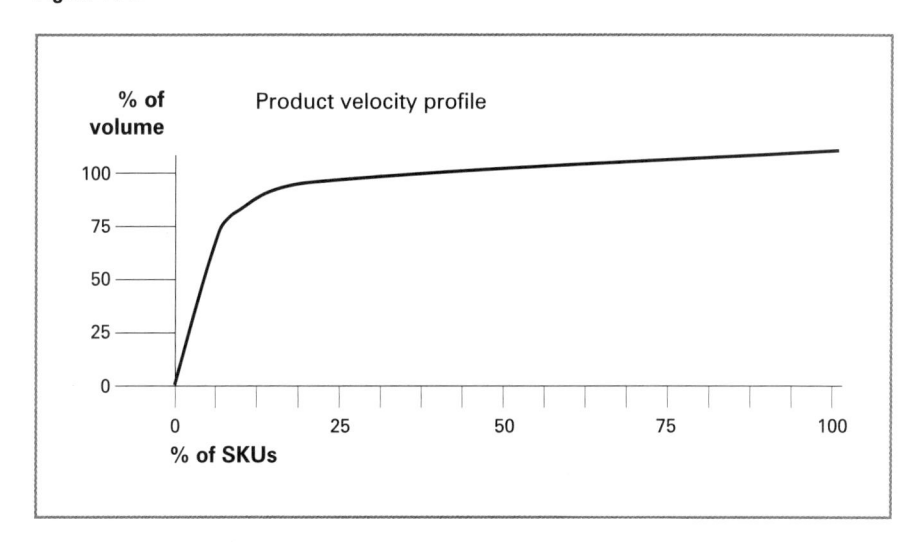

Product velocity profile

% of volume vs % of SKUs

aisles and staging areas, where it is readily damaged by lift truck traffic. When one item is stored in front of another, time is wasted rehandling items to retrieve the desired product.

Surprisingly little attention is paid to creating a capacity measurement system, probably because many feel the measurement system is impossible. If you store thousands of SKUs that range in size from a full pallet to a pencil, how can you create a workable system to measure warehouse capacity?

One approach is to divide the inventory into product classes based on storage characteristics. The warehouse is divided into sections or departments, each designed to handle a different class of freight. The typical warehouse might be divided into three departments devoted to three classes of inventory. One portion of the warehouse is open space designed for freestanding stacks; this space holds loaded pallets or similar units that can be stacked without artificial support. The second portion of the warehouse is reserved for rack storage; pallet racks capable of holding full or partial pallets are used to store products that are best handled in racks. The third type of storage is shelves or bins, which would hold the pencil-size items.

Consider this example:

Your warehouse has enough clearance to accommodate three-high stacks of pallets. Your storage bays are designed to hold deep rows four pallets deep on the north side of the aisle and short rows just one pallet deep on the south side. Honeycombing loss (see chapter 10) is incurred whenever any storage row contains fewer than 12 pallets (three high by four deep) in the deep rows, or fewer than three pallets on the short rows. Your first step to improve the situation might be to buy pallet rack in the short-row area, which would allow efficient storage of single-pallet quantities. Another option would be to divide the warehouse into a bulk storage area (deep rows) and an order selection area, sometimes called a pick line. A quantity of each SKU is kept in the pick line to allow order selection to be performed easily. Reserve stocks remain in other parts of the warehouse. When the warehouse is set up this way, your calculation of storage capacity must consider both the capacity of the pick line and the capacity of the reserve storage area.

The typical storage space calculation

This calculation is based on these assumptions: Your layout plan calls for 40 percent of the building to be used for docks, aisles and staging areas. Your calculated honeycombing loss is an additional 20 percent. You are storing a product packaged in cartons measuring 20 by 24 by 10 inches, and cartons are received in trailers each containing 1,000 units. The product can be stacked 15 feet high on a 48-by-40-inch pallet. The pallets contain layers two units by two, and five layers can be placed on the pallet. Stacking height is three pallets, or 15 layers of cases. Each storage pile, including pallet overhang, occupies 15 square feet. Figure 11-3 illustrates the space calculation that shows how you calculate that each carton requires a little more than half a square foot.

Alternatively, storage capacity can be measured in pallet loads. The first step is to examine the pallet rack area and count the number

Figure 11-3

Storage Space Calculation

Assumptions

A portion of gross space must be dedicated to aisles and staging, leaving 60% net space.

Honeycombing losses further reduce net space, leaving only 80% of the net space (48% of gross) available.

Calculations

Each pallet of product contains 5 tiers with 4 cases per tier, or 20 cases total.

Each stack of 3 pallets contains 60 cases.

Each stack is the size of one pallet plus one inch overhang on each of the 4 sides: 42 times 50 = 2,100 square inches or 14.6 square feet. Round this to 15.

Each stack consumes 25 gross square feet, or 15 divided by 60%.

Each stack, after honeycombing, requires 31.25 square feet, or 25 divided by 80%.

Each case takes up .52083 square feet, or 31.25 divided by 60 cases.

of pallet positions available in the racking. Then count the number of those positions that are filled to create a ratio of filled to empty space. Note that a partially empty pallet will take just as much space as a full one. Therefore, a capacity calculation figured on cases will be distorted by the presence of partially full pallets. The same procedure is used to calculate the percentage of empty space in a bin storage area.

Second, examine the freestanding storage area. Assume that it has a capacity of 4,500 pallets (300 rows of 12 each plus 300 short rows of three each). A physical check can show how many pallets are in stock at the end of each day. Again, the ratio of occupied units to capacity is calculated.

Using the steps just described, you can determine the capacity of each area of the warehouse daily.

Controlling the lift truck fleet

The most important tool for monitoring usage of industrial trucks is the hour meter mounted on the chassis of every piece of power equipment.

You can monitor usage of lift trucks with this simple three step procedure:

- Take engine hour meter readings for each unit at the beginning of each shift.
- After a day, week, or quarter, compare the meter readings of the trucks in the fleet.
- Divide operating hours by available hours to develop the utilization percentage.

A low overall utilization percentage will show that you may have more lift trucks than you need. However, such readings typically show that some trucks are overutilized and others are used hardly at all. That happens because warehouse people don't like to operate one or more of the trucks because of the design or some other feature.

More importantly, remember that not all hour meters work the same way. Some record the number of hours that the engine was running. Others record all hours when the ignition is on, whether the engine is running or not.

Therefore, it is essential to check with your lift truck vendor and verify that all of the hour meters on your equipment function the same way.

Figure 11-4

Usage per truck

Truck #	Capacity (hrs.)	Used (hrs.)	Use (% of capacity)
1	126.5	126	99.6
2	126.5	130	102.8
3	126.5	90	71.1
4	126.5	14	11.1
5	126.5	2	1.6
SUMMARY		**362**	**Average: 57.2%**

Some users have adopted a rule of thumb that the practical limit for lift truck usage is 75 percent of the time, or about 5.5 hours for a 7.5-hour shift. Figure 11-4 shows a typical truck analysis. Note that "favorite" machines are heavily used while others are nearly idle. When a warehouse supervisor requests an additional lift truck, you can use the information shown above to ask why trucks 4 and 5 have such light usage. Without such investigation, you might buy a new truck that has the same design problems that have caused trucks 4 and 5 to be neglected.

For operators of more than one warehouse, these records are especially valuable because an underused truck can be moved to another warehouse that needs more lift truck capacity.

Questions that solve problems

If you want to discover how well warehouse managers understand asset accountability and how well they measure utilization, here are a few questions to ask:

Q If we either use or offer third-party services, has the limitation of liability been precisely defined?
C Don't accept short answers on this one. Insist that your managers trace the details of liability limitation which exist today.

Q How is inventory velocity measured in our warehouse today?
C If your people have no inventory management tools, consider the value of becoming proactive in inventory control.

Q How full is our warehouse today, and how have we measured its capacity?
C No matter how your warehouse managers answer this question, go to each warehouse and ask for specific demonstrations of capacity measurement.

Q How many lift trucks do we have today? Is this too many or not enough? Why?
C Regardless of the answers received, be sure to discover whether the hour meters on each power unit are actually used. If inadequate controls exist today, it is not too late to establish a process.

Chapter 12

Reducing errors

In many warehouse operations, errors are the worst problem management faces. Errors mean lost customers — or worse: sometimes an error can be deadly. As long as human beings work in the warehouse, there will be some errors, and management's job is to reduce them as much as possible. In some warehouse operations, a decrease in errors is the best way to increase productivity. "Zero defects" is now widely regarded as a reasonable goal.

The cost of an error

The cost of errors varies widely, but you should try to get an estimate of this cost in your operation. If the wrong item is shipped, you will have an unanticipated stock-out when inventory is exhausted, with a corresponding overage in some other item. The undetected stock-out can cause customer relations problems when you are unable to deliver an item that showed on your book inventory.

Correcting the error includes the cost not only of receiving the return but also of shipping the proper item. In some industries, the shipper allows the receiver to keep a wrong item to avoid the cost of the return; the cost of taking back the wrong item and returning it to stock is many times the cost of a normal warehouse receipt. Part of this cost is the administrative burden of correcting a shipping error and handling a receipt of just one or a few packages.

But the most devastating cost of warehouse error is the creation of an unhappy customer.

Preventing warehouse errors

Many steps can be taken to minimize the possibility of error. One cause of errors is a misunderstanding when an order is taken by telephone. Such misunderstandings are minimized if the order taker repeats the order to the customer. Consider the procedure used by one fast-food company that makes home deliveries. This company asks for the caller's number, then the operator calls back to repeat the order. Besides eliminating prank calls, the second phone call catches a high percentage of errors.

With the wide variety of hard-copy transmission available today, probably the best way to prevent telephone errors is to prohibit or at least severely restrict oral communication for order placement.

A locator system prevents errors

Warehouse locator systems are used primarily to cut search time, but they have a second advantage: preventing shipping errors. If you have a locator system, the order picker will first be asked to go to a given location to pick a given item. Then, if the picker finds that the item is not there, you know there is either an error in the locator system or an error in the item specified. Order pickers who always question a mismatch between the locator system and the item provide an early warning of errors in the selection system.

Markings as a source of errors

A surprising number of warehouse errors are made because the labels or markings on packages are confusing or even misleading. Eliminate non-essential markings, and be consistent in the marking or labeling system.

A marking system usually includes the trade name, size, color, and item number. Some markings are too small to be read in normal warehouse light. Others are an ink color that does not show up under high-intensity lighting systems. If you have a high error rate, consider whether the marking on the packaging could be improved.

Another source of labeling error is the use of packages within a package. You may have a shipping case that contains inner packs, each of which contains three bottles. When terminology is unclear, the warehouse order picker may not know whether the customer wants one case, one pack, or one bottle. Confusion can result in unreported overshipments, which create a loss, or undershipments, which cause customer claims. Be sure that your system is absolutely clear in stating how many pieces the customer really wants.

Dyslexia and inventory errors

Physical inventory and picking errors are frequently caused by dyslexia, which reportedly affects nearly one-fifth of the population. One approach to controlling this is to give every employee a test that contains a list of twenty actual SKU numbers. The person taking the test is asked to copy those numbers onto blank lines on the test paper. Anybody who misses more than one or takes longer than 15 minutes should not be handling inventory transactions.

Picking documents

When multi-part forms are used, the picking document is frequently a copy that is fuzzy and difficult to read. Preventing errors requires picking documents designed for the order filler. The document should be as legible as you can make it, using the minimum number of characters required to identify the product. Eliminate unnecessary information that might distract the order picker.

A picking document might have four columns. The first shows the location of the product. The second contains its identification numbers. The third column is left blank for the order filler to place a check mark after picking the item. The fourth column lists the quantity to be selected. Any changes in the order should be marked only in the third column.

Use of bar coding

Bar coding will reduce both handling time and errors. Consider the receiving process as an example.

Without bar coding, the warehouse worker writes a receiving report while unloading each inbound shipment, then carries the receiving report and the accompanying packing list to the office for entry into the inventory system. A clerk compares the documents for discrepancies and then enters the information on the receiving report. After entry, the clerk might obtain the appropriate storage location for the merchandise. The report is then returned to the worker, who stores the stock in the assigned location.

With bar coding, the work performed by the clerk is eliminated. The warehouse worker scans a label on each item received and then uploads the information to the computer system. The system reveals any discrepancies by comparing what was scanned to the advance information transmitted by the client to the warehouse. A screen then displays the appropriate storage location for each unit scanned. After uploading, the process takes just seconds. Furthermore, the warehouse worker is faster and more accurate because there is no longer a need to copy information by hand.

Receiving — locking the barn door*

Every warehouse operator is aware of the critical nature of shipping. Emphasis on security, error reduction, and quality control is always directed to the shipping function. However, frequently receiving is undermanaged until something goes wrong.

Two dangerous things can happen with an uncontrolled receiving process. First, you may accept product damage that was not caused in your warehouse. Second, through either error or deliberate dishonesty, you may sign for merchandise that was never received.

A growing number of warehouses are demanding and getting advanced shipping notifications (ASNs) transmitted electronically. When the receiver knows everything that should be on the shipment, a more positive identification takes place.

It is essential to inspect merchandise carefully, paying special attention to products that are susceptible to damage. There may be vendors who are notorious for poor packaging, and receipts from them should be examined with special care. Effective receiving is both a materials handling and an auditing process.

To check or not to check?

A recurring debate among warehousing professionals is whether checking of outbound shipments is necessary.

---

* Adapted from an article by Daniel Bolger, The Bolger Group, Lancaster, Ohio.

The practice of checking originated at a time when it was presumed that warehouse workers were semiliterate and that a better-educated person had to keep the worker from making errors. As the process has grown in sophistication, someone decided that it was better to hire educated people and then hold them responsible for doing the job right the first time.

Today, technology has changed checking operations. Checking no longer involves judgement or arithmetic, since the "checker" does nothing but run items past a scanner and submit the results, just like the clerk at the checkout counter of your grocery store. As a result, the cost of checking is lower than ever.

Even with this technology, checking is still a waste of money at times. To determine when this is the case, compare the cost of errors with the cost of checking. When error frequency is low or the consequences of errors are minimal, the cost of performing the checking operation may be more than the benefit it can achieve.

As you look at checking in your warehouse, ask two questions:
- Have you applied state-of-the-art technology to minimize the cost of checking?
- Is the catch worth the chase?

Physical factors in the warehouse

The environment of your warehouse can invite order-picking errors. The most common problem is insufficient lighting. Minimum lighting may be adequate for bulk storage locations, but an order-pick area should have illumination of at least fifty foot-candles. The most popular and most frequently picked items should be at levels that eliminate reaching or stooping by the order picker — at least sixteen inches above the floor, but no higher than 6 feet.

Some products invite errors because of similar markings or similar appearance. Do not store such confusing items next to each other.

Personnel factors

The way you deal with people affects error reduction. Communicate your expectations so your people will know what you expect and will work to live up to those expectations. Your expectations may be in a written procedure, or they may be expressed in meetings dedicated to reduction of errors.

The first place to communicate your expectations is in the training of new people. Your trainers should review written procedures and discuss them with new hires. When you train new order pickers, use dry runs to teach them the importance of doing the job properly the first time.

Identification with work

People who identify with their work usually do it better. One method of promoting identification is to have each order filler sign each page of an order document after completing it. If the worker doesn't complete the order, then he or she initials each line handled.

Another means of encouraging worker identification is to insert a picking ticket into every order filled. This ticket should include the picker's name, not anonymous numbers. One picker's ticket reads: *This order was picked by Thomas E. Jones. If you find any discrepancy between the ticket and your order, please call 123-456-7890. Ask for the Claims Department and give my name when reporting the error.* A further refinement is to put the order filler's photograph on the ticket as well. This personalization has resulted in improved order accuracy. Using peer pressure to encourage more accurate order picking by listing each worker's accuracy rate on the warehouse bulletin board is often effective. The person making the most errors is at the top of the list; those with higher accuracy follow. Always be sure that workers are graded on errors as a *percentage* of total lines picked; otherwise the fastest order picker may falsely appear to be the worst error maker. If you post an accuracy rate list, be sure to recognize and praise those workers who achieve the lowest percentage of errors.

Pareto analysis and errors

The 80/20 rule (Pareto's law) can be applied to identify and reduce errors. It is likely that 20 percent of the workers will make 80 percent of the errors and that 80 percent of the errors will occur in 20 percent of the SKUs in the warehouse. This happens because certain people are error-prone and because some items are badly marked and thus subject to mis-picking.

By using Pareto analysis, management can discover which people and which items cause the most errors. When the key few are identified, management can find the root cause of the errors. As people are involved, the cause could be dyslexia or illiteracy. On the item side, the problem may be poor product marking. When the root cause is discovered, corrective action should follow. Error-prone people should be given other work where mistakes can be controlled. Badly marked products should be labeled more effectively in the future.

Rewards for the stars*

A perennial challenge in warehousing is to devise a way to reward star performers. One wholesale distributor has a quarterly award program based on four areas, three of which deal with elimination of errors:

- Inventory accuracy (when it is above 99 percent).
- Elimination of process errors (above 99 percent).
- Elimination of customer errors (fewer than 2 per 1,000 orders).
- Lines picked per labor hour — actual vs. budget.

A typical award will provide a day off with pay. The key to success in this program is broad-based and goal-oriented awards. The program is easily understood and visible to every participant. It combines merit with achievement of established goals. It recognizes individuals as well as the team organization.

---

* Based on information contributed by Edward Jurczek of Anixter, Inc.

Questions that solve problems

Since error reduction is a key step in quality improvement, you should question your warehouse managers frequently on this subject.

Q What was our error rate last month, and how did it compare with the same month of last year and with previous months of this year?
C If nobody has an answer, there is work to be done!

Q Can you think of anything that we could do to reduce the error rate?
C Look for some creative answers, and take careful note of the manager who says that nothing else can be done.

Q Have you read or heard of any new technology that would help us to lower our error rate?
C Keep an open mind when you hear the answers. New technology is likely to go beyond anything described here, since written descriptions of state-of-the-art devices are usually obsolete before the ink dries.

Chapter 13

Measuring performance

Warehousing is a service function, and a pervasive question among managers is how to tell exactly how well a warehouse is performing. Indeed, much of the great interest in benchmarking moves back to the question of how to measure performance.

The unique factors

Consider the unique aspects of a service business, features that may be ignored by managers who focus on production and marketing. Service industries have characteristics not found in most other business activities:
- The level of capacity must be set to anticipate demand.
- Workforce planning is extremely important.
- Competition is local, and the service is not transportable.
- Job responsibilities are poorly defined.

In a warehousing operation, capacity is fixed. The warehouse walls have no elastic, so storage capacity is a finite item limited by the size of the building. Although you can improve utilization of available space, at some point further improvement is impractical.

The skilled workforce in a warehouse can be stretched through overtime, but even that has its limits when workers would prefer free time to more pay. Shipping and receiving capacities can be extended through additional shifts, but once four shifts are in place there is no room for further expansion.

Warehouse operations require labor planning. No operator can keep a high-quality workforce if a significant number of people are frequently laid off. When labor is scarce, the best people will seek another job that offers more security. Yet failure to reduce labor cost when demand sags will cause the unit cost to increase.

Manufacturing is more portable than warehousing. An assembly operation can be moved across the Mexican border to achieve a lower labor cost. But warehouse locations are usually fixed by transportation requirements, tax advantages, or the availability of adequate space. Although warehouses can be and occasionally are relocated, they may not be moved as easily as manufacturing.

Job responsibilities in warehousing are more diverse, harder to define, and harder to supervise. The manufacturer can place inspectors at different points in an assembly line to check the quality of work. Because the warehouse worker is not in a static position on an assembly line, close supervision is virtually impossible.

Measuring effectiveness

All of these differences make warehousing more difficult to control and measure than other business functions.

Warehouse managers must distinguish between efficiency and effectiveness. A warehouse may appear to be operating with great efficiency, but the effectiveness depends on the ability to satisfy the customer. Therefore, the most important measures of warehouse effectiveness deal with customer service. This audit procedure can help to measure warehouse effectiveness:

1. Determine what percentage of deliveries last week were on schedule.
2. Report the percentage of deliveries that arrived damage-free.
3. Calculate the percentage of deliveries last week that arrived with no quantity discrepancy.
4. Compare each of those percentages with those from the same period last year.
5. Explain any increase or decrease.

How efficient is your warehouse?

Some have described the difference between efficiency and effectiveness as the difference between doing things right and doing the right things. If you do not do things right in customer service, your efficiency in doing the right things becomes unimportant because customers lose confidence in your warehouse.

Figure 13-1

Efficiency ratios

1. **Space utilization**
   Divide cubic feet of space actually used by total cubic feet available.
2. **Materials handling**
   Divide total pieces, pounds, or cubic feet handled by available worker hours
3. **Receiving productivity**
   Divide total pieces, pounds, or cubic feet handled by available worker hours (receiving).
4. **Order-picking productivity**
   Divide total pieces, pounds, or cubic feet handled by available worker hours (picking).
5. **Handling equipment utilization**
   Divide available equipment hours by the sum of hours shown on lift truck meters.
6. **Inventory fill**
   Divide lines requested by lines demanded.
7. **Employee turnover**
   Divide the number of employees hired in the past year by the total number of employees.
8. **Absenteeism**
   Divide man-days of absences by total days worked.
9. **Injuries**
   Divide number of reported injury accidents by total days worked.
10. **Warehouse damage**
    Divide cases damaged in warehouse by total cases handled.

Warehouse efficiency depends on the ability to utilize space and time. Any audit of warehouse performance should include an examination of ratios to measure efficiency. Figure 13-1 illustrates ten ratios that can be used in most warehouses. Other ratios may be added to fit peculiar conditions of your operation. Abrupt changes in any of these ratios will allow you to take action quickly to correct a defect that might otherwise be overlooked.

Quantifying space utilization

Every warehouse has a capacity, measured in cubic feet or meters. From the theoretical capacity you can deduce a practical capacity by subtracting space reserved for aisles, staging, and other support functions. However, management can influence the amount of space lost for the support functions. Therefore, the simplest way to measure capacity is to compare actual space and theoretical capacity.

The theoretical space capacity can never be reached. In a busy warehouse with many SKUs, the actual utilization will run between 15 percent and 30 percent. By maintaining such ratios over time, you can track storage performance and compare different warehouses that store the same product line.

Improving storage productivity

The payback for improved storage density is the avoidance of new construction or elimination of third-party warehouses. However, in many cases improved storage density causes an increase in labor costs.

Storage productivity is measured by the number of units that can be stored in each square foot of space. It is increased in at least four ways:

- ◆ Narrow-aisle lift trucks.
- ◆ Different types of storage rack.
- ◆ Improved packaging.
- ◆ Better inventory management.

Narrow-aisle lift trucks allow the aisle width to be reduced. The counterbalance lift truck normally operates in a 12-foot aisle. A turret truck with a guidance system will operate in an aisle of less than six feet. However, most narrow-aisle trucks are not designed for loading and unloading trailers, so a different crew (or at least a different truck) is needed when loading or unloading freight from trailers. In contrast, the counterbalance forklift can do the entire job.

A vital step in improving storage productivity is to determine how storage rack is used to increase storage density. Often more than one type of rack should be used. In some cases, storage improvement is made simply by buying taller rack uprights to allow merchandise to be stacked as high as the building allows.

Although many warehouse managers have little control over packaging, they need to understand how improved packaging increases storage density. Very few containers are strong enough to allow the product to be stacked to the normal ceiling height of a contemporary building. If the package could be strengthened, space utilization would be improved.

One of the most effective ways to improve storage productivity does not involve any investment in capital equipment. Better inventory management can reduce the amount of product kept in storage by eliminating the warehousing of items that are obsolete and will eventually be scrapped. Every warehouse manager should identify and kill off the FISH (first-in, still here) in the inventory. If your warehouse has become an attic rather than a distribution center, one of the best ways to gain improvement is to liquidate those items that have been stored long enough to gather dust.

Calculating a storage payback

When improved storage productivity avoids new construction, calculate the proposed square feet of new construction and price it at thirty dollars per square foot. When improved storage productivity eliminates third-party warehousing, you might use a projected cost of nine dollars per pallet per month. These rough calculations should be refined by developing detailed comparisons to fit your situation. Investments in capital equipment to improve storage productivity are therefore justified by calculating the costs that can be avoided by eliminating either plant expansion or third-party warehousing. These numbers can be used to create a justification that should be approved by your financial officer.

Quantifying handling productivity

Measuring productivity of people is more difficult than calculating space or equipment utilization. Benchmarks are rarer and less reliable. You should start by developing historical data.

For example, last year our warehouse moved 72,800 pallets. We employed five people, so each worker handled 14,560 pallets. Dividing this by a work year of 2,080 hours shows an average productivity of seven pallets per hour. We can thus compare this year's productivity with last year's. Management will at least know whether productivity is improving or deteriorating.

When you have different kinds of cargo, separate benchmarks are established for palletized products, single-case order picking, parts stored in bins, and other distinct categories. Materials handling hours are then separated by department.

Short-interval scheduling, described in chapter 9, allows you to make a fairly close estimate of the time required to do any warehousing job.

Justifying handling improvements

You can improve handling output in at least four ways:
- Scheduling longer service hours.
- Improving order-picking procedures.
- Reducing staging delay.
- Using technology to replace the checker.

Many warehouse operations have a 40-hour week, although there are actually 168 hours available. When facilities and equipment are used for more hours, the cost per hour of the capital investment is reduced. Therefore, increasing hours should allow you to avoid or delay acquisition of additional lift trucks or dock doors.

Because order picking is the most expensive procedure in most operations, improving its effectiveness will create the greatest results in controlling handling costs.

Staging is used in most warehouses. When staging is eliminated, handling cost is lowered. The simplest and smoothest operation is one that allows a single worker to unload a pallet from a trailer and put it directly into a storage stack or to reverse the process on outbound. When merchandise must be staged at the dock, the handling cost is naturally increased.

Most operators consider checking to be necessary to reduce errors. However, bar-code scanning can replicate the checking function with higher speed and greater accuracy.

Simulation in the warehouse

Until recently, computer simulation was too expensive and time-consuming to be justified for most warehouse operations. Simulating materials-handling systems before buying is somewhat like taking the test drive at an automobile dealership. Before spending big money for a new distribution center or a new handling system, it makes sense to take it for a test run. Computer simulation makes this possible.

Simulation is the process of developing a mathematical model to duplicate the performance of the design or operation. The model produces statistical outputs that deliver timely measures of system performance. It also includes graphic capabilities that allow the user to view the model as an animation on a screen.

Simulation can help answer the following questions:
- Are there enough dock doors in the warehouse?
- How many lift trucks are needed?
- How many order pickers are needed?
- Where should products be slotted?
- How should workloads be balanced?

You cannot use simulation if you are looking for results in a day. To do it right, the entire process requires a generous amount of time to develop the model and its programming logic. Depending on the software, a simple handling system from picking to shipping may require three days to a week to program. That does not include the time to gather and analyze data for input into the model.

The most significant result of simulation is the confidence that management will gain from visualizing the design. Simulation is no longer an exotic tool for scientists and engineers. Easier programming techniques and more powerful computers have made it accessible to everyone. In an age of increasing complexity, simulation in the warehouse should be considered as a management tool.*

---

* Adapted from an article by Maida Napolitano, Gross & Associates, *Warehousing Forum*, Volume 12, Number 1, ©The Ackerman Company, Columbus, Ohio.

Measuring performance by account

For nearly all third-party warehouse operators, and a growing number of private warehouses, the most difficult measurement is that of profit contribution for each customer or account. One way to do it is to establish targets for earnings per hour and earnings per square foot. When total earnings for time and space are above the targets, there is a contribution to profit. In any warehouse, there is time or space that is difficult to allocate, and it must be identified and tracked. When a given customer does not produce a satisfactory contribution, corrective action is obviously needed. Figure 13-2 shows a chart illustrating account performance and contribution.

Figure 13-2

Account performance and contribution

$30 HOURLY TARGET
$3.84 SQ FOOT TARGET PER YEAR

DATE	SQFT	HOURS	STRG	H$EARN	TOTREV	$/FT	$/HR	CONTRB	CONT%	CONT/FT
TOTAL	120,000	1,559	36,533	47,562	84,095	3.35	32.08	(1,085)	-1%	-0.01
May97	120,000	1,645	37,500	53,918	91,418	3.75	32.78	3,668	4%	0.03
Apr97	120,000	1,605	36,600	46,930	83,530	3.66	29.24	(3,020)	-4%	-0.03
Mar97	120,000	1,550	38,399	48,991	87,390	3.84	31.61	2,490	3%	0.02
UNALOC	9,291	66	0	0	0	0.00	0.00	(4,943)	0%	-0.53
May97	6,530	65	0	0	0	0.00	0.00	(4,040)	0%	-0.62
Apr97	8,765	32	0	0	0	0.00	0.00	(3,765)	0%	-0.43
Mar97	9,152	65	0	0	0	0.00	0.00	(4,879)	0%	-0.53
CUST A	28,835	461	9,224	16,523	25,747	4.11	35.60	2,685	10%	0.09
May97	24,428	475	8,196	18,021	26,217	4.03	37.94	4,150	16%	0.17
Apr97	23,498	458	8,123	15,540	23,663	4.15	33.93	2,404	10%	0.10
Mar97	24,171	489	8,863	16,636	25,498	4.40	34.02	3,094	12%	0.13
CUST B	20,390	122	5,422	3,451	8,836	3.19	38.43	(1,358)	-15%	-0.07
May97	22,466	128	5,355	3,812	9,167	2.86	29.78	(1,862)	-20%	-0.08
Apr97	21,160	117	5,601	3,470	9,071	3.18	29.66	(1,210)	-13%	-0.06
Mar97	19,941	108	5,302	3,558	8,860	3.19	32.94	(761)	-9%	-0.04
CUST C	8,841	71	2,643	1,927	4,562	3.50	30.01	(382)	-8%	-0.04
May97	8,582	73	4,034	1,947	5,981	5.64	26.67	1,044	17%	0.12
Apr97	9,383	61	3,435	1,597	5,014	4.39	25.89	182	4%	0.02
Mar97	9,897	84	3,421	1,906	5,327	4.15	22.69	(360)	-7%	-0.04

Monitoring several warehouse locations

A multicity operator should compare the performance of each warehouse with that of the others. The most obvious way to track service performance is to count the number of reported errors. However, errors should be compared with order volume, since a warehouse with high volume has a higher risk of error. Using the service performance report shown in Figure 13-3, you can compare the performance of warehouses in various cities.*

Figure 13-3

Service performance report								
	Orders	% of 6-mo. average	Errors	Service rating average	Through-put	% of 5-mo. average	Space use avg.	Space x1,000
Boston	1,870	105%	6	99.68%	67,521	101%	90%	78
Atlanta	1,746	85%	11	99.37%	105,879	87%	84%	105
Baltimore	1,571	98%	13	99.17%	95,072	102%	75%	98
Los Angeles	1,412	107%	21	98.51%	140,238	103%	85%	140
Chicago	1,268	97%	18	98.58%	117,816	99%	95%	125
Houston	900	95%	30	96.67%	130,956	89%	77%	127
Total	8,767	96%	99	98.87%	657,491	100%	83%	673

A sixty-minute warehouse evaluation

If you were given just sixty minutes to evaluate a warehouse, what things would you look for? The first priority is housekeeping. An orderly warehouse is a sign of good management. If trash is on the floor, ask who retrieves it and disposes of it. If damage is found, find out about procedures for dealing with it.

---

* Adapted from an article by John T. Menzies, Terminal Corp., *Warehousing Forum*, Volume 3, Number 8, ©The Ackerman Company, Columbus, Ohio.

Space utilization is another indicator of management. Always look up. See how much of the practical pile height is actually in use. Find out whether racking systems are designed to use all of the available space and whether all lift trucks have masts high enough to reach the highest rack position. Look at the locator system and determine how many locations are found for each SKU. Check on procedures to merge locations and save space. Does the locator system really work?

Since order picking is the most costly part of many operations, accompany an order selector and watch an order being filled. See whether the person doing the job has the right attitude as well as the right skill. Why is the order selected in the manner used?

As you look at the people in the warehouse, try to gain an impression of how they feel about the company. See whether they greet each other as they pass or remain silent. Look for any signs of friction. Are the people neatly dressed, alert, and apparently productive? Look for signs of pride in the work they do.

Within sixty minutes you should be able to evaluate housekeeping, space utilization, order picking, and the quality of the workforce.

Questions that solve problems

Your effort to audit warehouse performance can go in either of two directions. If you have a group of warehouses, you may wish to compare the results of one with the results of others in the group. Whether you have a group or only one, you may wish to consider the changes within one warehouse over a period of time. Therefore, in measuring performance, the first step is to decide whether you wish to measure changes over time or changes between locations, or possibly both.

Q What method do you now use to measure performance in the warehouse?
C If your manager has no measures, he or she will stumble over this one. Beware of the answer that appears to be improvised, since this is a sign that the manager wants to tell you something you would like to hear but actually has not effectively measured the progress.

Q Which of the various available measures is most important for our operation?
C A good manager can and always should emphasize customer service. Without good service, nothing else you do in the warehouse may save it from ultimate failure.

Q Of the ratios shown in Figure 13-1, which is most important for our operation?
C Again, this answer will show you the manager's priorities. If you disagree with those priorities, you have an opportunity to improve management performance through counseling.

Q Do we have any system for justifying the purchase of equipment to improve handling operations?
C If no justification process is described, then how or why were any expenditures approved in the past? The answers will reveal a great deal about the current financial approval process.

Q Do we have any means of measuring performance by account or customer?
C Compare the explanation given with the procedure described in this chapter.

Q How does current performance in this warehouse compare with the past?
C The answers will reveal much about how measurements have been done in the past.

Q Which warehouse is our best, and which is our worst?
C Again, the comparison of warehouses should be fact-based, and it will reveal much about the current measurement system.

Q Are we measuring any of the wrong things?
C This could be the opportunity to abolish unused reports or other activities that continue just through force of habit.

PART 3

Warehouse Management

Chapter 14

Finding the right people

No warehouse operation can be any better than its people. Whether you are starting a new operation or making the existing team larger, you cannot be too careful in selecting the people. Even if you're filling the vacancies of people who leave, the process represents an opportunity to improve the quality of the entire team.

Finding people in a scarce labor market

In the U.S. today, a growing number of metropolitan areas have full employment. When nearly all of the good people already have a job, it is more likely that some of the people available are also undesirable. Even when labor is not scarce, you may find a shortage of the high-quality people you want to work in your warehouse.*

Although there is no simple solution to the problem of labor scarcity, consider these steps to develop a recruitment program:
- Develop a labor requirements plan.
- Develop volume forecasts over several weekly periods.
- Use local labor recruiters, and reward them for quality, not quantity.
- Improve the working environment in your warehouse.
- Establish creative schedules to accommodate nontraditional workers: students, housewives, retirees, or the handicapped.

---

* Adapted from an article by Dallas Mulder, The Limited, *Warehousing Forum*, Volume 5, Number 7, ©The Ackerman Company, Columbus, Ohio.

Plans and forecasts provide enough lead time to allow your human resources people to do their jobs effectively. You should not ask your labor recruiter for five people on Friday and then expect five quality people to show up on Monday. When forecasts are made, your labor supplier has a chance to react and comment.

When the recruiters understand the jobs, they can do better at filling them. Recruiters should work at various jobs within the warehouse, if only for a few hours, to gain insight into the operation. They should always be urged to hire quality and not quantity. Never force recruiters into a position where they must deliver a number of workers without regard to the requirements.

Develop incentives so the temporary agencies send you only good people. One such incentive is to not pay for the first day's salary if the temporary worker doesn't meet your expectations. Don't permit the agency to replace dropouts during the week; insist that all temporary workers start on Monday. To receive maximum billing, the temporary agency will realize that it must send people who will remain through the week.

The working environment has much to do with your ability to attract and retain the best people. Design any task so it can be learned easily. Although increased automation may reduce the number of people needed, the skill requirement usually increases.

The ideal warehouse has just one job grade for all work assignments. That gives the manager maximum flexibility in assigning people to do any work that is needed. When new people are hired, part of their orientation should be to become familiar with the policy of reassigning people from one work area to another. When people are moved, it is extremely important for supervisors receiving these people to welcome them and express appreciation. When people are joining a new team, they need to feel welcome there.

Nontraditional employees

The best way to attract students and housewives is to provide flexible or part-time work schedules. Can you allow shorter hours for retired people who do not want to exceed a maximum annual earning? If you can provide a workweek of four ten-hour days, you will find that workers will prefer your warehouse because they will have an extra day off. You can use rotating shifts to provide five-, six-, or seven-day coverage even though each shift has a four-day week.

Some companies develop a reciprocating relationship among divisions. When your needs are great, another division may have excess labor, so you can loan out and borrow workers. Turning workers into "volunteer firefighters" does good things for their morale, since they get not only some variety but also a chance to show their talent to people in other divisions.

Don't overlook the need to provide competitive pay and benefits. Compare your pay scale with those of similar companies in your labor market every year. Wage surveys or data from a local chamber of commerce can be helpful. Some companies provide the opportunity for each worker either to have health coverage or to eliminate the purchase if a working spouse already has it. That allows people who already have the insurance to receive more take-home pay.

Retaining good people

Attracting and retaining good people go hand in hand. Good people need to see that there are opportunities beyond today's job. The best way to demonstrate that is in the manner in which you fill higher-level jobs in the warehouse. Developing people so that you can promote them and offer them better opportunities is the best way to make good people want to stay on your team.

The interview process

One of the biggest mistakes in the hiring process is a disorderly approach. Frequently when people are needed, management is under stress. It is easy to stumble in the selection process if you do not follow an orderly and careful program. A crucial part of that process is the job interview.

You can increase your skills as an interviewer by practicing techniques, just as a basketball player becomes proficient through practice. The interview process is shown in Figure 14-1.

The warehouse job is a series of tasks, and successful people accomplish those tasks in a predictable and appropriate manner. Ask yourself what tasks each candidate must perform to be successful. Then consider which skills, abilities, and knowledge are needed to perform those tasks. Finally, ask yourself how a successful person would accomplish each task.

Figure 14-1

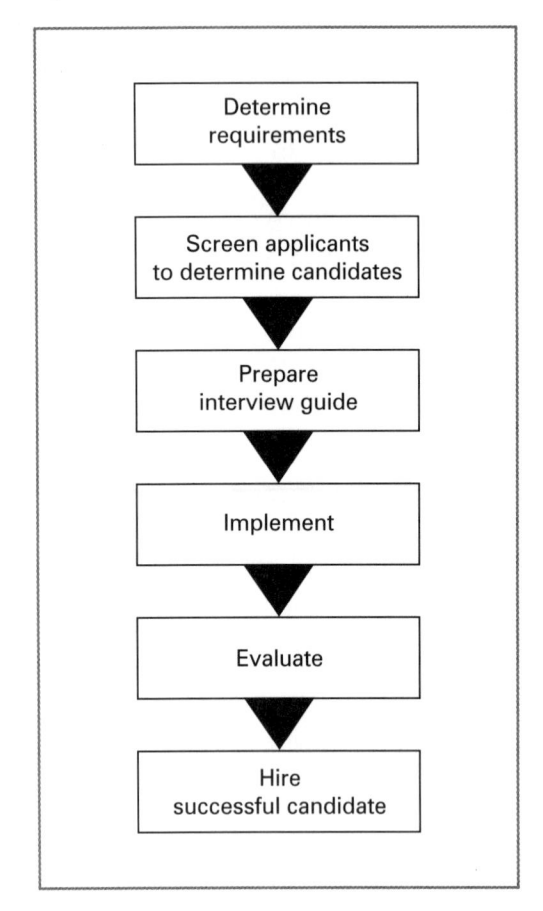

```
┌─────────────────────────┐
│ Determine requirements  │
└─────────────────────────┘
            ▼
┌─────────────────────────┐
│ Screen applicants       │
│ to determine candidates │
└─────────────────────────┘
            ▼
┌─────────────────────────┐
│ Prepare interview guide │
└─────────────────────────┘
            ▼
┌─────────────────────────┐
│ Implement               │
└─────────────────────────┘
            ▼
┌─────────────────────────┐
│ Evaluate                │
└─────────────────────────┘
            ▼
┌─────────────────────────┐
│ Hire successful         │
│ candidate               │
└─────────────────────────┘
```

One of the best ways to outline your requirements is to profile a successful person. Think of someone in your warehouse doing the job now who has been quite successful. Why is this person successful? What does he or she do, or not do, to contribute to that success? How does that successful individual deal with other people? Answering those questions helps you identify the requirements necessary to build a profile of the successful candidate.

Once you have an established list of requirements, develop a pool of qualified candidates. When the labor market is tight, recruitment may become the toughest part of the process.

Keep your ultimate objective in mind: to hire a person who will be successful. Try to screen in, not screen out. Don't risk losing a good candidate because of one blemish on the application.

Review the resume with the intention of finding indicators that the person has necessary knowledge, skills, and abilities. Try counting the things you like on each resume you read. Look for indicators that the person will be successful in your warehouse. Review your requirements list, and compare it with the resume. Management skills should be indicated on a resume, but initiative, flexibility, and problem solving are less evident. Those need to be researched in an interview.

Once you have narrowed the list, write an interview guide with a list of questions in the order you will ask the candidates. The question list is important for two reasons: first, you can ensure that you do not forget to ask something; second, you can concentrate on listening instead of worrying about what to ask next. The questions should be in chronological order, in a format that allows you to follow an applicant through his or her career. This method helps you learn whether there is a pattern of growth or lack of growth, whether that person has reached a plateau or will continue to progress, and how easily and often the candidate learns new skills. Develop questions that will provide insight into the applicant's knowledge, skills, and ability.

Much of the conventional wisdom about interview questions is misleading. Avoid open-ended, nonspecific questions such as "Tell me about managing your warehouse" or "What is the best way to control warehouse expenses?"

You should also avoid theoretical questions such as "What would you do if …?" Instead ask, "What did you do when …?" This takes the question out of the future and generates facts about past performance. Factual questions require the person to respond with a fact. They might include the following:

- How many people did you supervise?
- What type of equipment did you use?
- What kind of warehouse management system did you use?

The answers help you determine an applicant's knowledge, skill, and ability.

Action questions require the candidate to describe performance in a specific situation. "Step me through the way you implemented your quality control program": This question requires the applicant to explain actions. The answers help show how that person will act in your warehouse and whether he or she will be successful.

Here are some good questions for management interviews:*

- Tell me about your role at your present (last) company.
- Do you believe you have an opportunity to grow with your present company?

---

* Adapted from an article by Dan Bolger, The Bolger Group, *Warehousing Forum*, Volume 12, Number 11, ©The Ackerman Company, Columbus, Ohio.

- Who specified the work standards that you use today?
- What do you like best about your present job?
- How has your education experience helped you?
- What are the management skills needed in your job?
- Whom do you report to?
- Tell me about your experience.
- What is your earnings expectation for next year?
- When you discover evidence that one of your employees is on drugs, what do you do?
- What do you need to do to cope with the differences between your present job and the requirements of our company?
- Is there anything else you want to tell me about your ability to handle this job?

The face-to-face interview is a critical point in the process. Begin with an opening designed to put the candidate at ease. The goal is to establish rapport and reduce anxiety. You might discuss something interesting you saw on a resume. Once you have asked all the questions on the interview guide, you may wish to describe the company and to sell the applicant on your company. However, you don't know whether you need to sell the job until most of the interview is completed. Close the interview by making sure each candidate knows what will happen next and when. Finally, end the interview on a positive note.

Evaluation

Return to your list of requirements and create charts similar to the one shown in Figure 14-2. Rate each candidate against each requirement. Candidates must all be measured against the same standard: your requirements list. Establishing that standard satisfies the primary legal requirement of equal-opportunity laws and prevents you from hiring the best of the worst — a person who may look good next to other candidates but still does not really meet your requirements. A candidate who is missing an important requirement will probably fail on the job.

Figure 14-2

MATRIX EVALUATION

Requirements	CANDIDATES			Comments
	A	B	C	

KEY ✔ Meets requirement.
     − Does not meet requirement.
     + Exceeds requirement.

Reference checks*

Many people assume that all references today will be positive and that respondents are afraid to provide negative feedback. But the manner in which the following questions are answered will tell a lot

---

* Adapted from an article by Dan Bolger, The Bolger Group, *Warehousing Forum*, Volume 12, Number 11, ©The Ackerman Company, Columbus, Ohio.

about the attitude of the reference being asked:
- How do you know the candidate?
- How would you rate that person's skills in supervising people?
- How well does he interact with other managers?
- Can you give me some examples where this person has shown creativity?
- How would you rate his ethics?
- What overall rating in business would you give this person?
- Would you like to add anything else?
- Would you (re)hire this person? Why?

Probation

Most warehouses have a probationary period of one to three months before the new employee becomes a permanent member of the workforce. It is preferable to complete all pre-employment investigation before the new worker is ever put on the job. That averts the possibility of injury or damage caused by a person not suited for the job, as well as the expense and pain of dismissing an unqualified employee. However, no matter how careful your investigation, the risk of error always exists.

For that reason, it is important to observe a new employee closely during the probationary period. No investigation can always reveal attitude problems that will show up only in the workplace. By eliminating unfit workers during the probationary period, the warehouse operator gains a second chance to ensure quality in the workforce.

Proficiency tests

Pre-interview tests may eliminate a percentage of applicants. There is no need to waste interview time on people who cannot pass your tests or do not have appropriate backgrounds. One human-resource consulting firm developed some pencil-and-paper tests for candidates. They include a three-part checklist with the following:
- Questions to determine the candidate's interest and willingness to do the job.
- Questions to determine which of a list of job behaviors best describe the candidate.

♦ A critical-choice exercise that asks the candidate to choose between courses of action.

Scoring of the tests is done by the consultant, who faxes the results to the client within a few hours.

Here are some samples of the questions used for a grocery warehouse order selector. Question 14 is from the checklist for interest and willingness:

14. Safely and properly stack boxes and other items to prevent damage.
A. Has little experience.
B. Has some experience.
C. Has considerable experience.
D. Willing to accept.
E. Unwilling to accept.

In the critical-incident section, a sample question is No. 27:

27. You are operating a forklift with a high load. You are unable to see over the load while driving forward. Which one of the following is the best thing to do?
A. Honk your horn to warn others.
B. Get a coworker to walk in front to direct you.
C. Drive backwards so you can see.
D. Drive slowly so if you hit something it won't cause any damage.

Figure 14-3 is a test that will measure basic skills and arithmetic. Since nearly all warehouse workers must count and check the products they handle, this skill is an essential part of many warehouse jobs.

All of these tools should help you increase the odds that you will always select the best people. There is no process more critical to the success of any warehouse operation.

Figure 14-3

Test number 5
Suggested time: 6 minutes   Score _____

The following problems require a combination of thought and figuring. Read each one carefully and, here again, do not spend too much time on any particular problem. Do your figuring on the back of test no. 4, scratch paper, or the margins of this page.

1   A store requires a 10 percent down payment on all merchandise. What would   _____
    the down payment be on a television set priced at $345.00?

2   If Dr. Jones receives $30 each month from Mrs. Smith, how much will he re-   _____
    ceive in a year and a half?

3   Mr. Brown pays us $9.47 on one of his accounts and $6.52 on another ac-   _____
    count. How much change will he receive if he gives us two fives and a ten?

4   Before making the two payments above, Mr. Brown owed us $102.56 on one   _____
    account and $73.49 on the other. After we apply these payments, what is the
    total of his new balances?

5   Harry's salary is $4,420 per year. How much does he make a week?   _____

6   Mary types 430 words in 10 minutes. If she maintains this same rate of   _____
    speed, how many words will she type in half an hour?

7   If pencils are selling at 4 for 15 cents, how many can you buy for $1.35?   _____

8   Sally has four apples. Jane has half as many as Sally, and Arthur has two and   _____
    a half times as many as Jane. How many apples are there?

Questions that solve problems

The manner in which the following questions are answered will show whether your warehouse manager appreciates the need to hire and develop the best people in order to improve warehouse performance.

Q Can we say yes to these questions about the working environment in this warehouse?
- Is the warehouse safe?
- Is it clean?
- Is the workplace temperature comfortable?
- Do we have attractive eating and lounge areas?
- Are our parking lots lighted and safe?
- Is security adequate, both inside and outside the warehouse?
- Do we provide lockers to secure personal valuables?
- Can we provide flexible working hours?

C If any of these questions does not elicit an affirmative answer, probe the reasons why and steps that might be taken to improve the situation.

Q Have we taken any steps to attract and retain nontraditional employees

C Compare the answers to the opportunities described on page 150.

Q Do we chart and compare worker turnover with other warehouses or with our performance in the past?

C Your ability to retain good people is a quantifiable feature. If no measure is in place, it is not too late to start one.

Q Describe proficiency tests and other procedures used to evaluate people before they are hired.

C Compare the quality of this answer with the features described in the section on proficiency tests.

Chapter 15

Management productivity

Success in warehousing depends on leadership of people. Managers are constantly searching for easy means to solve problems with people management. The latest book or seminar offering a quick fix is picked up and forgotten. The "quick diet" approach of management development just doesn't work. Managers are not taught in school how to lead a group of people, and they don't learn it by reading a book. Learning how to manage people to achieve results requires training, effort, and practice.*

The three most important jobs for every manager are the selection and recruitment of good people; the training, development, and promotion of those who are hired; and the dismissal of those who do not make the grade.

A successful manager is able to get things done through others. How do you find the people who will make your job a success? Many managers have little experience in attracting, training, and developing the people they need for their team.

In the warehouse, it is not uncommon for an outstanding lift truck operator to be promoted into management. Yet the promotion decision is frequently made because of superior work effort, not because that person has any experience or skill in leading other people. If the newly promoted supervisor fails, the effect on the warehouse crew can be severe. At times, the failure is marked by excessive turnover of hourly workers, absenteeism, or even more serious problems. In one

---

* Adapted from an article by the late Richard E. Rogala, Rogala & Orr, *Warehousing Forum*, Volume 12, Number 6, ©The Ackerman Company, Columbus, Ohio.

case, the result was that the new manager was dismissed because the warehouse operation seemed to be getting worse each day. It was apparent that the new manager had failed to obtain the respect and support of the people working in the warehouse.

The hallmark of good warehousing is well-motivated and effective people. The recruiting and retention of such people is a prime function of a warehouse manager.

Success factors

Leading a group of people is more than organizing and planning. It is more than being a good salesman, a good accountant, or a skilled lift truck operator. Learning the basics of managing people requires the development of three basic skills:

- Selecting competent people.
- Developing those people.
- Motivating those people.

Underlying these activities is your need to develop a genuine understanding of people, how they work, and what motivates them.

Some people have keen insight into behavior. With that insight they are in a good position to learn the technicalities of managing people. Others may lack that insight, and they need to be formally trained in the causes of behavior and how they are manifested in the workplace. Either way, whether acquired intuitively or through training, your skill in understanding people needs to be focused on how you will identify and select competent people as well as how you will develop and motivate those people today and in the future.

You must do six things to select the right person for the job:

- Clearly define the job, the tasks to be accomplished, and the setting within which the job exists.
- Review academic and work experiences, even though by themselves they do not tell you how well the candidate will do.
- Agree on a list of the central behaviors required for this job.
- Through the interview, identify the behaviors of the candidate.
- Match the behaviors of each candidate to the job requirements.

- Select the best candidate, the one whose behaviors and skills match the needs list you created. Do not settle for the best person in a mediocre group.

Motivation

Your program to motivate people should include these steps:
- Discover and then utilize the internal incentives that are important to each person. This requires a clear understanding of what motivates each individual.
- Reward each person with an enthusiastic response when you see effective behaviors. Be sure you lead the cheering section when you see a good performance.
- Provide tangible incentives for jobs well done. Maintain and constantly refine a reward program.

Because warehousing frequently allows promotion from within, a good warehouse manager can raise morale by identifying and using the leadership capabilities shown by some individuals in the crew. Recognition of outstanding performance will inspire each worker to improve, and when an outstanding person is successful in making the transition from lift truck operator to supervisor, others in the group realize that anyone with talent can advance in the organization.

People development

Developing people means giving every person an opportunity to perform on the job and to risk mistakes. As you develop your people, you must do these things:
- Communicate your expectations.
- Provide feedback — tell people how they are doing, as well as the reasons why you think they do less (or more) than expected.
- Discuss and give advice on future training, career planning, and goals.

Management's ethical responsibility

The ethics of each manager can be measured by whether the worker can respect and trust the boss.

At a corporate level, the last years of the 20th century saw an epidemic of downsizing or re-engineering. This included the shutdown of warehouses and the release of workers and managers who had done a good job. No one could claim that all restructuring is unethical, but the way it is done can create questions about ethics and trust. Three traits instill one person's trust in another:

- Ability to get results.
- Integrity.
- Concern for people.

All restructuring is designed to get results, but when workers do not see any improvement in what they are doing, they lose confidence in management.

Integrity is doing what you say you will do. Those who handle layoffs or shutdowns in a devious manner lose the confidence of the employees.

Concern for people seems to be rare today. People are still talking about the New England textile mill that in the 1990s kept all workers on the payroll after the plant was destroyed by fire. The owner explained that he needed to repay the loyalty that his workers had always shown to him. The ethical warehouse manager will show that it is possible to cut costs without cutting concern for others.

At the line management level, workers will perform best for a management team that has earned their respect. The manager who preaches about improving productivity while failing to set a personal example is soon exposed as a phony. The manager who demands austerity while receiving a large bonus or salary increase should not be surprised if workers react negatively.

Ethical conduct in warehousing begins with management. Ask yourself whether you have considered any action that would erode the confidence of your workers or customers. This is more than a human-resources issue; high trust can be a competitive advantage in warehousing. Trust is not awarded; it must be earned.

Generation management in warehousing

Consultant Brian Joiner defined four stages of management in his book *Fourth-Generation Management*.

- The first generation is management by doing.
- The second generation is management by directing.
- The third is management by results.

- The hallmarks of the fourth generation are quality and the ability to work as one team.*

Management by doing is not really management in all. A common problem for warehouse workers newly promoted to supervision is a tendency to do jobs that should be delegated. (For more about delegation, see Chapter 15.) For some, this is the result of perfectionism — the belief that no one can do the job as well as you can. For others, it is the result of inexperience or fear. The insecure manager fears that a more talented subordinate might be his replacement. If you walk through your warehouse and see a supervisor doing work that hourly people should be doing, you should always find out what is going on.

Management by directing is the "straw boss" approach to warehouse supervision. The foreman provides exact instructions to workers, telling them not only what to do but also how to do it. If the instructions are given precisely, proper standards will be maintained. Many warehouses have this kind of management.

Management by results does not provide workers with every detail of how to do their jobs. A typical instruction is, "Here is a pile of orders — we need to get them out by the end of the day." Each worker is judged by ability to achieve the result, but the manner in which the work is done is not standardized or closely supervised. Management by results fosters independence and creativity among the people in the warehouse. However, lack of standardization frequently creates difficulties in serving the customer and may produce wide variations in warehousing quality.

With fourth-generation management, quality and productivity are two sides of the same coin, not opposing forces. Viewing the organization as a system should reduce waste and inefficiency. The warehouse supervisor becomes a teacher and a coach, not a straw boss. That supervisor gathers and understands data, finds out what will delight customers, studies the process, and is constantly engaged in coaching and training. That supervisor should spend a significant amount of time talking to warehouse customers and sometimes to the customer's

---

* Adapted from an article in *Warehousing Forum*, Volume 10, Number 3, ©The Ackerman Company, Columbus, Ohio.

customer. The fourth-generation manager also spends time overseeing and improving the training process.

The fourth-generation warehouse manager must optimize the system, recognizing that overemphasis on one part could hurt another. For example, the manager who concentrates on the warehouse might neglect transportation. Yet the customer is interested not in shipments but in getting each shipment on time and in good condition. For the customer, warehouse management is not really important. If the delivery segment of the system fails, the customer is unhappy. As a manager, you are being judged by performance of the entire logistics system, which includes transportation.

Quality management has become a standard requirement for today's workplace. The best way to define quality is to ask the customers. A third-party operator should ask major clients two questions:

- What do you like about dealing with us?
- What don't you like?

Warehouse managers should ask similar questions of the customers who receive shipments from them.

Warehousing is a service business, and superior service depends on dedicated people. Your people must share your dedication to quality. Much depends on how they feel about their jobs and their bosses; your employees are unlikely to treat the customers any better than their company treats them. If your people have an abusive supervisor, don't be surprised if they are hostile to customers. A key ingredient is "all one team," which requires a single-minded dedication to quality service. You cannot achieve it in a warehouse unless everyone is pulling together.

Maintaining service expectations*

Warehouse managers are expected to maintain service, and yet the actual service function is often poorly defined. To meet the customer's service expectations, a warehouse manager needs five things.

---

* Adapted from an article by Richard J. Price, Venator Group, *Warehousing Forum*, Volume 10, Number 3, ©The Ackerman Company, Columbus, Ohio.

The first is commitment. The manager who does not demonstrate a personal commitment to providing superior service is not the kind of manager you want to retain. If attitude is not there, technical performance will eventually suffer.

The second is creativity. Good managers are self-starters. They develop solutions to problems and opportunities as they arise. Excellent managers are willing to think "outside the box" in developing and improving warehouse services.

The third element is cost control. Customer service comes at a price, and providing a service that is unneeded and perhaps even unwanted could break the budget for the warehouse operation. Within commonsense boundaries, each manager must exercise cost control.

The fourth is technology. We have technical capabilities today that were undreamt of a few years ago. The successful manager uses technology to improve service.

Finally, the service-oriented manager should have a willingness to "walk the talk." This manager does what he says he will do, makes promises and keeps them, and demonstrates an ability to lead by example.

Improving your managerial skills

Much is written about improving products, but less is known about the importance of improving yourself. Successful warehouse managers have four traits in common:

- They know their strengths and weaknesses. It may take counseling to recognize what you are good at. Tasks that you are not good at should be delegated to others who like to do them.
- They recognize the inevitability of change. Like the dinosaur, those who cannot accept change may be destroyed by it.
- They never stop growing. When mental growth stops, decay soon follows. Growth includes creativity, both in yourself and in those who report to you.
- They keep score on themselves.

The importance of communication

Successful warehouse managers communicate clearly. Clear communicators genuinely understand what they are trying to convey. They use appropriate words to phrase the ideas, and they choose an effective way to put them across. They also listen effectively.

Some people take courses in public speaking, yet they fail to realize that the most important speeches made in a business setting may have an audience of just one person. The ability to express your ideas clearly and effectively must be practiced and improved.

In today's age of information, a growing number of communications are made in writing, often with e-mail. Be sure your writing is clear and easily understood. Work to develop and improve your writing skill.

The hardest communication skill to acquire is listening. There is relatively little training material about listening.

Listening requires concentration. Choose a place that is relatively quiet and comfortable to share information. The effective listener minimizes the likelihood of interruptions. Offering frequent feedback is a good way to be sure that you have listened effectively and gotten the correct message. A manager who is a poor listener may find that people on the team avoid communication because they are frustrated by the results.

Running effective meetings

Meetings remain a primary medium of corporate communication, yet poorly organized meetings are a constant curse of corporate life.

Whenever you call or a meeting or are called to one, the first question to ask is whether the meeting is truly necessary. See whether there is another way to accomplish the same results without the meeting. If the meeting is necessary, is your presence equally essential? If not, consider whether it makes good sense to attend or whether you might use your time more productively.

A successful meeting requires a detailed agenda, participation among all those present, and sufficient trust to allow each participant to express ideas without fear of negative feedback. The successful meeting is one that gets results. Results are found in meaningful changes, not necessarily in well-written minutes.

Some successful warehouse operations have a brief meeting every day at the beginning of the shift or at a coffee break. Holding a five-minute meeting each day allows the supervisor to describe current events and look to problems that affect the day's work. Each person attending feels as if he or she is "on the team" because of information shared during these daily meetings.

Transition from worker to manager

The field of warehousing has always been notable for its upward mobility. A significant number of warehouse supervisors begin their careers as hourly workers. Outside of the military, few fields have more upward mobility.

Even so, many people in warehousing don't know how to manage the transition from worker to manager. As a result, many people teach themselves as they strive to become warehousing professionals.

In most warehouses, the prime criteria for promotion from worker to manager are skill and good attitude. Unfortunately, neither skill nor attitude guarantees success in making the transition. The supervisor requires other skills to succeed as a manager, and these skills may or may not exist among those who are promoted from the ranks:

- Leadership.
- Dedication.
- Mentoring.
- Management support.
- Continuous learning.
- Time management.
- Ability to find and develop other leaders.

In spite of much writing, leadership remains a mysterious process. Some say that leaders are born and not made. Yet effective leaders have traits in common. All have superior communication skills. They also have a vision. They have a sense of what must happen in the future, and some idea how to get there. The best leaders also have a common touch, the ability to put people at ease and gain the confidence of those they work with.

Effective supervisors use language that demonstrates their dedication — or lack of it. Speaking about "my work" is a clear sign of dedication. Equally obvious is the lack of dedication shown by a person who describes his company as "they." When anyone refers to his own team in the third person, he shows a lack of ownership.

In the warehouse, the most important task of a leader is to be a mentor or teacher. As people move up from the ranks, the ability to teach is an essential part of warehouse supervision. In third-party warehousing, acquisition of each new account requires new learning. In private warehousing, changes in systems, products, or procedures all require additional teaching and learning.

No supervisor can be effective without the support of senior management. Sometimes the supervisor has to work to win support when it is lacking. Your boss may not realize that warehousing is a craft that is becoming a profession. How you improve that awareness and gain the support is vital to your success. One way is to set the example for learning by being active in one or more professional societies or trade associations that deal with warehousing.

The mark of a true professional is constant practice of the basic skills. Where does the warehousing professional go to practice? One answer is publications, and there are plenty of materials covering the field of warehousing. At least two professional societies in warehousing and logistics management publish significant amounts of material concerning warehousing. The successful supervisor needs to constantly update skills in the management of warehouse space and time.

Successful managers have a reputation for getting things done and for getting them done on time. Are you known for being well organized? Seek help when you need it. None of us can get everything done alone, and the most successful time managers are those with the ability to build a team to get the job done.

Developing future managers

Effective managers plan to be replaced so they can be promoted. That means they develop and train successors. The insecure manager may fear that training a successor will threaten his job. In fact, the opposite should be the case, since a person who has developed a successor is most ready to accept a bigger job. The road to the top requires effective successors, and this kind of planning is found in the best warehousing organizations.

Moving from hourly worker to supervisor is not an easy task. It requires training, practice, and hard work. Those responsible for the management development process must be sensitive to the question of whether the potential trainee has "the right stuff" to succeed in a more responsible position. Your ability to handle this process can have a great deal to do with your personal success as a warehousing professional, as well as the success of your entire organization.

Questions that solve problems

Q How do we measure employee turnover, and what do our measurements now show?
C If no measure of turnover exists, your warehouse manager is ignoring a crucial factor in management productivity. High turnover is a clear sign that the management program is not working.

Q Who is ready to replace you in the job you hold today?
C If your warehouse manager does not give a definite and credible answer to this question, this may be a sign that your managers are unwilling or unable to train and develop people.

Q What evidence do we have that our warehouse workers are happy with their jobs?
C By focusing on the positive rather than the negative, you are likely to get a better answer, but any hesitation in answering this question may mean that your manager has not thought much about motivating people.

Q What evidence do we have that our warehouse maintains the highest ethical standards?
C Again we focus on the positive, and failure to provide examples may mean that your managers have not given this important point much thought.

Q Which of Joiner's four generations of management best describes the situation in our warehouse?
C The way this question is answered may say as much as the actual answer.

Q What method do we use to help newly promoted workers make the transition from worker to supervisor?
C If no program exists, you will get a very short answer to this question.

Chapter 16

Training for excellence

Teaching and training may be the most important activity in a successful warehouse. Indeed, the teaching function may spell the difference between failure and survival of any business. Corporate analysts have discovered that a prime cause for small-business failure is lack of management succession. That means that the people who start the business never take the time to develop people to carry on after they have retired.

Today, when there is growing concern about the state of public education, training is one way to compensate for the functional illiteracy found among many workers. Some companies have created classes in reading, writing, arithmetic, or English as a second language.

We are required by law to provide training to ensure safe operation of lift trucks. Although the law does not require us to correct the faults in our education systems, a voluntary effort to do so can upgrade the quality of your warehouse crew.

Turning your company into a learning organization can be an effective way to raise the morale of your people and to improve your company's competitiveness in warehousing.

Managers as teachers

Your warehouse people arrive at work each day ready to observe how you teach and implement the culture of your organization. They measure how you exercise the standards your company claims to honor. If you don't meet their expectations, they punish you with substandard quality. In effect, warehouse productivity may be a measure of how your people rate your performance.

As a manager, you are also a teacher. If your warehouse has high absenteeism, low morale, high turnover, or a "cover your butt" attitude, this could be a reflection of your failure to inspire those who work in your operation.

Managers influence their employees less by what they say than by what they do.

Training goals

Training should not be a pep rally. Workers don't need a cheerleader, they need a coach who helps them go through the process of learning to do jobs that are new to them.

The first step in developing a training program is to define the goals. Why are we conducting the program? What results do we expect from it? How will we measure the success or failure of the trainees? In other words, how will we give grades? Will those who fail the training course be dismissed, reassigned, or given additional training? Who will be trained, and when?

Effective training does not tell people what to do; it helps them discover what they are able to do and shows them how to do it better. Effective training is a bit like an Easter egg hunt. If you tell the children where the eggs are, the hunt isn't any fun. When they discover the hiding places on their own, they get confidence in their ability to discover more eggs as they search further.

There are no magic formulas for running a successful warehouse, just as there are no formulas to ensure success in managing a supermarket or a bank. An effective training program gives people a tool and teaches them how to use that tool to manage better than they did before. That is what the trainee should expect, and that is what the instruction must deliver.

Orientation

Some companies do little more for the new employees than explain who the boss is and where the restroom is. But every new employee will be "filled in" on the company by somebody. If management does not control the process, the orientation will probably be done by an informal leader, and it probably will not be done in a way that management would approve. Orientation is best provided by the supervisor, but the procedure for guiding the new employee must be outlined in detail and scrupulously followed. Having a supervisor handle the process gives every new employee the chance to become acquainted with the boss and establishes the supervisor as the best source of information about the company.

In nearly every organization, there are three information sources: the supervisor, the shop steward, and the grapevine. These information sources are competitive, and any evidence of one source's unreliability will discredit that source. If employees are to accept supervisors as the best source, the orientation process must be handled skillfully.

The most vivid impression that a new employee gets of the company is the one received during the first day on the job. First impressions are made just once. Find out what impression your company makes on a new worker on the first day.

Many warehouses neglect orientation programs. Some simply hand new workers the company rulebook, show them the time clock, and start them on the job. A "bull of the woods" foreman may show authority by giving the new worker the dirtiest job in the warehouse. Others may over-orient a new employee by drowning that person in more information than one can possibly absorb.

The goal of an orientation program is to make newcomers feel welcome and to communicate the expectations of the supervisor and the company. Every orientation program should:

- ♦ Introduce the company. Tell about the history, goals, and objectives of the organization; explain the mission statement or other corporate credos.
- ♦ Describe all company benefits, even repeating earlier descriptions to ensure a total understanding.
- ♦ Introduce fellow workers. Others in the crew should be encouraged to welcome each newcomer.
- ♦ Provide a complete tour.
- ♦ Demonstrate confidence. The orientation is your chance to show the new employee that you are certain of his or her success.

Done correctly, the orientation program creates a positive image that inspires loyalty and goodwill. Those impressions go beyond the opening day and should be the foundation for future management development.

Mentoring

Mentoring is the process of pairing a new employee with an experienced one who serves as a tutor. The mentor is a leader who is familiar with company policies but is also a recognized people person. Ideally, a mentor should work with only one trainee at a time.

Formal mentoring programs may follow a six-month schedule during which the mentor visits the trainee every two weeks for three months, then once a month for three more months. The formal schedule should not prohibit informal visits at any time. Confidentiality between mentor and trainee is essential. The role of the mentor is to provide advice on company procedures, but the mentor may provide personal advice when asked to do so.

Mentoring is a time-consuming process. It requires frequent interaction and could result in a short-term drop in productivity. If mentoring is not available to all employees, it could be a source of resentment among those not invited to participate.

The transition from worker to manager

Many warehouse supervisors or managers begin their careers as hourly workers. As people move up from the ranks, the ability to teach becomes an essential part of warehouse supervision. Your warehouse needs to chart a process of growing from worker to supervisor and from supervisor to manager. Those who are in training to be supervisors should be required to submit frequent action plans. These reports should include short- and long-term goals, as well as a description of current accomplishments. Trainees who have difficulty in submitting effective action plans are sending a signal that their lack of communications skills may make it difficult or impossible for them to succeed as supervisors.

The fine art of delegating

Management is getting things done through other people. Getting things done through other people requires delegation. Delegation, like most human activities, is effective only when done in proper proportions. People newly promoted to management often underdelegate, retaining many of their former duties. Some do so because they enjoy them; others can't believe anyone else will do them properly. A few fear that a subordinate will do them better. The successful manager understands that long-run success depends on the ability to develop skills through delegation of tasks.

However, successful delegation requires competent people to delegate to. Therefore, you must select people in whom you have confidence. They will grow only when you give them tasks that challenge and excite them.

Delegation includes responsibilities. A manager should never delegate without looking back; if the subordinate never receives correction, he or she never has a chance to grow and profit from errors. The effective manager must provide feedback on performance and ask for feedback from team members as well.

A seldom-discussed trap for managers is delegating too much. Some things simply cannot or should not be delegated. If you are concerned about the possibility that you have delegated to much, ask yourself these questions:

- Will it really take less time if I delegate it?
- Is the delegated job a challenging one for the delegatee?
- Can I live with the outcome?
- Does the delegatee have the skill to do the job well?
- Have I delegated the jobs I love and do best?

Proper delegation is like walking a tightrope: it requires constant balance and correction. Look at the jobs you delegated last week. How many of those delegations were successful?

Leadership by example

The successful warehouse supervisor needs more than power and discipline to get the job done. Supervisors exercise leadership, and that is often done by setting an example.

Why does every good warehouse supervisor pick up trash found on the floor? By picking up things that never should have been there in the first place, the supervisor demonstrates that he or she will do something that hourly people neglected. Setting this example shows that good housekeeping is really important.

The effective supervisor holds frequent dialogues with people on the warehousing team. If that supervisor does not allow open exchange of ideas, good communication in the work crew will soon be lacking. Today's warehouse supervisor must have four skills:

- Openness to change.

- Problem solving.
- Customer orientation.
- Teamwork.

In the 21st-century warehouse, the traditional autocratic supervisor has no place. On the other hand, the sensitive leader who has all of the above skills will always be successful.

Training lift truck operators

No one is born with the skill to operate a lift truck. When lift trucks were first introduced to warehouses, nearly everyone had to learn by doing. Today, federal law requires lift truck operators to be trained. In 1999, the Occupational Safety and Health Administration (OSHA) published new rules to govern training programs. One part of those regulations relates to the trucks themselves, and the other relates to the workplace. The truck topics include vehicle capacity and stability, operating limitations, and familiarity with controls and instrumentation. Workplace topics include service conditions, hazardous locations, ramps, and ventilation. Refresher training is required whenever there is an accident or a near miss, a change in the workplace, or reassignment of a worker to a different type of truck.

The best training schools are run as profit centers, but the trainer is there to teach safe and productive operation, not to promote any single brand of equipment. Many of the schools are run at a dealership training site, but some trainers offer to hold the course at the customer's facility, using the customer's lift trucks.

Trainers should emphasize that people on lift trucks are operators, not drivers. Many feel that operating a lift truck is like driving a car, so a first step in training is to point out the significant differences between an industrial truck and an automobile.

Training should emphasize the causes of accidents and how they can be avoided. The number one cause of accidents is operator inattention. Most courses emphasize that additional training will be needed when the operator moves from a conventional forklift to a specialized truck.

The handling maneuvers for a truck equipped with a carton clamp or push/pull attachment are more complex than for the conventional forklift. When palletless handling is introduced to a warehouse, workers may react with fear or uncertainty. A training program provides the motivation needed to successfully implement a new system.

In today's scarce labor market, people with no familiarity or experience are seeking warehouse jobs. Some of these people have never seen an industrial lift truck before, let alone operated one. Managers have found that a good training program for unskilled employees creates operators who do not have to unlearn bad habits acquired in a previous job. As a result, those workers may be more effective than others with warehousing experience.

Training for superior performance

Whether you are teaching new workers to operate lift trucks or developing skilled workers into tomorrow's supervisors, effective training can make your company more competitive. The people who will run your company in the future may be working in your warehouse today. Designing a training system to identify and develop those people may be the most important management task you face.

Questions that solve problems

The best way to evaluate your training activity is to talk to the students. Start with hourly people, since they are the most important students of all. We suggest that the questions below all be asked of employees who have been with the company for thirty days or less.

Q How did you find the orientation received on the first day of your employment with our company?
C Keep probing until you get a full description of the orientation program. Any response that is less than enthusiastic could indicate a problem with the program.

Q How do you feel about the safety training you received?
C Again, keep probing until you find whether the new employee has had enough training in all aspects of work safety, including lift truck operation.

Q Do you have any questions about the company today that were not answered in our previous orientation and training programs?
C This is a good chance to open a dialogue that will reveal the degree of satisfaction shown by a new employee.

Q What experiences have you had with our company that were different from any previous job?
C Again, the emphasis should be on the positive, but watch for any negativity that may surface. The answers may also point out opportunities to improve orientation and training programs.

The following question should be asked of managers, not hourly workers:

Q How effective do you feel that you are at the task of delegating work to those who report to you?
C Be sure there is a clear understanding of what you mean by delegating, and be sure that the question is asked in a positive way that promotes a penetrating dialogue on this subject.

Chapter 17

Motivation, discipline, and continuous improvement

When business is good and labor is scarce, a prime concern of management is creating the motivation and retention programs that will keep good people working in your warehouse for many years. When business conditions are turbulent, the motivation program is focused on maintaining morale even if your company or your competitors are in a crisis. The success of any warehouse depends on the motivation and discipline of the people who work in it. What can you do to build the highest-quality team in your industry?

Motivation and retention programs*

During 1999, members of Warehousing Education and Research Council responded to a survey asking about programs to motivate and retain warehouse workers. The techniques described can be divided into five categories:
- Group activities.
- Services.
- Workplace environment.
- Rewards.
- Other techniques.

Group activities include athletic teams, picnics, catered luncheons on company time, and group outings.

---

* Adapted from *Effective Motivation and Retention Programs in the Warehouse*, Thomas W. Speh, WERC ©1999.

Services include day care, transportation, laundry, gymnasiums, cafeterias, professional help with financial planning and career counseling, personal counseling, and stock purchase plans.

Workplace environment includes flexible schedules, incentives for safety and attendance, and a company newsletter.

Rewards are divided between monetary awards and a wide variety of recognition and nonfinancial prizes.

Programs classified as "other" include tuition reimbursement, scholarships, merchandise discounts, and structured advancement programs.

Monetary awards are considered the most effective but also the most costly. Group activities are the least expensive, although athletic teams have often been discontinued because of the risk of injury. Some companies have rejected employee-of-the-month recognition programs because they are perceived as popularity contests that benefit few workers and are therefore not effective as a motivator.

Flexible work schedules

The survey mentioned above described flexible scheduling as "a technique with untapped potential." It was rated as highly effective, but most respondents do not use it. This suggests that the biggest problem with a new kind of workweek is resistance to change.

Yet one distributor has attracted the best people in its community by offering a four-day workweek with longer workdays and three days off. The four-day week is so popular that the best workers in town seek employment at that warehouse because they appreciate a long weekend and a reduction of travel between work and home. For some workers today, the trip to and from the workplace is the most frustrating task of the day.

As you consider alternatives to the 5/8 week, notice the change in the makeup of many warehouse jobs during the past few decades. Once all warehouse work was physically demanding and fatiguing, but many warehouse tasks today are easier than ever. Increased unitization, better use of power equipment, and improved ergonomics have all combined to reduce the physical effort in warehouse work. While yesterday's order picker may have been exhausted at the end of an eight-hour shift, today he or she may work ten or even twelve hours without undue fatigue. Furthermore, the nature of the work is changing. Today's warehouse worker is likely to operate a computer terminal as well as a lift truck. The dividing line between clerical and materials handling tasks is less distinct than ever.

But what about customer service? The fastest disappearing act in warehousing is the operation with a forty-hour week. Few customer expectations today can be met with a 9-to-5 schedule. With a continuing emphasis on short order-cycle times and better service, forty hours is simply not enough. At the same time, we recognize the difficulty of managing people on second and third shifts. Those late shifts are where we find the greatest frequency of accidents, substance abuse, and other disciplinary problems. Three of the worst accidents of the late 20th century — the nuclear accidents at Three Mile Island and Chernobyl and the explosion of the Challenger space shuttle — were traceable to fatigue of night-shift workers. Long hours are necessary to cut the order cycle time, and this creates the need for creative scheduling to allow round-the-clock operations that still attract good workers. Therefore, a big problem facing warehouse managers in the 21st century is to maintain motivation and quality while keeping the warehouse open for more than forty hours a week.

One warehousing company has created a 7-day, 24-hour schedule with four shifts as shown in Figure 17-1.

Figure 17-1

Four-team work cycle: Team work schedules

Team:	Team 1	Team 2	Team 3	Team 4
Sun	6:00a – 6:00p	6:00p – 6:00a		
Mon	6:00a – 6:00p	6:00p – 6:00a		
Tue	6:00a – 6:00p	6:00p – 6:00a		
Wed	6:00a – Noon	6:00p – Midnt	Noon – 6:00p	Midnt – 6:00a
Thu			6:00a – 6:00p	6:00p – 6:00a
Fri			6:00a – 6:00p	6:00p – 6:00a
Sat			6:00a – 6:00p	6:00p – 6:00a

Each worker has three full days off plus a short shift on one of the four workdays, and management says that this schedule has helped to attract and retain good workers.

Some warehouse operations use people who seek part-time work to supplement another job or to finance their studies. These part-time workers may be eager to work on nights or weekends. Such people can be accommodated by a shift concentrated on the weekend. Another accommodation for the part-time worker would be a short shift of five hours, which allows working mothers or students the freedom to handle their other activities.

Countless variations to the schedules can be developed once you recognize that the traditional 5/8 workweek is not a necessity. Whether shifts of varying lengths will be popular with your workforce is a question you should test by asking your people whether they would like to try it.

Many managers worry that changes such as these will be disruptive. Yet there is ample evidence that most hourly workers would welcome a job that does not call for five eight-hour days. If you doubt this, ask the people who work in your warehouse.

New approaches to work

Telecommuting is a creative solution to the travel problem for some office workers. Advances in communications equipment and information processing make it possible for some people to do at least part of an office job by using equipment based in a home office.

Some warehouses have resolved labor shortages by hiring people with physical handicaps. One apparel manufacturer uses deaf-mute workers for order picking with considerable success. By tapping the ranks of the handicapped, you may find workers who try harder because they have a strong motivation to succeed.

Traditionally, hourly labor in warehousing has been a young person's game. When the work is strenuous, those who get older tend to look for an easier job. Yet today's workforce is getting older. Projections show that by 2001, people ages thirty-five to fifty-nine will be in the majority in most workplaces. One warehouse operation hires workers in their seventies. Absenteeism and turnover is lower than with younger workers. Because the over-sixty segment is now the fastest-growing group in the country, it will be a growing part of the warehousing workforce.

This brings both benefits and costs. Health-care coverage costs start to expand as people move out of their forties, so fringe benefits will cost more if the workforce is older. People over sixty-five have half as many workplace accidents as younger people but take longer to recover when they are hurt. Some companies try to redesign jobs if they are to be done by older people.

Six ways to motivate warehouse workers

There are six things you can and should do to motivate the people in your warehouse:

- Be sure they are part of the family.
- Hire the best people.
- Measure and appraise.
- Empower your workers.
- Celebrate success.
- Create coaches, not traffic cops.

In some companies, the people in the warehouse are considered a lower form of life. They are not treated the same as sales, production, or office people. Sometimes this happens without direction from management and even without management's knowledge. But the effect on morale is devastating. If your company treats the warehouse as the "back room," you need a change in attitude.

In contrast, one retailer emphasizes the importance of warehouse people by providing superior amenities such as lunch rooms and break areas. The chief executive tours the warehouses frequently, and there are constant reminders that the warehouse is the key to success in that organization.

Standards for hiring warehouse workers should be at least as high as those for other departments. When people who have failed in other departments are reassigned to the warehouse, the effect on morale is severe. There is no excuse for suggesting that the warehouse will be a haven for subnormal performers.

But it isn't enough just to pick the best; it is equally important to pluck out bad apples. If you have someone in the warehouse crew who is not performing or who shows a poor attitude, the mechanism must be in place to urge that person to either improve or get out. When management demands the highest standards, everyone on the team will recognize that only the best can stay. A selection process that emphasizes quality will raise morale rather than lower it. Nobody likes to work next to a loser, and warehouse workers are no exception.

Conduct an appraisal interview at least once a year with everyone who reports to you. This meeting should be separated from any review of compensation. The appraisal process is difficult, and some managers avoid it because they do not want to deliver negative feedback. Yet everyone needs to receive grades. Good managers give them, whether they are positive or negative.

Developing incentive pay for workers has always been difficult. Wide variance in work content makes a fair incentive system nearly impossible. There are many other ways to provide recognition for a job well done; the size of a reward may be less important than the recognition it brings. There are two simple and proven techniques:

- Say "Thank you" frequently.
- Tell your people what they are doing right, and always be specific and consistent.

A good supervisor is a source of training and counseling. Workers need to bring their problems to a sympathetic leader, but they also need to feel that the supervisor will get something fixed. A person who dispenses tea and sympathy without achieving any change will lose the workers' respect. A foreman who drives rather than leads will find that workers will look for a job with less pressure. A warehouse supervisor serves as a bridge between workers and management. That supervisor needs a good relationship both with those above and below. Communications with both management and workers must be effective. A well-motivated warehouse work crew is nearly always headed by an effective supervisor.

Managing performance*

Warehouse operators have used a variety of techniques to manage the performance of their employees. Some accomplish little except to

---

* Adapted from an article by Robert E. Ness, ODW Logistics and A. J. Stinnett, The Stinnett Group, *Warehousing Forum*, Volume 11, Number 9, ©The Ackerman Company, Columbus, Ohio.

create resentment and strife. There are two steps to ensure that performance management is a successful process:
- Describe responsibilities in a written position description, and use that description to assign duties. It must be specific enough to assign accountability, yet general enough not to restrict autonomy.
- Examine and evaluate the performance of each manager.

In the warehouse, there is daily and sometimes hourly interaction between managers and employees to issue and receive work, solve problems, answer questions, and monitor progress. This also includes those work processes that provide or assign work to employees. The result is a rule of performance. For example, a typical rule for a forklift operator would read as follows:

The product is stored where it belongs. The product is properly stacked. Stacks are damage-free. Partial-unit loads are in front. The storage area is clean. The receiving document is correct and on time.

Once employees understand what they are expected to do, you tackle the difficult task of making certain they really accept the rules of performance, or those conditions that will exist when a job is done right. Informing, teaching, and persuading workers to do their job right the first time requires unrelenting yet gentle treatment by every member of management. This is the first crucial step of the performance management process.

The next part of the process is to observe performance and be certain that workers are clear about what they are to do. The intent here is to allow workers to make the decisions and to hold them accountable for quality and discipline.

The next step is to record performance. Figures 17-2 and 17-3 illustrate forms that can be used to record incidents involving work performance. In this warehouse, managers are expected to complete the performance record by the end of each Friday.

Finally, the manager reviews each performance record with each worker at least once per quarter.

The review meeting requires three steps: First, schedule the discussion at least one day in advance to give the worker a chance to think about the review. Second, plan the discussion by reviewing rules of performance and the employee's performance since the last meet-

Figure 17-2

```
Ohio Distribution Warehouse Corporation
Performance Record
Name:  Jones, Joe              Qtr: 1st      Yr: 2002
```

1/5	1/12 Good week!	1/19	1/26	2/2
2/9	2/16	2/23 Backed into stack, damaged 3 cases.	3/1	3/8
3/15	3/22	3/29		

Remarks:

Initials: KBA
Date: 4/2/2002

ing. Third, review plans for that worker's future development.

As you review performance, be candid and specific. Mention first the good work and then the poor work, if any. Encourage full participation in the discussion. Discuss areas that need to be improved and any needed training. Then re-establish by negotiation the rule of performance that you expect this worker to meet in the future. Finally, answer all questions and close the meeting by thanking the worker.

When good performance is discovered, a recognition procedure should be in place. When poor performance occurs, the manager should first determine whether the work process needs adjustment to enable the employee to perform properly. The intent is to fix the *process*, not to fix the *blame*.

Workers are satisfied with the process because they know where they stand and how they are expected to improve. Most importantly, they are treated equitably and consistently.

Figure 17-3

OHIO DISTRIBUTION WAREHOUSE CORPORATION
Performance evaluation — Nonmanagement associates

1. **Quality**: How well the associate performs.
Does he/she consistently do the work right the first time?

Improvement required	Sometimes	Usually	Almost always
1	2	3	4

2. **Quantity**: How much work the associate completes.
Does he/she consistently do as much work as needs to be done?

Improvement required	Sometimes	Usually	Almost always
1	2	3	4

3. **Attitude**: The associate's feeling about the work and the company.
Is he/she consistently positive about the company, willing to do what needs to be done without direction, and committed to the welfare of other associates?

Improvement required	Sometimes	Usually	Almost always
1	2	3	4

4. **Housekeeping and safety**: The extent to which the associate practices good housekeeping and follows safety guidelines.
Does he/she maintain a clean and neat work area and consistently follow safety procedures and practices?

Improvement required	Sometimes	Usually	Almost always
1	2	3	4

5. **Attendance**: The extent to which the associate is present for duty.
Does he/she work the required days and hours, report on time, and respond willingly to overtime requests?

Improvement required	Sometimes	Usually	Almost always
1	2	3	4

Evaluation summary
- Quality _____
- Quantity _____
- Attitude _____
- Housekeeping/safety _____
- Attendance _____
- Evaluation score _____

Pay adjustment recommendation and justification:
_____

Training or improvement needed for present job
- Quality: _____
- Quantity: _____
- Attitude: _____
- Housekeeping and safety: _____
- Attendance: _____
- Training needed for next logical job: _____
_____

_____   _____   _____
Signed and dated by associate, evaluator, and reviewer.

Maintaining warehouse discipline

A well-managed warehouse is also a well-disciplined warehouse, one where people play by the rules because they know that to do otherwise will harm the warehouse and their jobs. A well-disciplined warehouse exhibits these traits:
- Managers and workers cooperate in achieving housekeeping excellence.
- Errors and damage are minimized.
- When things are done wrong, workers receive feedback.
- When new workers drag down the operation, the rest of the crew pulls together to improve quality.

The best supervisors do not rely on punishment to control their workers. They know that positive reinforcement for following rules is more effective than a negative response for breaking them. In a warehouse with good discipline, workers know what is expected of them. There is a formal or informal understanding of what level of productivity is expected. Procedures are clear, and everybody follows them.

Warehouse discipline is not easy to define, yet experienced operators know it when they see it. When it is lacking, the signs are equally obvious.

Discipline by peer review*

Traditional methods of discipline may foster an attitude of "us against them." This can create a perception that the company does not resolve workplace disputes fairly. Some companies use a dispute resolution process known as peer review.

Peer review systems replace the traditional grievance arbitration process by allowing an employee to appeal disciplinary actions to a committee that includes coworkers. Normally, all disciplinary actions are subject to peer review, and the employee may challenge either the discipline itself or its severity. Some companies have narrowed the scope of their peer review system to cover only specified actions, such

---

* This subchapter was adapted from an article by Theodore J. Tierney, *Warehousing Forum*, Volume 3, Number 4, ©The Ackerman Company, Columbus, Ohio.

as involuntary terminations, overtime, or the proper application of the layoff procedure. Where peer review systems are limited in coverage, companies usually maintain an open door for other review issues.

The peer review process begins when a worker lodges an appeal. The process is initiated within seven days. The supervisor reviews the discipline and tries to resolve the complaint. However, if the employee remains dissatisfied, he or she may take the appeal to the peer review board. The typical board has five members: the aggrieved employee selects two, management selects two, and those four select the fifth. When the board convenes, the issue is presented in an informal setting. The board may ask questions or call additional witnesses. In addition, the board reviews personnel records. Then the supervisor and the employee leave the room while the board deliberates.

In considering the case, the board decides only whether there has been a violation of company policy. It is not empowered to change company policy. The board may uphold the discipline, reduce or increase its severity, or overturn the discipline entirely.

Majority rules, and the board's decision is final in most companies. In some companies, a unanimous decision is required. If such a decision cannot be reached, both majority and minority reports are given to a manager, who then renders a final decision.

In companies that use peer review, both employees and management comment upon it favorably. Such systems allow employees to participate in management decisions that affect them directly. Employers find that board members take their responsibility seriously and do not abuse or undermine the process. In fact, peers on the board are often more stern with rule violators than management would be.

A peer review program can help you in five ways:
- It raises employee morale by giving workers a voice in disciplinary matters.
- It discourages unionization by removing a common source of discontent.
- It reduces expensive arbitration.
- Its supports the company's position in subsequent litigation, such as EEOC charges.
- It maintains control by keeping workplace disputes in-house.

Continuous improvement

The concept of *kaizen* or continuous improvement is associated with Japanese manufacturing. But the real originator of the concept was W. E. Deming, a teacher of statistical quality control who worked with Japanese managers in the 1950s. Deming's 14 points can be applied in today's warehouse:

1. Improve product and service.

The warehouse manager needs new methods to deal with tomorrow's requirements. Job descriptions must be altered to describe tomorrow's jobs, but today's training for supervisors must be adjusted to create the attitude necessary for success in today's workplace.

2. Adopt the new philosophy.

Quality is now the centerpiece of management philosophy in warehousing. Dedication to quality is no longer unusual, it is assumed. The warehouse that neglects quality will probably not survive.

3. Eliminate mass inspection.

In warehousing, inspection is done to prevent shipping and receiving errors. With improved controls such as bar code scanning, errors should be discovered before the picking or receiving process is completed. Use of the advance shipping notice substitutes for inbound inspection.

4. Stop awarding business on price.

This point has application in choosing third-party warehouse suppliers. The "lowball artist" is rapidly becoming irrelevant. The only cost that is important is the comparison between the cost of outsourcing and the cost of keeping the product in-house. Today's buyer should know enough about warehousing to recognize a lowball price when it is presented.

5. Constantly improve the system.

The warehouse manager who is satisfied with things as they were yesterday is an endangered species in the 21st century.

6. Keep on training.

When workers don't know as much as they should about their jobs, high quality is not possible. In warehousing, the team must learn new skills every time a new client comes to a third-party warehouse or new product comes to a private warehouse.

7. Encourage leadership.

There is a difference between management and leadership. The best supervisors are those who are true leaders. Because warehousing cannot be closely supervised, leadership is even more important than it is in manufacturing.

8. Drive out fear.

When people are afraid their jobs may be eliminated, they may also be afraid to do their best, ask for help, or point out problems. In the warehouse, the best way to drive out fear is through daily communication with everyone in the organization. Consider a short meeting at the beginning of every workday, and be sure the meetings involve everyone on the shift.

9. Break down barriers.

In some warehouses, it is difficult to get teamwork between the people on the floor and those who work in the office. When things go wrong, one group blames the other. Warehousing quality requires that every worker be on the same team.

10. Eliminate slogans and targets.

Empty slogans and unrealistic targets cause resentment because they suggest that workers could do better if they tried harder. The manager who lectures people but ignores the need to replace worn-out lift trucks will be perceived as a person who does not know what's going on and doesn't care enough to find out.

11. Don't rely on quotas.

In today's distribution center, the goal is to improve customer satisfaction. Anything less than 100 percent is not as good as it might be.

12. Promote pride of workmanship.

In some warehouses, people are not doing a good job because they are not encouraged or even allowed to do it. When sloppy housekeeping, improper stacking, or excessive damage are tolerated, workers form the impression that management does not care and that therefore they don't need to care either.

13. Emphasize retraining.

Warehousing is a changing business, with constant introduction of new equipment and new processes. Your people must be ready to contribute as the company improves its methods and equipment. They can accomplish this only through constant re-training

14. Use the PDCA (plan, do, check, act) cycle.

This cycle is just as important in warehousing as in manufacturing.

Even though these 14 points were designed for manufacturing, they work equally well in warehousing. They can help you build a team of respected leaders and dependable followers, a work crew of reasonable stability, and an emphasis on continuous improvement rather than a "quick fix" philosophy to solving problems.

Questions that solve problems

The ability to retain people and reduce turnover is a quantifiable measurement. Other aspects of employee motivation are harder to quantify, but some questioning will at least reveal the degree of interest shown by warehouse managers.

Q How does worker turnover in this operation today compare with the turnover last year and three years ago?
C Failure to improve employee retention is a clear sign of a problem, either internal or external.

Q Which kind of program has proven most effective to motivate our warehouse workers?
C Failure to comprehensively answer this question is a good indication that your manager has not given much thought to a motivation program.

Q Do all of our people work an eight-hour, five-day week?
C Again, failure to consider flexible scheduling is a sign that your management has not considered creative scheduling alternatives.

Q How often do we conduct appraisal interviews?
C The answer to this question might be accompanied by an audit of the appraisal process.

Q Have we installed a performance management system or a peer review system?
C If the answer is no, as it probably will be, explore the willingness of your manager to consider changes in discipline systems.

Q How well can the fourteen points of W. E. Deming be applied in our warehouse operation?
C Ask for specific examples on each of the fourteen points, except those that clearly do not apply to your warehouse operations.

PART 4

Security

Chapter 18

Controlling the inventory

For most warehouse operators, the most valuable capital asset under their control is the inventory. Usually the inventory is worth more than the building and far more than the equipment in the warehouse.

Today, that inventory is turning faster than ever. Not long ago, everyone assumed that the sure sign of a recession was a buildup of inventory and a shortage of warehouses to hold these bloated stocks. But in today's information era, the old rules no longer apply. As inventory velocity continues to increase, the importance of good inventory controls is not always recognized.

In one reader survey by an inventory newsletter, almost half of the respondents were aware of inventory theft in their facilities. The best way to combat a theft problem is to tighten inventory control to the point where stolen inventory will be missed soon after the theft takes place. Preventive measures include cycle counting, controlled access, and switching of duties among various warehouse employees.

Physical inventories*

Why do people take physical inventories? Finance people are concerned about accountability, and public accountants are retained to verify the internal recordkeeping. A physical inventory is one way to correct accuracy failures in the process of receiving, shipping, and re-

---

* Part of this chapter is based on an article by W. G. Sheehan, in *Warehousing and Physical Distribution Productivity Report*, Volume 16, Number 11, ©Alexander Research and Communications, Inc., New York.

cording of transactions.

The annual physical inventory is not unlike an annual checkup by a physician. Both provide an early warning about problems and an opportunity to correct past errors. Considering the impact that the physical inventory can have on operations, it deserves more attention than it receives. Inaccurate inventories can impair a company's ability to plan materials requirements and cause uncertainty in financial planning. An inaccurate inventory leads to lost sales, lower fill rates, and lost productivity.

How often should a physical inventory be taken? Your auditors or bankers may influence this decision. Bear in mind that loss of assets is not the only damage you may suffer when the physical inventory and book inventory are badly out of balance.

Preparing for the physical count

An efficient physical inventory starts weeks before the actual inventory date. You may wish to assign an inventory coordinator for each of the physical inventories to be conducted. This appointment pinpoints responsibility and establishes a sole source for information flow.

A first step is training. Thankfully, inventories are not taken every day; that means, however, that the people who do this job may lack experience or may have forgotten things they knew when inventory was taken before. Therefore a key step in preparation is training people on the proper procedures for taking an accurate count. Employees must be taught how to fill out inventory tags and whom to talk to regarding problems with the count.

A second step is organization. An annual wall calendar marked with inventory dates is helpful. Get rid of obsolete items, waste or excess material before the physical inventory. About two weeks before the inventory date, bring key personnel together to discuss responsibilities, availability of workers, equipment requirements, and supplies required.

Decide whether the inventory should be pre-tagged or tagged during the first count. Your computer system should produce inventory tags preprinted by location. If these tags have everything filled out except the quantity, the physical count will take less time. Damaged goods and items in the repacked area should be counted in advance.

Good housekeeping is an absolute requirement for an efficient physical count. If there are mixed pallets, mixed stacks, or products stored in aisles or staging areas, the count will take much longer.

Anticipating problems

Five common pitfalls can be prevented by advance awareness:
- Failure to correct problems from a previous inventory.
- Poorly motivated people on the inventory team.
- Inadequate checking of discrepancies.
- Failure to account for all of the paperwork.
- Inadequate procedures.

The end of the count is not the end of the inventory, because the process is not complete until all counts have been reconciled and inventory records updated. This important last step is sometimes handled poorly, and failure to reconcile means that the imbalances found at one inventory will still be there at the next one.

Counting stock is not fun. One warehouse incentive program provided money prizes to each member of the team that counted the most items or turned in the most inventory tickets. Another prize went to team members who achieved the most accurate count. One criterion, however, was that the winners in each category had to rank in the upper third in the other category. The team that counted the most tickets also needed to have a reasonable level of accuracy, with the most accurate team also needing to achieve a high level of productivity. Achieving efficiency through motivation can significantly improve the counting process.

Proper control of inventory tickets is a necessity. This control begins with having each inventory ticket bear a unique serial number. The tickets should be handed out according to zones and should be placed on the product in sequence. This maintains an audit trail, and it expedites further counts, since the checker will know precisely where to find each inventory ticket that is in question.

Each inventory team must turn in all tickets and verify that every ticket is accounted for at the conclusion of the inventory. Missing paperwork is a clear sign of an incomplete count.

Carefully developed procedures are the key to success in any inventory counting operation. A cutoff date for receipts and shipments must be established for accurate reconciliation after the count has been completed. Material received after the cutoff date must be omitted from the count. Similar treatment is necessary for other activities taking place after the cutoff.

Notes should be taken regarding the time required for the inventory, the equipment used, and the items counted. This information is useful in planning for the next inventory and in reviewing the effectiveness of this one.

Cycle counting*

A growing number of warehouse operations use a cycle count to supplement or replace the full physical inventory. Cycle counting is the counting of a small percentage of the inventory on a regular basis. Since you are continually counting, when errors are identified you can define the cause of the error and take corrective action. The immediate objective of cycle counting is not only inventory accuracy but also the identification and elimination of errors. A byproduct of identifying and eliminating errors will be a more accurate inventory in the future.

Cycle counting begins with a determination of what items to count and when to count them. Many operators rely on a Pareto or ABC analysis in determining what and when to count:

- The A items are typically 80 percent of the dollar throughput and only 20 percent of the SKUs.
- The B items are 15 percent of throughput and 40 percent of the SKUs.
- The C items are 5 percent of throughput and 40 percent of the SKUs.

A cycle counting plan would then call for the A items to be counted more often than the B items, and the B items more frequently than the C items. The typical cycle count plan might involve counting 6 percent of the A items, 4 percent of the B items, and 2 percent of the C items each week.

---

* This subchapter is by James A. Tompkins, Ph.D., Tompkins Associates, Inc., Raleigh, North Carolina.

Every item should be counted when it is easiest and cheapest to get the most accurate count. There are at least four ideal times to count:
- When the inventory balance is low.
- When an item is re-ordered.
- When the inventory balance is zero or negative.
- When a large order is received.

Cycle counters should be assigned to the job on a permanent basis, but that does not mean that cycle counting is necessarily a full-time job. It does mean that the workers assigned to cycle counting should be on a permanent team.

The realistic productivity standard is that a cycle counter can process 40 SKUs per day. These counters must be familiar with the stock location system, the layout, and the items being counted.

The counting team must recognize the possibility of crossovers. When a count reveals an overage on one item, the counters should identify and check other items that may be confused with the one that is not in balance.

Most of the controls described earlier for physical inventories will also apply to cycle counting. Valid cutoff is critical because cycle counting takes place without affecting normal operations. This calls for careful coordination of counting and transaction processing. Any transaction that takes place after the inventory balance is reported and the actual count is made must be isolated so that an accurate reconciliation takes place.

Figure 18-1

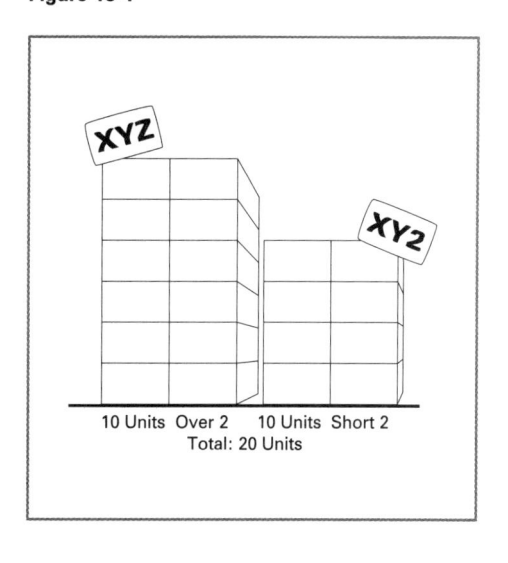

10 Units Over 2   10 Units Short 2
Total: 20 Units

The cycle counting document is forwarded to a reconciler, a team member who did not take this particular count. The reconciler compares the count with the inventory record and determines whether the count is valid. Validity is determined by compliance with a standard of tolerance. Tolerance is based on monetary value of the item being counted. A typical count tolerance limit would be fifty dollars; that is, if the cycle count is within fifty dollars of the inventory record, the count is acceptable. When a bad count occurs, the item is recounted. The recount will determine whether the original count was bad or the item count is actually within the tolerance limit.

It is important to recall that a prime objective of cycle counting is the identification and elimination of errors. Therefore investigation of each bad count is a critical process. If the counted quantity is verified as less than the inventory record, there are two possibilities, which are easy to check:

- ◆ A request for this item was filled without recording the transaction.
- ◆ A sales or production order was incorrectly subtracted from inventory.

If the variance shows that the count quantity is higher than the book record, replenishment orders should be reviewed to see whether product was received and improperly recorded. Recent sales or production orders should be checked for erroneous subtractions from the records.

At the end of each month, prepare a rating for the cycle count process. This might be a ratio of good counts to total counts.

Acceptance of cycle counting

A monthly newsletter, *Inventory Reduction Report*, surveyed its readers and reported that cycle counting has made substantial inroads as an accepted inventory management process. Reduction of inventory cannot begin without confidence in the accuracy of inventory records. It is common for companies using cycle counting to report accuracy rates of 99.8 percent for the total inventory. The corrective action feature for investigating inventory errors tends to improve communication between sales and manufacturing. All departments appreciate the benefits of discovering errors through the cycle counting process.

Some report that greater inventory accuracy keeps customers happy. A customer who has been hurt by inventory inaccuracy will obviously welcome any step that keeps this from happening on a regular basis.

Many report that physical inventories have either been eliminated or reduced in frequency by introducing cycle counting practices. Some indicate that they can reduce safety stock levels because of greater confidence in inventory accuracy.

With the growing acceptance of cycle counting, the 21st century may be the time when physical inventories are totally replaced by cycle-count procedures.

Questions that solve problems

Inventory security is a key element in controlling a warehouse operation. Therefore, these questions should be asked not just of your warehouse managers but also of your financial officer and your public accountants.

Q What steps have been taken in the past year to verify the accuracy of our warehouse inventories? How often have we counted, how have we counted, and what were the results?

C If you don't get similar answers from all three of the parties that receive these questions, there is a problem that requires additional investigation.

Q Have we used cycle counting to supplement or replace physical inventories?

C Failure to consider cycle counting suggests that your managers are not in touch with state-of-the-art inventory control methods.

Q Is our inventory accuracy better or worse than it was five years ago?

C Signs of deterioration could highlight serious problems. Failure to control inventories is a sign that the warehouse is slipping out of control. A management team that loses control of the inventory probably needs to be replaced. Because of the critical nature of inventory control, it is imperative to ask questions such as these on a regular basis.

Chapter 19

Theft and mysterious disappearance

Any product that moves through warehouses can be stolen. However, the products most likely to attract thieves are valuable, marketable, or both. Most thieves consider marketability more important than value.

Some commodities have become more attractive to thieves over time. The early computers were very expensive but difficult to sell. As the cost per cubic foot of computer product has gone down, the marketability and specific theft risks of this product has risen dramatically. If you want to know about theft risk, law enforcement officials or your insurance company can provide current information.

Many warehouse operators apply selective security standards, establishing more secure areas within the warehouse for those products that represent the greatest risk.

Responsibilities of the warehouse operator

For the third-party warehouse operator, responsibility is limited by the Uniform Commercial Code. Under this and English common law, a third-party bailee is responsible only for the degree of care that a reasonably prudent owner would exercise. If your goods are stored in a third-party warehouse, your own insurance coverage should provide primary protection, since the third-party operator is liable only when security measures can be proved to be substandard. On the other hand, the manager of a private warehouse is ultimately responsible for the security of everything stored in the building.

Two kinds of losses

Warehouse thefts fall into two categories. The first is mass theft, which might involve the hijacking of a truck or a break-in at a warehouse. The second is pilferage, also called *mysterious disappearance*.

Mysterious disappearance may involve collusion theft in either shipping or receiving. It may also involve the clandestine removal of small amounts of merchandise over a long period. Small products of high value may be taken out in lunchboxes, handbags, or pockets — or they may be put into a trash container or other outdoor location for later removal.

There are two ways to defend against mass theft and pilferage. The first is to develop physical deterrents in the warehouse that make it difficult for thieves to breach the security of the building and remove products. The second defense requires that you confirm the honesty of all employees.

Controlling collusion theft*

Lately the nation has seen a significant increase in collusion theft. In the warehouse, collusion theft is usually accomplished by a partnership between a truck driver and a warehouse worker. This is the most difficult warehouse crime to control, since no electronic or paperwork system will always expose collusion when it exists.

Furthermore, collusion thefts are frequently quite large. One survey indicated that 40 percent of warehouse thefts are by employees at that warehouse. Obviously, the best way to avoid collusion theft is to be certain that you hire honest people, but that has become more difficult with a tight labor market in recent years. Once the use of a polygraph (lie detector) test was permissible, but federal law now prohibits polygraph use as a hiring practice.

Confirming employee honesty

A major factor in collusion theft is a perception that management lacks concern for security. A primary failure is lack of pre-employment

---

* Adapted from an article by Daniel Bolger, The Bolger Group, *Warehousing Forum*, Volume 11, Number 5, ©The Ackerman Company, Columbus, Ohio.

screening. It is difficult to screen applicants to include only those people who are absolutely honest, have the required skills, and are drug-free. Yet hiring the wrong person can easily cost thousands of dollars.

There are many ways to do pre-employment screening. Personal interviews, drug screening, reference checks, and background reviews are all necessary steps.

Pre-employment tests can help you screen candidates for the job. The cost is low, ranging from twenty-five to fifty dollars per candidate.

Researchers at the University of Iowa studied more than forty tests and a half-million testees. They reported that the tests will identify disciplinary problems, disruptiveness on the job, tardiness, and absenteeism. It is difficult for dishonest people to fake honesty. Thieves will expose bad habits in the tests, partially because they tend to believe that "everybody does it" and that it would be implausible to claim that they never do it themselves.

A growing number of experts have demonstrated a significant correlation between people who fail these tests and steal from employers. Other professionals are concerned about the large number of "false positive" people who are honest but are incorrectly identified as dishonest because of test scores.

London House (a division of the McGraw-Hill companies) and Reed Psychological Systems are two suppliers of honesty tests. Both consider their questionnaires sensitive and will not allow them to be published. Figure 19-1 shows a sample assessment report.

The test designers provide instruments that are in compliance with all federal and state laws prohibiting discrimination on the basis of race, color, religion, age, sex, national origin, disability, or record of offenses.

These surveys are designed to be easily given and administered. The tests can be completed in less than an hour and can be scored with the aid of a personal computer. Raw scores are faxed to the testing company or processed by telephone.

The handling of references

A growing number of people are wary of giving negative reports about a former employee. Facts offered in good faith or opinions hon-

Figure 19-1

Significant behavioral indicators

Interview questions

Scale: Work values
514: You've indicated that you're not always very prompt. What types of situations typically cause you to be late for work?

Scale: Supervision attitudes
614: Your response indicates you frequently break rules to do the job right. Please describe some situations in which you did this.
621: Based on your response, you've occasionally gotten into trouble for fooling around at work or school. Please describe some examples.

Significant behavioral indicators

Positive indicators

Scale: Honesty
In recent years, has never thought about stealing money 89
Thinks he or she will never take something of value
from future jobs without permission 88
Believes he or she is definitely too honest to steal. 39
Has never taken company merchandise or property
from jobs without permission............................ 96
Has not taken any money, without authorization,
from jobs in the past three years 110

Scale: Drug avoidance
Believes that someone who drinks alcohol is unacceptable 115
Believes that someone who uses uppers (amphetamines)
is very unacceptable 116
Believes that someone who uses marijuana
is very unacceptable 118

estly held are a solid defense against defamation claims.

When you check references, your most important question is, "Would you rehire?" The Society for Human Resource Management estimates that nearly one-fourth of all resumes and applications contain at least one serious fabrication. Reference checking will reveal such dishonesty even if the person giving feedback is trying to avoid anything negative. You are more likely to get a useful response if questions are in the form of a choice between two options. For example, "Would you consider this individual to be more technically inclined or a more people-oriented person?" It is best to ask the most interesting questions first, finishing the interview with basic verification of employment dates, salary and title. Reference checking is time consuming and therefore expensive. Large companies indicate that they spend about 10 percent of their hiring time checking references, and the cost of hiring each employee is about $9,200. That may seem expensive, but consider the potential losses resulting from hiring a dishonest employee.

Other collusion theft controls

One proven deterrent for collusion theft is random tests on loadings for outbound vehicles. Choose one or two outbound loads at random each month, and call the trucker back in for the load to be completely rechecked. When potential thieves learn that this kind of surveillance is under way, they may conclude that it is too risky to steal at your warehouse.

Another key to controlling collusion theft is excellence in inventory management. If employees get the idea that management does not know how much material is in the warehouse, they may conclude that if something disappears it will never be missed. On the other hand, when inventory discrepancies are regularly and carefully checked, the message is out that management can and will control the stock in the warehouse.

Collusion is difficult to control, but it will be minimized if you take care to hire honest people and demonstrate that management is committed to protecting the property in the warehouse.

Undercover investigations*

An undercover investigation should be considered whenever a warehouse has an unexplainable inventory shortage. Receipt of a reliable tip that there is a theft problem will also be good reason to place an undercover worker inside your warehouse.

Americans dislike spying. The right to privacy is an American heritage, and undercover investigation could be called invasion of privacy. However, collusion theft can become an almost unsolvable puzzle in a large distribution center. You may need to use undercover services in spite of a dislike for the practice.

Undercover services are provided by large detective agencies as well as some specialist consultants. The undercover investigator is hired as an ordinary employee, and that person does everything possible to be a typical worker and blend into the work crew. By befriending various members of the crew, the operative gradually discovers the causes of problems. This is a delicate and dangerous occupation. Total confidentiality is essential, both to secure success of the project and to protect the safety of the agent. Using an undercover investigator involves six steps:

- ◆ Selecting the operator.
- ◆ Preparing the cover.
- ◆ Bringing the undercover agent into the warehouse.
- ◆ Establishing rapport.
- ◆ Collecting information from the investigation.
- ◆ Concluding the operation.

The first step in selecting the operator is to find an agency that you can trust. The selection process is complicated by the fact that many agents refuse to list recent clients as references, for obvious reasons. Once an agency is selected, the agent must be evaluated as an individual. Does that person have the intelligence, maturity, and common sense to get the job done? Does he or she have the physical appearance and skills necessary to blend in with the other workers and per-

---

* Adapted from an article by Barry Brandman, Danbee Investigations, *Warehousing Forum*, Volume 6, Number 10, and Volume 11, Number 2, ©The Ackerman Company, Columbus, Ohio.

form the assigned task? Selecting both the agency and the individual is critical to the success of the project.

Once the operator is selected, a carefully prepared cover story is developed. This must include job references that will hide the agent's true background and add credibility to the undercover role. The undercover operator follows the same interview and selection process used for other employees. That person is also paid in the customary manner. A thief who is already in your warehouse will be highly suspicious of any new people.

The process of establishing rapport will take some time, perhaps four to six weeks. The agent must win the confidence of fellow workers without appearing overly inquisitive or aggressive. This could involve participation in company athletic leagues or sharing a few beers in taverns frequented by fellow workers.

Undercover service companies usually provide written reports of the investigation. They are prepared daily and mailed to the home of the executive who hired the operator. The reports are written so that even if they fell into the wrong hands they would not identify the author. They are designed to provide information about potential criminal activity.

Concluding the operation can be as delicate as starting it. In one case involving drug dealing, the operation ended with confrontation and dismissal of nearly one-third of the workforce. The undercover operator was fired along with the drug dealers to preserve the cover.

The warehouse manager must recognize that the undercover agent is in a dangerous job. Breaking that agent's cover could pose a significant risk. For that reason, as few people in management as possible should know about the undercover investigation. The cover should be preserved even after the investigation is over.

Security audits

Management must actively combat theft, focusing on the three aspects of defense: physical, personnel, and procedural. No one of the three will be effective without the other two, and a "Maginot Line" complex can be as fatal in warehouse security as it was in military history. The greatest enemy of security is complacency. An outside security audit is a good way to guard against such complacency.

Physical deterrents

Electronic alarm systems are more reliable than watchmen, but it is important to remember that any system designed by one human can be defeated by another — especially if the theft ring includes a former employee of an alarm company. Some alarm companies use subcontractors to install equipment. While the alarm company may have honest and bonded employees, the subcontractor may not. A dishonest electrician can defeat many alarm systems.

Closed-circuit television is sometimes used primarily as a psychological deterrent. Television seldom prevents theft. Dishonest employees quickly find that no one closely watches the monitors. Even if someone watched them for hours each week, they would overlook a collusion theft because it looks exactly like normal materials handling.

Many electronic alarms are designed to protect only doors and windows. Such a system will not stop the thief who is willing to cut through the warehouse wall. The walls of most contemporary warehouses are not load-bearing. Whether they are built of metal, concrete, or masonry, a thief needs little time to cut a hole large enough to allow a mass theft. Because of the vulnerability of warehouse walls, the best electronic alarm systems include a *wall of light* surrounding the building interior. The thief who penetrates a warehouse wall will still sound an alarm when entering the wall of light.

Cargo seals are serial-numbered metal strips that are broken before a truck or container is opened. Properly used, the cargo seal is a physical deterrent to cargo theft. Because thefts from interstate commerce may be investigated by the FBI, the presence of a seal was once sufficient to discourage unauthorized entry. Today, bolder thieves may not be deterred by the threat of an FBI investigation.

If a railroad car or a truck is broken into while at the shipper's warehouse, the carrier has a legal right to disclaim responsibility because the vehicle was not under its control. Electronic systems that extend coverage to trailers are available, and under certain conditions they must be used.

Restricted access

Only warehouse employees should have access to storage areas. Customers in a bank are not offended by barriers that prohibit them from walking behind teller counters; warehouse users should not be offended if their movement is restricted in the same manner. Even warehouse employees should be permitted to enter only those areas involved in their own work. Despite the good sense of this approach, many warehouse managers have no physical restriction to prevent people from wandering at will. They do not prevent visiting truck drivers from walking or loitering in storage areas.

One way to reduce losses of theft-prone products is to place them on the upper levels of storage racks, where they can be removed only by a lift truck operator. Denying access to unauthorized people improves both security and storage productivity.

Customer pickups and returns

Customer pickups create an unusual theft risk. One way to control that risk is to have merchandise for pickup pulled from stock by one person, with delivery to the customer made by a different person. This procedure is based on the fact that usually only two people are involved in collusion thefts.

Customer returns present a different security problem, particularly if the merchandise is returned in high volume or in nonstandard cartons. Be sure all customer returns are checked thoroughly and promptly. If your returned-goods processing is not current, you're inviting pilferage.

Security procedures

Personnel policies can encourage or discourage honesty. Establishment of a policy on the acceptance of gifts is one example. If truckers can obtain a convenient unloading appointment by making a "gift" to a receiving manager, the moral atmosphere that encourages pilferage will also be promoted.

Cargo seals should be applied or broken only by a supervisor. The system should show which supervisor performed such tasks and the time that the seals were checked.

Every empty container is a potential repository for stolen merchandise. An empty trailer left on a dock could be the staging area for a theft. The same is true of empty trash containers. Empty freight vehicles should be kept under seal or inspected as they are removed from the warehouse. Such inspections should be covered by a written record of the time and place.

Control of documents is as important as the handling of cargo. Fraudulent bills of lading or parcel bills can be used to divert shipments. Supervisors should control the issuing of all documents.

Many workers on warehouse crews have lunch or coffee breaks all at the same time, with no employees available to control exposed docks or entrance doors. With staggered rest breaks, a few people can always be on duty to protect the warehouse against unauthorized entry.

No one should park personal vehicles near the buildings or loading doors. Never permit vehicles to back into any slot unannounced. Retain all cargo seals until the unloading is verified, and then make sure the seals are mutilated so they cannot be reused. Broken seals should never be discarded on the warehouse property.

When the entire warehouse crew understands that security is essential for survival, you can create a team spirit that is strong enough to drive out dishonest employees.

Questions that solve problems

Some warehouse managers remain in a state of denial with respect to the potential for theft or pilferage. Even when there is evidence that it exists, some are unable to face the issue. Therefore, when you question warehouse managers about security, your questions must be particularly incisive to demonstrate your personal interest in security.

Here are some of the questions you should ask:

Q What evidence do we have to confirm that there is no theft problem in our warehouse today?
C Be sure the answer is supported with facts that demonstrate comprehensive inventory accuracy. If this question is not answered convincingly, you probably need to probe further into security situations in that warehouse.

Q Of those employees hired in the past three years, what evidence tells us that they are honest?
C The answer should include a description of the current system of security checks.

Q When did we last audit our security system, through independent investigation or some other audit procedure?
C If nothing has been done in the past three years, you should probably order a security audit.

Q When did we last test our burglar alarm system to be sure that police respond properly?
C The answer to this will tell about how involved management is in controlling theft security.

It is important to constantly search for new ways to protect warehouse inventories, primarily through better procedures to screen people and discover those who are not honest. It is equally important to constantly investigate new physical protection procedures as well as better audit procedures to determine how well security is maintained today.

Chapter 20

Protecting your people

Those who understand warehousing recognize that management of *things* is far less important than the management of *people*. A warehouse is only as good as its worst employee. Therefore, an excellent warehouse is more than a beautiful building and modern equipment; it must be a greenhouse that grows the highest-quality people. Workers cultivated in the best warehouses are both healthy and honest. They have a sense of ethics, which comes from examples set at the top. They perform well, and they also look good.

Personal appearance and housekeeping

Housekeeping is a leading indicator of quality among those who judge warehouses. The review of housekeeping typically refers to neat stacks, clean floors, and clear aisles. However, never overlook the importance of the personal appearance of warehouse workers. Do your people look like professionals?

One way to control personal appearance is to issue uniforms to everybody in the warehouse. Uniforms may be less acceptable in the American culture than in some other parts of the world. Many individualists feel stifled by any requirement to wear a uniform. Requiring some people to wear uniforms but not others may be divisive; one way to solve this problem is to issue uniforms to everyone in the company. At one auto assembly plant, everybody on the production floor wears a white shop coat. A member of management in the plant replaces his or her business suit coat with the white shop coat. At one grocery warehouse in South America, green uniforms are issued to workers who are licensed to operate a lift truck, blue uniforms to everyone else. Thus the uniform will reveal any violations of operating authority.

Companies using uniforms often find that the economic value of the uniform as a fringe benefit is positive. The cost of rented industrial clothing is not high, and the supplier usually takes responsibility for cleaning, alteration, repair, and replacement.

Whether you have a uniform program or not, be sure to praise workers who dress with a professional appearance. Workers who see the well-dressed people garnering praise will get the message.

Safety*

Injuries and accidents are expensive, whether they happen on or off the job. Since warehousing involves lifting, pushing, holding, and working with power equipment, the potential for accidents is high.

A federal study indicates that injured warehouse workers are typically not the newcomers. Those with five or more years' experience are more likely to be injured than those with less. In fact, those with less than one month's experience are the least likely to be injured. Apparently experience causes carelessness, which in turn leads to injuries.

The same study indicates that extreme fatigue may not be a factor in accidents. Twenty-nine percent of accidents occur after only two to four hours on the job, and an additional 23 percent occur during the first two hours on the job. Only 8 percent occur after eight or more hours in the workplace.

The most dangerous work in a warehouse is loading and unloading of freight vehicles. Warehouses reporting the most accidents are wholesalers and retailers, who account for 68 percent of all warehouse injuries, as contrasted with only 8 percent in warehouses devoted to transportation and public utilities. Presumably most third-party warehouses are in this smaller category.

Here are four more statistics about safety that may surprise you:
- ◆ Workers are more likely to be injured in larger warehouses; 82 percent of injuries occur in warehouses with

---

* From *Injuries to Warehouse Workers*, by U.S. Bureau of Labor Statistics.

eleven or more employees.
- ◆ Older workers are safer; 74 percent of those injured are thirty-four or younger.
- ◆ Most warehouse workers do not wear protective equipment. The most commonly used protectors are gloves and steel-toed shoes; hard hats and safety glasses are less frequently used.
- ◆ Although safety training is common and sometimes mandated by law, many workers never receive proper training; only 28 percent of injured workers had received training in proper manual lifting.

When workers are asked why accidents happen, 54 percent blame factors other than workplace conditions. However, 22 percent say that lack of space in the workplace was a factor. Some feel that working too fast or in an awkward position was the contributing cause.

A common problem in warehouse safety is the stacking of corrugated-cardboard boxes. Humidity in a warehouse can break down the corrugated material and cause collapse. Therefore, merchandise piled high should be regularly inspected for any sign of carton failure, and leaning stacks should be taken down before they fall.

The metal or plastic bands used to seal containers are a common source of injuries. When banding is cut, it can fly back and cause cuts or eye injuries. Used banding left on a warehouse floor can cause workers to slip and fall or get tangled in a forklift truck.

Federally mandated training

Long-awaited federal regulations governing training of operators of industrial trucks took effect in 1999. Before that time, the Occupational Safety and Health Administration (OSHA) had required training for lift truck operators, but no standards were published governing how that training should be given. The 1999 regulations were intended to provide a standard. The new rules require any worker to be trained before using a lift truck. The ruling is specific about what topics need to be addressed: some relating to the trucks themselves and some relating to the workplace. It also requires refresher training whenever an operator has a near-miss situation, a change to a different type of lift truck, or a change of workplace.

Research performed by OSHA in connection with these regulations revealed one surprising fact. According to a 1992 study of workplace injuries, lack of training is in sixth place as a cause of accidents. The number one cause is operator inattention, followed by vehicle overturning, unstable loads, operator struck by a load, or a fall from an elevated truck.

Ergonomics and safety*

Ergonomics is the study of job demands from the perspective of what tasks workers can safely physically perform. It is also the science of designing machines, tools, furniture, and work methods for maximum human comfort and efficiency. Good ergonomics is also the business of helping people work smarter rather than harder, arranging the work so people will minimize the possibility of fatigue or injury.

Unfortunately, many managers today look at ergonomics as just a way to stay out of trouble with the federal government. A more important motivator should be the improvement of your company's accident and safety record and a reduction in health benefit costs. On-the-job injuries are expensive, and one trade group reports that the average medical cost for a back injury is $30,000. If good ergonomics can significantly reduce your injury record, that should be a stronger motivation than fear of federal regulators.

Perhaps the most important motivator is a gain in productivity. When people work smarter, they are more productive. When management arranges the workplace to reduce fatigue, your people can do the same amount of work with less effort and thus move more pounds of freight every day. Good ergonomics can and should have a payback in improved productivity.

The most obvious way to improve ergonomics in the warehouse is to avoid conditions that cause an awkward or strained situation in manual handling of merchandise. The worst strain may be that caused by twisting, a motion referred to by technicians as the asymmetric multiplier. Avoiding situations that require workers to twist while lift-

---

* Adapted from an article by Eugene Gagnon, Gagnon and Associates, *Warehousing Forum*, Volume 10, Number 5, ©The Ackerman Company, Columbus, Ohio.

ing could avoid or at least minimize situations that require the worker to stoop to the floor or reach overhead while handling heavy cases. Place merchandise so that the distance walked in selecting orders is minimized. Reduce repetitive motions that can cause injury, sometimes referred to as cumulative trauma disorder (CTD). People working with keyboards may repeat certain motions enough to cause a CTD such as carpal tunnel syndrome.

The best way to avoid the awkward motions that cause injury is to carefully plan the arrangement of stock in the warehouse. Those SKUs that move fastest or are most strenuous to handle should always be placed in the "golden zone," between belt and shoulder height. That allows the order picker to grab and move the case without stretching or bending. Since it is impossible to place all merchandise in the golden zone, at least the fastest movers should be there.

Several practical steps will improve ergonomic conditions. At one grocery warehouse, two extra pallets are always placed on the floor beneath the first loaded pallet. That puts the lowest case eight to twelve inches higher than if the extra pallets were not used, and thus reduces the risk of strain from leaning down to pick up the lowest case. In some warehouses, order selectors use a case hook to pull cases from the back of second-level slots. The hook allows the selector to avoid climbing up on equipment or product.

Common sense can reduce walking. If order picking is done in a zigzag pattern, the picker selects from one side of the aisle and then immediately selects merchandise directly across the aisle. When a pallet jack is used for order selection, the pallet should be positioned three feet from the merchandise to be picked. If it is farther away, too many steps are needed. If it is closer, the picker will need to twist while moving from storage to the pallet.

Rotating jobs every few hours has several advantages. It allows workers to do different tasks and therefore reduces the possibility that a repetitive motion might cause injury. It has other advantages such as cross training and developing new skills, as well as avoiding job boredom.

Sometimes injury is related to fatigue. Uncontrolled overtime can contribute to injuries and accidents. Scheduling and judicious use of part-time workers enables warehouse managers to reduce overtime.

Tasks should be designed for small breaks, and workers should be trained to use these breaks to avoid undue fatigue and to plan ahead. They should be encouraged to periodically stop moving, study the remaining work, and plan the best way to get the job done. In other words, warehouse workers should be taught to work smarter and not harder.

Training and job review are essential. Have all of your order pickers been taught the best way to select orders without undue fatigue or wasted motion? Are your supervisors trained in ergonomics so that they know how to teach workers the best way to get the job done?

Proper slotting is essential to improved ergonomics. How do you ensure that the right merchandise remains in the golden zone? Unless management controls the put-away function and keeps the right materials in the golden zone, there is no assurance that an ergonomically correct stock layout will remain that way.

Exercise can be as important as training to keep your people in shape to avoid injuries. Some warehouses start the day with aerobic exercises done as a group by the entire warehouse crew. In one situation, management and even visitors join in the exercise session. Although the exercise program is not mandatory, most users find 100 percent participation.

Try to learn as much as possible by observing the work and asking the workers how they are doing. Whether you use a consulting engineer or do the job yourself, the form shown in Figure 20-1 will help you record observations.

Reducing manual handling risks

The manual handling of cargo has always contained an element of risk. At a time when government safety authorities are monitoring this situation closer than ever before, it makes sense to consider three ways to control the risk:

- ◆ Redesign the job.
- ◆ Train workers in better techniques.
- ◆ Improve the employee selection process.
- ◆ Change the layout so that the average worker can meet the physical demands more safely. In effect, that is what ergonomics is all about.

Figure 20-1

Employee observation form

Employee name		Date	Observer name		Employee ID	
Area	Shift	Job code	Previous performance			Equip #
Start	Actual	Goal	Performance this job		Document #	
Employee: Does the job just completed represent your normal assignment?					Yes	No
Employee: Do you feel you have the normal skills required to do the job just observed?					Yes	No
Employee: Do you feel you need additional training in the methods for this job?					Yes	No
Employee: Do you feel, while performing the job just observed, that you worked faster, slower, or equal to your normal work pace? Explain:					Faster	Slower
Employee: Do you feel the pace at which you worked was reasonable?					Yes	No
Employee: Do you feel that you could maintain this pace for an entire shift?					Yes	No
Employee: In your opinion, what could be done to create a more productive work environment? Comments:						
Observer: Were any equipment problems, barriers, or significant delays encountered? Comments:					Yes	No
Observer: Was the job function performed safely? Comments:					Yes	No
Observer: Was the quality of work performed acceptable? Comments:					Yes	No
Employee signature:					Date:	
Observer signature:					Date:	

The idea that injury risk goes with the job should be discarded. Show your warehouse workers how to take the time and precautions to perform a job safely. Training should be used to make employees aware of the dangers associated with various tasks performed in the warehouse. The effectiveness of your training program can be measured by comparing injury rates after the training with those before.

Reducing the three risks of manual handling tasks should be viewed by the warehouse manager as an investment in worker safety, morale, reduction of workers' compensation costs, and increased productivity. Instead of protecting workers from hazards, change the emphasis to the removal of hazards from the workplace.

Substance abuse in the warehouse

Substance abuse is an unpleasant and emotionally charged subject. Most people feel pain when they read or hear about such problems. Nearly all of us live with memories of substance abuse that afflicted people close to us. Because those memories are unpleasant, we would rather not hear about this subject, and we react the same way we do to information about terminal illness and death. However, it is vitally important for you to be proactive in dealing with substance abuse in the workplace.

If you have more than ten people in your warehouse crew, you probably have substance abuse problems. In a tight labor market, up to 50 percent of people who are looking for a job have a substance abuse problem. The substances under consideration include more than illegal drugs; alcohol and even prescription drugs, when abused, are just as dangerous. The abuse problem is aggravated by the fact that work done in today's warehouse is more exacting than it was in the last century. A growing number of today's warehouse workers must be computer literate. This means that impairment could result in distorted information fed into your warehouse information system as well as faulty cargo handling. Therefore, the potential loss from tolerating substance abuse is higher today than ever.

The starting point for controlling substance abuse is to create and publish a company policy on this subject. If your company has no policy, your people probably do not understand your position. Fortunately, most people do not abuse substances and would prefer not to work with those who do. A policy statement is the first step in creating an understanding concerning this significant problem. Here is a model policy statement:

Our company is committed to providing our employees with a safe workplace and an atmosphere that allows people to protect merchandise placed in our care. Our employees are expected to be in suitable mental and physical condition while at work to allow them to perform their jobs effectively and safely. Whenever use or abuse of any mood-altering substance interferes with a safe workplace, appropriate action must be taken. Our company has no desire to intrude into its employees' personal lives. However, both on-the-job and off-the-job involvement with any mood-altering substance (alcohol and drugs) can affect the workplace and our company's ability to achieve its objective of safety and security. Therefore, employees are expected to report to the workplace with no mood-altering substances in their bodies. While employees may make their own lifestyle choices, this company cannot accept the risk in the workplace that substance abuse creates. The possession, sale, or use of mood-altering substances at the workplace, or coming to work under the influence of such substances, shall be a violation of safe work practices. Violation may result in termination of employment.

This policy does several important things. It relates your position on substance abuse to health, safety, property protection, and quality control. Everyone understands that these are essential to any effective warehouse operation. The policy sets standards of conduct. But what if your company already has a substance abuse policy? First, be sure that everybody is aware of that policy. Second, be sure the policy is actually enforced.

When considering substance abuse offenses, remember that there are three violation levels, which differ markedly in their impact. The first level is the employee who reports to work while under the influence of a substance consumed off the job. That worker may be unsafe in the warehouse and therefore a threat and a nuisance to fellow workers.

A more serious offender is the employee who comes to work in possession of mood-altering substances. Possession suggests that the substances are being consumed in the warehouse and that the offender is under their influence.

Most serious of all is the worker who brings substances to your warehouse for the purpose of selling them to others in the work crew. This offender may or may not be consuming these substances, but your warehouse is being used as a market. The third level of offense deserves the strongest discipline, and the second is far more serious than the first.

Much has been written about the symptoms of substance abuse. The most important thing to remember is that no single sign of substance abuse might not also be caused by something else. It is therefore impossible for any warehouse supervisor to observe a worker and conclude that substance abuse is present. Unless the active consumption is also observed, there is always a reasonable doubt.

The issue of testing or screening has generated widespread controversy, particularly among those who believe that screening infringes traditional rights of privacy. Warehouse workers can cause death or injury if they are reckless in their work. Your failure to screen to eliminate applicants with substance abuse problems might be considered a failure to properly care for the healthy people in your warehouse crew who are entitled to a safe workplace.

The most difficult challenge in handling substance abuse is the method of intervening when a warehouse employee exhibits suspicious signs on the job. A proven answer is to use the services of your company physician, or any competent physician your organization can retain. You have the right to question the health of any employee who appears impaired while on the job. That includes the right to require that this employee immediately visit a doctor for a checkup to find out what is wrong. When you do so, you have an obligation to pay for the time spent during this process, and you should control transportation for that employee to and from the doctor's office. Any physician can tell whether the signs are caused by substance abuse. Thus this is the most effective means of dealing with the problem. If the employee refuses to visit a doctor, dismissal for insubordination is the available remedy.

Four steps are necessary for successful implementation of a substance abuse prevention program:

- Publication of a policy.
- A detailed screening program for all new hires.
- Training and retraining of supervisors and managers to recognize and intervene when there are behavior problems that might be related to substance abuse.
- Most important, a rehabilitation and discipline program used when problems are uncovered.

Warehousing ethics — a matter of trust

Whether business ethics are improving or declining at the start of the 21st century is debatable. Whether conduct in your operation is getting better or worse, ethics are particularly important in warehousing. Exploration of the ethical process in warehousing has value for these reasons:

- The warehouse manager is responsible for property that belongs to others.
- A failure to keep promises regarding warehousing can have serious consequences.

- High employee turnover in the warehouse is usually accompanied by low trust.
- Margin pressure among competitive third-party warehouses causes some to engage in unethical behavior in buying or selling services.

In today's world of supply chain management, just-in-time deliveries and vendor-managed inventory, a failure to keep an operational promise can do significant damage. If your warehouse is supporting an assembly line, failure to make a timely delivery or delivery of the wrong product can cause a plant shutdown.

Keeping promises also involves a relationship between workers and management. If a significant percentage of workers are absent on the first day of hunting season, for instance, management may be unable to keep commitments made to customers. People who arrive late or not at all contribute to the inability to maintain a reliable schedule.

Warehouse managers also rely on other companies to keep service promises. If your warehouse uses truckers that are not part of your company, the truckers' failure to maintain a promised schedule affects your reputation as well as that of the transportation supplier.

Unlike manufacturing, warehousing work does not lend itself to tight inspection and control. It is not practical to follow the route of every warehouse order picker. A careless or unscrupulous warehouse worker may select the wrong item, ship damaged merchandise, or engage in collusion theft. When workers no longer care about the future of their employer, they may lose the incentive to be honest.

How does management maintain the trust of workers? A key part of the process is to treat them with compassion and respect. The manager who shows that he cares usually receives quality work from those who report to him. The second way to generate trust is through frequent contact. Management by walking around (MBWA) has long been praised for its effectiveness in a warehousing environment. MBWA is the best way to get to know the people who report to you.

The lowball proposal is an old practice in third-party warehouse marketing, and unfortunately it has not disappeared. The hungry warehouse operator submits a low price for new business, hoping that the price can be adjusted once the customer has moved into the warehouse.

Ethical lapses don't always happen on the vendor side of the table. An ancient ethical lapse is the buyer who is on the take, receiving kickbacks from a vendor of warehousing services. Another buyer may collect a group of warehousing proposals, receiving free advice from vendors who are eager to demonstrate their skills. In the worst cases, none of the proposals is accepted, and the buyer uses the ideas gained from the bidding process to improve a warehousing operation.

As the relationships between third-party warehouses and their customers has moved from a transactional business to one of long-term relationships, there is a growing realization that ethics and the ability to play fair have become an essential part of the process.

Protect your people by demanding the highest standards of ethics and honesty in warehouse management. In return, the majority of your workers who are honest people will help you find and eliminate dishonesty. The best way to protect your people is to set an example for ethics and honesty that demands that they respect each other and the company that employs them.

Questions that solve problems

When you appraise your management's ability to protect the hourly people in the warehouse, it may be well to question workers rather than the warehouse manager. Find out how they feel about their jobs and the security of their workplace. Here are a few questions you can use:

Q How do you feel about your work here? Is there anything we could do to make your job more enjoyable?
C This open ended question will help learn about any concerns your people have about quality of work life. Although some people may not want to discuss things that are troubling them, the answers to this question will tell you whether to look for trouble in the workplace.

Q Have you seen any safety hazards in your job that changes in work practices might prevent?
C Even if your warehouse has safety committees or safety meetings, your hourly people will appreciate your concern.

Q Can you suggest changes in layout or work methods that would make your job easier to do?
C Many of the best ideas about ergonomics come from workers who see things that engineers or managers might miss. If one of your people provides a useful suggestion to make the job easier or safer, be sure to provide a reward for submission of a good idea.

Q How do you feel about our substance-abuse policy?
C Obviously, asking this question presumes that you have a published policy, and asking about it will help demonstrate whether your workers really understand it. Asking about this may also illustrate your attitudes towards substance-abuse prevention.

Q Do we convey an image of honesty and upright conduct?
C Listen carefully to the answers to this one. Not every worker will tell you what you want to hear.

Chapter 21

Protecting the property

Three kinds of major losses could affect your property:
* A business interruption could interfere with the ability of the warehouse to function normally. This includes anything that makes it impossible to ship, receive, or move materials.
* A casualty loss could affect the building and contents.
* Other losses may damage just the warehouse structure.

Power failure

The dependability of electric power is so generally accepted that warehouse operations seldom have a comprehensive plan for power failures. Yet nothing will paralyze a warehouse as completely as a power failure. Even if the warehouse has internal combustion lift trucks and skylights, failure of computer systems alone will stop most operations. As warehousing becomes a global function, managers are moving into parts of the world where long power failures are a frequent occurrence. Therefore, a growing number of facilities need backup systems to provide power.

One warehouse complex has an emergency generator to provide enough power to maintain computer operations and provide 25 percent illumination in the buildings.

Electric power is not the only critical resource for warehouse operations, but it is the one that will cause the greatest paralysis if interrupted.

Casualty losses

The most catastrophic casualty loss is fire. A warehouse fire, once out of control, can destroy both the building and its contents.

Windstorms are a common threat to warehouse buildings. The modern warehouse is particularly vulnerable to windstorm damage because its wide expanse of flat roof is readily damaged by high winds. When roofs are built with asphalt as an adhesive, insurance carriers limit the amount applied to reduce risk of fire. When you reduce asphalt to cut fire risk, you increase the risk of damage by windstorm.

The risk of water damage includes both floods and sprinkler-system malfunction. Sometimes ill-trained emergency fire brigades may set off the sprinkler systems, and the leakage can cause as much damage as a fire.

Overloading of the building, structural failure, or earthquake all may cause a building to collapse. The risk of explosion is influenced by the products stored in or near the building.

Vandalism and malicious mischief clauses in insurance contracts cover losses caused by sabotage or other acts of malicious destruction. A more general risk is that of *consequential loss* -- the losses that may come as the result of an earlier event. One example is a power failure that disables the refrigeration system in a freezer, with spoilage of stored products as a consequential damage.

Fire

One of the best ways to control fire risk is to buy both insurance and loss-prevention advice. The more progressive insurance companies have continuing research and development on loss prevention. Those companies control losses by making every employee aware of how to prevent fires.

Sprinkler systems

Means of controlling the risk of fire vary in different countries, but in the United States today the most widely accepted method of fire risk reduction is the automatic sprinkler system. The automatic sprinkler is a series of pipes installed just under the ceiling carrying enough water to extinguish or contain a fire. In most of the world, sprinkler systems are considered unacceptable because of the danger of water damage, but in the United States, such systems are required by building codes in all but the smallest warehouses. The two widely used types are dry-pipe and wet-pipe systems.

Dry-pipe systems

The dry-pipe system uses heated valve houses, each with a valve containing compressed air that keeps water out of the sprinkler pipes. When the air is released, water is permitted to flow. Dry-pipe systems must be used in unheated warehouses or in outdoor canopies where temperatures fall below freezing.

Sprinkler heads are installed on the pipes at regular intervals. Each head has a deflector to aim the flow of water and a trigger made of wax or a metallic compound that will melt at a certain temperature. When heat reaches that temperature, the trigger snaps and allows water to flow through the system and onto the fire.

Most systems include a water-flow alarm that will ring a bell and send an electronic signal to summon the fire department. The electronic signal is particularly important for controlling a false alarm or an accidental discharge.

Wet-pipe systems

In the wet-pipe system, water fills all the pipes up to the sprinkler heads, which means the entire warehouse must be kept above freezing. The wet-pipe system works faster than dry pipe because compressed air does not have to be released first. That makes it a safer system for fire control. Furthermore, the wet-pipe sprinkler is less susceptible to false alarms than the more complex dry-pipe systems.

All sprinkler systems are equipped with master control valves, which present two risks: accidental closure and deliberate shutoff by a vandal. Nearly one-third of dollar losses from fires occur because the control valves were closed.

Other protection against fire

Fire extinguishers are an important first response for fires. A portable extinguisher often prevents a small blaze from becoming a large fire. The best way to be sure that fire extinguishers will be used effectively is to have periodic training and drills.

Most fire protection systems also include fire hoses for use before the fire trucks arrive. Fire drills should include use of hoses. Many large fires are prevented by teams trained to act effectively the instant a fire is discovered and well before the fire department can arrive.

The warehouse operator's proficiency in loss prevention is usually reflected in the rate insurance underwriters assign to the facility. Some public warehouse operators will advertise their fire insurance rate, knowing that it reflects their success in loss prevention. Fire underwriters measure both management interest and employee attitudes toward fire protection. They recognize that loss risks can be increased by smoking, poor housekeeping, or even troubled labor relations.

A new type of sprinkler system

Underwriter approval of the early-suppression, fast-response (ESFR) sprinkler system is one of the most significant advances in the long history of sprinkler systems.

Two developments of the past few decades have made sprinkler system protection more complicated: the increased use of storage racks and the introduction of more products that contain volatile or poisonous chemicals.

Protection experts consider rack storage hazardous because a typical rack arrangement leaves vertical spaces that act as a flue in the event of a fire. The insurance underwriters' solution to the problem has been to require installation of intermediate sprinkler heads within the rack.

That has brought cries of dismay from warehouse owners, because intermediate sprinklers are expensive and destroy layout flexibility. Racks equipped with intermediate sprinklers are expensive to adjust or move. Furthermore, it is relatively easy to accidentally hit the in-rack sprinkler heads while handling freight. For these reasons, many warehouse operators have stubbornly resisted underwriters' requests for in-rack sprinkler systems.

Elimination of the need for in-rack sprinklers is the primary virtue of the ESFR sprinkler system. The ESFR has two unique features: a quicker response time and a heavier sprinkler discharge. When enough water is dropped onto a fire early on, the fire will be suppressed before it presents a severe challenge to the building itself. Furthermore, the ESFR system typically opens fewer sprinkler heads than a conventional system and thus reduces water damage. Reducing the size and duration of the fire will also reduce smoke damage.

There are two ways to deal with fire: Suppression and control. Standard sprinkler systems operate on the control principle, ESFR systems on suppression. The standard sprinkler system allows a fire to develop but retards its spread by opening twenty to thirty sprinkler heads. This widespread discharge soaks surrounding storage piles so they will not ignite. The water discharge protects the building by cooling the steelwork and preventing structural failure and collapse. Suppression is left to firefighters.

The ESFR system is designed for suppression rather than control. The goal is to apply enough cooling water to a heat source before a fire plume can develop.

Windstorm losses

Certain parts of the country encounter hazardous storms. Gulf Coast areas are notable for hurricanes, and parts of the Midwest have problems with tornadoes.

Probably no economical warehouse design could withstand a direct hit from a tornado or hurricane. However, certain kinds of construction have proven more resistant to such storms.

A pre-engineered metal roof, for example, has greater wind resistance than a built-up composition roof, simply because the metal roof does not rely on asphalt or any other chemical adhesive. Overhanging truck canopies should be avoided in high-wind areas, since they are particularly susceptible to wind damage.

Causes of cargo damage

Nearly every occurrence of cargo damage within the warehouse can be attributed to one of the following factors:
- ◆ Biological change.
- ◆ Chemical reactions.
- ◆ Contamination.
- ◆ Temperature.
- ◆ Foreign odors.
- ◆ Physical damage.
- ◆ Prolonged storage.

Biological change may occur in food and other products because of bacterial action, mold, or fermentation. Sometimes this includes the rotting of packaging, which may cause package failure and falling stacks.

Some merchandise is spoiled because of chemical reactions within the container. Such reaction may be beyond the control of the operator.

Food products may become unsafe for consumption because of contamination by insects or rodents.

Inadequate temperature control or improper changes of temperature will cause some products to deteriorate.

Some articles are susceptible to absorbing foreign odors that make them unattractive or unsafe.

Physical damage may be caused by improper handling or by one of the casualty losses described earlier. This kind of damage is easy to detect.

Many products will deteriorate simply as a function of age. Errors in inventory control may cause some items to stay in storage beyond their reasonable shelf life.*

Flood and leakage

One way to control the risk of loss from flood or leakage is to be sure that no merchandise is stored directly on the warehouse floor. The use of storage pallets or lumber dunnage will keep all merchandise a few inches above the floor and therefore provides a measure of protection in the event of leakage.

Mass theft

Warehouse managers should never assume that a protection system will always prevent mass theft.

You should deliberately breach the security system periodically just to learn how fast the police will respond. Holding this kind of burglary drill is potentially dangerous, and managers who do it must

---

* Adapted from an article by Sergio Ledesma, Aloccidente, *Warehousing Forum*, Volume 10, Number 5, ©The Ackerman Company, Columbus, Ohio.

be sure that they do not become victims of a police accident. One way to reduce this risk is to inform the police chief, but not the alarm company, that a drill is taking place.

Since the technology for electronic protection is constantly being improved, the alert warehouse operator should always look for equipment that is better than the system already installed. But all such equipment should be *failsafe*, meaning that it will ring an alarm if wires are cut or power is interrupted.

Outside lighting is an important deterrent to mass theft. Intense outside light will make a thief feel conspicuous. Rather than run the risk of being seen, most burglars will select a less well-lit building.

Vandalism

Vandalism, sabotage, and other deliberate destruction are difficult to control. The most serious vandalism risk is the intentional closing of sprinkler valves. There are electronic devices to counter this. Also, it is possible to apply a seal that shows at a glance whether a valve has been closed. The risk of vandalism increases during labor strife, and management should be especially alert at those times.

Surviving an insurance inspection

The insurance inspector is far more concerned about the materials in your warehouse than the building itself. With few exceptions, warehouse buildings are fire resistant. If you are fortunate enough to be warehousing noncombustibles, and if those materials are stored in bulk with no combustible packaging, then you have a very safe warehouse. However, almost every warehouse is filled with products that contain some paper or corrugated packaging, plastics, wood, and combustible chemicals.

The insurance industry rates combustibles in five classes:

- A **special-hazard product** is one in which the plastics content of packaging and product is more than 15 percent by weight or more than 25 percent by volume. Expanded or foamed plastic packaging, such as that used to protect computers and television sets, is particularly hazardous.
- A **Class IV commodity** can be any product, even a metal product, packaged in a cardboard container in

which non-expanded plastic is more than 15 percent of the product weight or expanded plastic is more than 25 percent of the product's volume. An example is a computer with plastic parts that is protected by a foam plastic container.
- A **Class III item** is one in which both product and packaging are combustible. An example is facial tissue.
- A **Class II product** is a noncombustible item stored in wood, corrugated cardboard, or other combustible packaging. Although the contents will not burn, the package will. Examples include refrigerators, washing machines, and dryers.
- A **Class I item** is the least hazardous commodity: A noncombustible product stored in noncombustible packaging on pallets. The pallets themselves will burn, but if nothing else on the pallet is combustible, it is rated as Class I.

The fire inspector will consider the quantity of material in your warehouse in each of the five classes and the manner in which you store materials. From a protection standpoint, solid-pile storage — free-standing stacks that are snugly against each other — provide the least hazardous storage arrangement. The exception would be a commodity that is itself quite dangerous, such as a flammable chemical.

The fire inspector will also look at the number and width of your aisles and the height at which goods are stored. Nearly all underwriters request that goods be at least 18 inches below sprinkler heads; with more hazardous materials, even more space between product and sprinklers will improve the ability of the sprinkler system to control a fire.

The greatest risk with high-piled storage is a chimney or flue effect. If you have a thirty-foot stack of combustible boxes with a six-inch space between rows, a fire will move up the thirty-foot flue like a blowtorch. The flame at the top will be extremely hot and violent, and the heat can expand the steel framework and cause a collapse.

Storage racks can be made safer from the underwriter's point of view by allowing a vertical space between rack structures, to permit sprinkler water to run down into the racks. Pallet racks or installations that use metal grates are considered safer than solid-steel shelving, because they have openings to allow water to flow down through the levels.

Fire safety for the most dangerous materials is improved with ample aisle separation. If the hazardous products are separated from the rest of the merchandise by wide aisles, the chance of controlling a fire is increased. In some cases, extremely hazardous materials are put in a special-hazard building isolated from the rest of the facility. A fire in that building will then not threaten the larger warehouse.

Plant emergency organizations

An emergency plan can greatly reduce the risk of serious loss. For this reason, casualty underwriters strongly recommend highly trained plant emergency teams.

The emergency team functions after an emergency is discovered and before the fire department or other professionals arrive.

The emergency organization should always include representatives of plant *maintenance* or *engineering* departments, since these people are the most familiar with the protection systems, control panels, and circuit breakers. The plant emergency team should know how to operate all protective equipment and be trained to react with confidence and accuracy.

The most important aspect of training is practice drills. Such drills should include sounding the alarm, moving to a prescribed emergency station, and handling fire hoses, extinguishers, and sprinkler system controls. The last of these is the most complex, since a large sprinkler system usually has many valves as well as a booster fire pump. A good emergency organization also is schooled in first aid, since the first priority is to save lives.

Emergency teams need regular drills and preparation. When emergency plans are made and then forgotten, the team rapidly becomes disorganized and useless.

Reviewing protection procedures

Property protection systems are now so common that warehouse managers frequently overlook the importance of a review.

In most U.S. cities, building codes require the installation of an automatic sprinkler system in any warehouse with more than 50,000 square feet. Codes also require installation of fire hoses, portable extinguishers, hydrants, and fire doors. Because all of this gear is required, a manager may fail to confirm that it is all in working order.

Your insurance carrier may insist on a periodic review of the condition of the protective systems in your facility. However, if the carrier does not demand it, common sense does. If tragedy strikes, your failure to provide review and training in this area could be more than an embarrassment, it could be the cause of litigation.

Questions that solve problems

Insurance people are particularly curious about whether senior management is actively involved in loss prevention. Therefore, you should never be too busy to ask questions about your company's protection systems. Here are some points of inquiry that will demonstrate your active involvement in protecting the property:

Q **Have there been recent inspections by fire underwriters or other protection authorities? If so, have copies of their reports been sent to me?**
C No matter how busy you are, you should receive these reports if warehousing is your responsibility.

Q **Has the company suffered any casualty losses during the past year? If so, is there anything we might have done to have prevented them?**
C If you had to ask the first question, you may be too far removed from operations. However, asking the second is a legitimate exploration of ways to improve protective procedures and systems.

Q **Have we considered installation or retrofit of the new ESFR sprinkler systems?**
C Even though this technology was introduced several years ago, many people are still not aware of it.

Q **Are there any unusual hazards associated with any of the materials stored in our warehouse?**
C You can't ask this one too often, since the introduction of any new product into your warehouse could represent a new and possibly unrecognized risk.

Q **What drills are rehearsed to teach our people how to be safe in case of windstorm, flood, or fire?**
C The answer will provide some indication of the quality of your emergency planning.

PART 5

Handling of Cargo

Chapter 22

Receiving, put-away, and storage*

Nothing can be distributed until it has been received and that receipt has been processed. Therefore, any study of warehouse handling logically begins with the act of receiving.

Receiving is the process of accepting material into the warehouse. Receiving is also the transfer of possession from shipper or carrier to receiver. This may or may not involve the transfer of title, but it always indicates a transfer of responsibility to the warehouse operator. Because this acceptance of responsibility includes a financial risk, the process requires an audit trail. Receiving deserves more care than many warehouse operators give it.

Ask any group of warehousing professionals what the most important aspect of their job is, and they usually mention order picking. A close second is the process of getting shipments out on time, because all of the marketing pressure is directed at outbound movement. One result of this is that the inbound function is substantially neglected. This neglect manifests itself in several ways. The first is lengthy staging at the receiving docks. The second is a substantial time lag between the moment materials are unloaded and the moment they are available for shipment. A third is the loss of opportunities to cross dock merchandise even when it is logical to do so.

The most frequent cause of poor product flow is a need for inspection of inbound merchandise. Sometimes goods are held until the in-

---

* The first two subchapters are adapted from an article by William J. Ransom, Ransom and Associates, *Warehousing Forum*, Volume 7, Number 7, ©The Ackerman Company, Columbus, Ohio.

spector is able to come to the dock. The result is a waste of time and space in the receiving area.

Some companies measure the time from "dock to stock," the total time between receipt and storage of merchandise. However, those who measure this closely are the minority, and some who do so still tolerate a slow dock-to-stock time.

Many receiving departments have no way of identifying opportunities to cross dock goods. In spite of the popularity of cross docking as a concept, many receivers lack an information system that would identify cross-dock opportunities. Thus every item received is put into a storage location, even material that might be immediately used to fill customer orders.

Physical aspects of receiving

Receiving begins with the arrival of a vehicle at your dock. You unload the material, count and confirm the quantity with shipping documents, and inspect for quality assurance. Inspection ends with a decision to accept or reject the load. If it is accepted, the merchandise is moved to a storage area. There are three options in receiving material, listed in order of efficiency:

- Unload product from a carrier and move it across the dock for outbound. This is the simplest method because it requires no storage.
- Unload product and take it directly to a storage slot. Also known as a live unloading, this is the second-best receiving method and requires no staging or rehandling.
- Place unloaded material at a staging or temporary storage area near the receiving dock. This step is taken if the material requires additional checking or processing, if storage space is not immediately available, or if a different lift truck is used for storage.

The third option is least preferred, because it requires rehandling the material. It also requires storage or staging space on the dock to hold unloaded product until it is moved to storage. Sometimes pallet racks are used for staging to reduce the amount of space needed.

When the physical aspects of receiving are not closely supervised, you may be charged with damage for which you are not responsible.

Through accident or dishonesty, you might sign for material that was never actually received. As you examine your receiving operation, consider how many opportunities there are to change the system to allow materials to be cross docked from one vehicle to another, or to be live-unloaded from truck directly to storage.

Receiving as a process

The receiving process has six steps:
- A carrier calls and makes an appointment for delivery.
- Before the vehicle arrives, the receiver verifies that an advance shipping notice (ASN) is available for the inbound load. If it is not, the shipper is contacted and asked to provide ASN information by fax or e-mail.
- The dock door is assigned for the inbound load.
- The vehicle arrives and is properly secured with wheel chocks or similar safety devices.
- The cargo seal is broken in the presence of the truck driver, and the inspection of the load is completed.
- The load is removed from the truck.

The unloading process has three options:
- A lift truck removes unitized or palletized material.
- Loose or floor-loaded material is stacked on pallets.
- Material is removed by conveyor to a staging area.

The first is usually the most efficient, and every effort should be made to require unitized loads from those who ship materials to your warehouse.

Check-in requires absolute accuracy. The best way to achieve this is by using bar-code scanning to compare a bar code on each package with information that tells what should be received. Where bar codes are not used, a blind receiving process is preferred. A checker writes down the received quantity without reference to an ASN or packing list. A third option is to give the receiver a listing of the items, and the receiver records the quantity of each on the load.

Checking is the most important step in the receiving operation. Receiving is not complete until discrepancies between the ASN and the goods received have been resolved or documented. Damaged material is either moved to a recoopering area or returned to the carrier.

The growing use of the ASN has improved the receiving process. See Chapter 12.

Put-away

The final step in receiving is the placement of merchandise in a permanent storage location. How is that location chosen at your warehouse? Who does the selecting? In a surprising number of cases, the location decision is made by the lift truck operator, and he or she makes it by finding the closest open bay so that the put-away can be finished quickly.

If you allow that to happen, storage locations soon become a hopeless mixture of SKUs without rhyme or reason. However, when locations and the put-away process are systematically controlled, the need to rewarehouse product later can be avoided. Space will be saved because empty locations are planned rather than discovered.

Your warehouse should have at least one person designated as a storage planner. That planner should know where empty storage locations are, where additional space can be created by rewarehousing, and what inbound loads are expected.

The planner scans the identity of items on the inbound loads to budget space for each item in transit to the warehouse. With this information, the planner should develop specific instructions for each item on every arriving load of freight.

Stock locator systems

A key element in space planning is an effective warehouse locator system. The locator system is primarily designed to reduce lost time during order picking when the picker searches for misplaced merchandise.

Most warehouses today have a computer-based stock locator system. Although locator systems are not new, some warehouse operators still question their value. When such systems are not used, the operator relies on a "biological database," which may work satisfactorily until the key person is absent because of illness or vacation. As the inventory grows in complexity, the biological database eventually breaks down.

If your warehouse contained only one SKU, you would not need a locator system. You might get by without one if you had as many as

two or three SKUs. But warehouses with more than three items gain at least seven advantages by using a stock locator system:
- Saved space. When an item is stored in several locations, partial stacks can be consolidated to free space for additional SKUs.
- Saved time. Order pickers do not have to search for a place to put inbound merchandise, and they don't have to search for an item needed to fill an outbound order.
- Improved control. The best order-pick system instructs the operator to first go to a specific location and then to find a given item. When location and item do not match, this is a clear signal that something is wrong with the system.
- Faster and less expensive order picking. The pick list can be designed to show the shortest travel path to select an order.
- Better and easier control of FIFO (first in, first out). Always list the location that holds the oldest stock, and use it for the first outbound shipment.
- Improved product quarantine. A location can be locked to enforce the quarantine.
- Control of individual production lots to ensure proper product recall. When each lot is recorded in a separate location, control of the materials is greatly improved.

Installing and maintaining a locator system

How detailed do you want your system to be? The most precise locator system could isolate each item to a given flow rack slot, a specific position on a bin or shelf, or a single pallet position. A less precise system may isolate a single bay of the warehouse as its location, which requires the worker to search within that bay for the specific item. Depending on the layout and nature of your inventory, you may decide that a detailed system is not necessary; one that isolates the general area will suffice.

Effectively using a locator system begins with planning for inbound merchandise. The system should identify empty locations available for storage. It should also show how new empty locations can be created by consolidating partial pallets, partial shelves, or bins.

When goods are shipped, the pick list should show the location first, then the SKU number. If the order picker finds another item in the indicated location, the discrepancy must be reported and corrected. The space planner should make regular location checks throughout the warehouse to discover errors as well as opportunities to save space by relocating stock.

If your locator system is to work effectively, you must demand precise communication and immediate correction of errors. When a physical inventory is taken, the locator system provides a time-saving control over the counting process.

Your warehouse layout

To some extent, the layout should reflect your company strategy. If the business is growing, the layout must be designed to adapt to growth. If the number of SKUs is expanding rapidly, a layout with fixed locations will soon cause trouble. However, if your business is shrinking or if the number of SKUs is receding, you will make very different decisions on layout.

A necessary step in looking at layout is to first consider the broad assignments of space before getting into detail. Some warehouses handle finished goods and replacement parts. The storage and handling characteristics are usually far different for parts than for finished products. How much space is allotted to each? These macro questions must be decided before the detailed layout is developed.

If you are building a new facility, the layout should be developed before the building is designed. The best warehouses are designed from the inside out. If you must work within existing buildings, the boundaries of those buildings will limit your options in layout.

One way layout influences building design is in the placement of aisles. Aisle placement also will influence construction, since lighting for the storage areas should be placed over the aisles. Lack of planning in this area can become very expensive. In one new building, the owner spent more than $20,000 to correct a lighting error that never would have happened if the warehouse layout had been part of the construction plan.

Another limiting factor in layout is product flow. As merchandise moves through the warehouse, at what locations will it be received and from where will it be shipped? Dock locations may be a limiting factor for the warehouse layout.

Four inventory characteristics will influence layout decisions:
- Security.
- Stock-level variation.
- Physical characteristics.
- Packaging strength.

Security includes the risk of fire as well as theft. An effective security layout places theft-prone merchandise where it cannot easily be stolen. Hazardous materials are stored in areas designed to isolate or control the extra risk. For example, aerosol containers are typically kept in an isolated explosion-resistant room.

Inventory-level variations occur when certain items are popular in one season and inactive in another. Other items create a surge because they are on a promotion sale. These variations must be considered as the layout is planned.

Physical characteristics of each item should be analyzed in order to group together those items with similar size and storage characteristics. For example, tubing, piping, vinyl siding, ladders, and other extra-long items might be stored in cantilever rack or a lean-to storage area designed to store them on end. Similar considerations should be given to other items of unusual size or shape.

Packaging strength must be considered by the storage planner who seeks to maximize use of available space. High block stacks with no racking are the most economical arrangement for merchandise that is packaged well enough to support this kind of storage.

The limiting factor in high stacking is usually packaging rather than clearance. When packaging is weak, storage rack is the most common means of achieving efficient space use. The knowledge of stacking capability of each package is essential in layout planning.

The affinity factor

Affinity is the degree of attraction between two SKUs. For example, if a pail of adhesive is sold with nearly every order of floor tile, it makes sense to store tile and adhesive side by side. Data analysis will reveal these and other affinities.

However, affinities may also be negative. If floor tile orders almost never include ceiling tile, there is no reason to keep those items close to each other.

Load characteristics

At times, the manner in which products must be loaded should be the guiding factor in how the stock is arranged and picked. For example, in the shipment of plumbing supplies it is necessary to separate heavy items such as metal piping from lighter and more fragile items such as plastic pipe. An additional separation is needed for "china," easily damaged porcelain plumbing fixtures. The pick list must recognize differences in loading characteristics, and storage locations should be arranged to make order picking as effective as possible.

Special operations

Some warehouses include special operations. These might include repacking or refurbishing damaged or returned goods, assembly, kitting, or packaging. The layout must provide space in the best location to support these special operations.

Planning for changes

The prime objective of warehouse layout is to use available space effectively and to handle materials at minimum cost. The layout planner must allow maximum flexibility to deal with future changes, and some of these cannot be anticipated. Developing a layout is really a process rather than a formula. Once you understand the process, you can develop a layout that will work well today and can be readily adapted tomorrow.

Questions that solve problems

As you appraise the effectiveness of receiving and storage, you should ask your managers a few questions about how they get the job done.

Q Can you describe in detail our existing receiving procedure?
C You might want to follow the question with an inspection to learn how receiving *actually* takes place.

Q What steps have we taken to improve receiving accuracy?
C If your warehouse managers aren't considering bar coding, find out why not.

Q Who decides where inbound products should be stored?
C If you don't hear a storage planner described by name or function, you are missing an opportunity to improve operations. If you have a storage planner, find out how that person works.

Q Can you describe to me how our stock locator system works?
C If there is no system, you have identified an opportunity for improvement. If there is one, and responsible people don't know how it works, it's possible that the system exists only on paper.

Q How many storage locations do we have for item XYZ?
C Choose one of your most popular items. If it is stored in many locations, this may be a sign of a poor locator system or none at all.

Q Are you satisfied with our warehouse layout? How could it be made better?
C Don't ask this until you have time for a long answer and considerable discussion. A manager who is satisfied, or has no ideas for improvement, may be either out of touch or complacent.

Chapter 23

Order selection and cross docking

Order-picking operations make up the largest expense category in most warehouses. Selection of orders is also the most important function performed. If this job is not done right, little else can make up for it. Therefore, when we consider order picking and cross docking, we are considering the most costly and critical functions in the typical warehouse.

The influence of velocity

Throughout the last quarter of the 20th century, warehousing professionals noted a steady increase in the velocity of inventory turns. While warehouses once served as a place for storage, today they are increasingly dedicated to the constant flow of materials. Two conditions created this change. The first was a significant increase in the cost of money and a recognition of the fact that asset turnover not only can conserve capital but also may provide the most accurate measure of corporate success. Second, the information age has allowed a degree of inventory control that was not possible earlier. Supply chain managers have both the incentive and the ability to turn inventories faster than ever.

Cross docking is the ultimate in high-velocity turnover, since it involves moving merchandise in through one dock door and immediately out through another.

Order picking in your warehouse*

Because order picking is both expensive and prone to error, the goal of every warehouse operator is to design a system that reduces travel and thus reduces costs while at the same time reducing the possibility of errors.

One way to reduce travel is to create an order pick line consisting of pick slots (locations) where product is available for selection. The pick slots should be in places that are easily identified and physically conducive to low-fatigue and error-free picking. One way to achieve this is to put the fastest-moving items between waist and shoulder level, known as the "golden zone."

Variances in package size and configuration, picking quantities, stocking quantity, and inventory requirements often necessitate more than one picking system. There are three picking options:

- Full pallets are the minimum amount selected (unit load picking).
- Full cases are the minimum amount selected (case picking).
- Individual items are removed from cases (broken case picking).

Order picking can be manual, power assisted, automatic, or any combination of the three. A manual system might use grocery carts or four-wheel hand trucks that are pushed through the pick line and loaded. A powered system might use order-picking lift trucks to transport and elevate the worker through the pick line. An automatic system might use a stacker crane or an automated picking device to replace the warehouse worker.

---

* This subchapter is based on writing by William J. Ransom, Ransom & Associates.

Varieties of order picking

The first and most common way to pick orders is called *discrete picking*. A single person takes a single complete order, moving from top to bottom of the pick sheet and selecting one line or SKU at a time. Discrete picking is the simplest way to select orders and therefore the most popular.

Discrete picking has these advantages:
- It is the most easily understood option.
- It provides the fastest response to the customer.
- Because only one person is involved, responsibility for speed and accuracy is readily established.

Discrete picking also has some disadvantages:
- Travel time may be higher than other methods.
- When orders are small, productivity is lower than with other methods.

Zone picking requires that the warehouse be organized into distinct zones, with one or more workers assigned to each. The order picker isolates all the SKUs on the order within his or her zone and selects that part of the order only. When this selection is completed, the product is brought to an order consolidation area to be combined with merchandise picked from other zones to make up the complete order.

There are two subvariations of zone picking. Simultaneous zone picking selects from all zones at about the same time, with consolidation of the order as soon as all zones are completed. Sequential picking moves the order from one zone to another, with picking from the first zone completed before the order moves to the second one.

Zone picking has some advantages:
- It works better when your inventory contains substantial variation of product requiring different handling equipment, such as a mixture of large appliances and small repair parts.
- It reduces travel time by keeping fastest movers in the most convenient zones.
- It reduces congestion by careful arrangement of stock in different zones.

Zone picking also has a few disadvantages:
- Order selection is more complex than with discrete picking.

- Response will be slower for emergency orders or customer pickups because more people are involved.

Batch picking involves a single worker handling a group of orders all at the same time. A batch pick list may be prepared that shows the total for each SKU found in the entire group of orders.

There are two subvariations for batch picking. In one, the entire batch is gathered together and brought to a staging area for segregation by individual order. A second and better method is to use a batch picking cart that contains bins or spaces for each order in the batch. When this method is used, the order selector segregates by order as the product is picked.

Advantages of batch picking include:

- Travel is significantly reduced because the worker can visit one location and take everything needed for a group of orders.
- The more orders in the batch, the greater the productivity gain (up to a point).
- When segregation is performed at a staging area, there is a second check on accuracy.

There are also two disadvantages:

- The process is more complicated than discrete picking, so there is a greater risk of error.
- Since batch picking obviously won't work for single emergency orders, it cannot be the only method used.

Wave picking is the separation of orders by time. In a typical warehouse shift, there are several waves or periods that are handled at specific times of the day.

The prime advantage of wave picking is that it can be used to provide better coordination of the picking and shipping functions. For example, it may be more efficient to pull the orders for the most distant delivery points first, allowing those outbound trucks to leave earlier in the day. The closest destinations might be selected last. Wave picking is also used to separate parcel orders from other shipments, coordinating the parcel wave with the pickup time for the parcel carrier.

Wave picking, like the zone and batch picking methods, is more complex than discrete picking and therefore requires more precise control. Like the others, it is abandoned when an emergency order takes priority over the original schedule.

These variations are sometimes combined. Zone-batch picking is a feasible combination. Within each zone, the worker selects a group of orders rather than a single one. Zone-wave picking might be used to handle each wave within a separate zone rather than throughout the warehouse.

The bucket brigade*

In the days before fire engines, the bucket brigade was a standard method of moving water to extinguish a fire. A group of people lined up and passed buckets of water from one to another. The same principle governs a new method of selecting orders. The bucket brigade technique requires no capital investment, little change in warehouse management systems, and minimal effort to retrain workers. The technique has been implemented in enough industries to confirm that it really works and improves productivity.

In traditional zone picking, each worker selects orders from a specified area. The problem is balance. A faster worker will finish the job and spend time waiting for slower workers to catch up. Some of the imbalance comes from the orders themselves. One order may have a heavy volume from one zone and virtually nothing from another. As a result, one picker is busy while another is idle.

When the bucket-brigade system is installed, zones are abolished. The fastest picker is stationed at the last zone of the pick line, and the slowest picker is at the first zone. The bucket brigade is a pull system. Each order picker moves forward until the person ahead takes the work, and then the picker goes back to get more work. No one is permitted to go back until another picker takes the work, and no one is permitted to pass another picker. The slowest worker starts the new orders, and the fastest worker completes each order. Therefore, the size of each zone is determined by the speed of the picker. Since the workers are sequenced from slowest to fastest, the fastest one is the lo-

---

* Adapted from an article by Professor J. J. Bartholdi, III, Georgia Institute of Technology and Professor D. D. Eisenstein, Graduate School of Business University of Chicago, *Warehousing Forum*, Volume 11, Number 9, ©The Ackerman Company, Columbus, Ohio.

comotive that pulls the train. The fastest picker covers the widest area, and the slowest one covers the narrowest area, so the line balances itself spontaneously.

A significant advantage of the brigade is the ability to have narrow aisles. No worker ever passes another, so passageways need not be wide enough to allow two people to pass. Another advantage is improved team discipline. The speed of each team member becomes obvious as one observes the amount of pick line covered by each worker. Occasionally a team may ask management to remove one team member who is abnormally slow.

Management's hardest job is to rank pickers according to talent, but this becomes easier once the people are well known. The production rates can be changed by increasing or decreasing the number of pickers.

A team approach is an essential part of the bucket brigade. The team leader is typically the fastest worker, who paces the entire system. In some cases, team members are supplemented by temporary workers.

The bucket brigade can be used with batch picking as well as single-order picking. If orders are picked on a batch system, the influence of order variance is reduced.

Cross docking

The distribution system in which freight moves in and out of the distribution center without ever being stored is called cross docking. On occasion, other services such as repackaging or kitting may be included in a cross-dock operation. Cross docking has almost as many flavors as ice cream, and the flavor you choose has a great deal to do with the cost.

An inbound load that is marked and separated by outbound order equals plain vanilla, the simplest and least costly method for the warehouse operator. The operator pulls the separated orders and stages them for outbound shipment.

A more expensive flavor is an inbound load sorted by SKU but not segregated by outbound order. Here the operator must receive the load and then make up outbound orders according to a separate manifest. This takes more time and space than plain vanilla.

A still more complicated flavor is one in which the inbound load is labeled by outbound order but not sorted or segregated. Here the operator must first unload the merchandise and then segregate by noting the destination labels and matching them with a shipping document.

Another flavor requires that the inbound load be handled in combination with other merchandise already in storage at the warehouse. The operator must blend stored merchandise with cross-dock merchandise, again a more difficult operation than plain vanilla.

The most complex and expensive flavor of all is one in which goods are not separated by SKU nor by outbound order but are loaded at random on the inbound vehicle. Now the operator performs two sorting operations, one to segregate SKUs and a second to fill customer orders. This might be a low-cost operation for the shipper, but it is the most expensive option for the cross-dock operator.

Whether you are buying or selling cross-dock services, it is important to recognize all five flavors and to appreciate the differences in cost and complexity of each variation.

Success factors in cross docking*

The most important success factor in cross docking is the need to keep it simple. If you get carried away, you may create a highly sophisticated and unprofitable cross-docking operation.

Since cross docking is not storage, a third-party operator should charge an additional fee for any product that is in the facility more than three days. Otherwise, the user receives storage services without paying for them.

The three most important ingredients for success in cross docking are time, communications, and accuracy. Regarding time, it is essential for the cross-dock operator to receive detailed information about the load before the vehicle arrives. Failure to submit advanced information will usually wipe out the cost advantages of cross docking.

---

* Adapted from an article by Jesse Westburgh, Florida's Natural Growers, *Warehousing Forum*, Volume 10, Number 9, ©The Ackerman Company, Columbus, Ohio.

Communications quality is as important as timeliness. The operator must know exactly what freight is scheduled to be received, when it will arrive, and when the outbound loads must be shipped. If the details are not accurate, the advantages of the operation are again destroyed.

Accuracy includes sortation and communication by the cross-dock operator. If the documentation of handling of both inbound and outbound moves is not accurate, the cross-dock operation will not succeed.

Six forms are used to document and support a cross-dock operation.

Figures 23-1 (left) and 23-2 (right)

Pick Ticket

Product Code _____

Customer	Case Qty
Chain A	_____
Chain B	_____
Chain C	_____
Chain D	_____
Chain E	_____
Chain F	_____
Chain G	_____
Chain H	_____
Chain I	_____
Chain J	_____

Old Inv.	
Ttl Cs	
Amount Rcvd.	
New Inv.	

Loading Tally

Trailer Number _____ Loaded _____
For Delivery _____

Driver: This load must be checked by piece count and product code number at time of unloading. Please report any discrepancies to the Dispatcher on OS&D form and return this tally to your office.

B/L [Pallet]
1. Store

B/L [Pallet]
2. Store

B/L [Pallet]
3. Store

Stop Offs

Nose _____
2 _____
3 _____
4 _____
5 _____
6 _____
7 _____
8 _____
9 _____
10 _____

Special Instructions:
_____
_____
_____

A pick ticket is prepared for each product code. It lists customers receiving merchandise and the quantity going to each destination. A sample is shown in Figure 23-1.

A loading tally accompanies each bill of lading and is used to control the outbound shipments. It shows where each order is within the trailer, starting with the nose and ending at the rear. Figure 23-2 shows a sample.

A pallet record lists the number and type of pallets received and shipped; the purpose of this form is to control pallet exchange. Customers are warned that they will be billed for the cost of pallets if they are not returned.

The other three forms: receiving tally, bill of lading, and invoice are similar to those used in other warehouse operations.

An effective cross-dock operation provides timely and accurate distribution of cargo without the need of storage. If everything is not done accurately and on time, the results will be disappointing. Information handling is as important as freight handling. The whole operation depends on the performance of well-motivated people.

Reverse order picking*

Reverse order picking, a variant of cross docking, is a simple system that combines receiving with the makeup of outbound customer orders. The unloading crew makes up all available outbound orders as the product is received, thus saving a second order-picking operation and restaging.

For reverse order picking, a recap sheet (Figure 23-3) contains a column representing each item on the inbound load. The order outlines list each outbound order by number and by customer name. A ticket is made for each stock item. For example, product code 17315 (see Figure 23-4) lists shipments destined for five different cities. Using this ticket, the receivers segregate the merchandise for each of the five outbound orders as they unload the truck. Once these five orders are on separate pallets, each pallet is labeled with the name of the

---

* Adapted from an article by Jesse Westburgh, Florida's Natural Growers, *Warehousing Forum*, Volume 1, Number 4, ©The Ackerman Company, Columbus, Ohio.

Figure 23-3

	15045	16116	17315	17354	18518
434718 Grocer 1		10	200		25
434732 Grocer 2	30			50	10
434744 Grocer 3		25			
434740 Grocer 4	40	30	400		
434745 Grocer 5		15	200	25	
434729 Grocer 6	40			20	10
434741 Grocer 7	15	20	10		
434728 Grocer 8	200	50		25	15
434728 Grocer 9	10	10		100	200
434731 Grocer 10		15	30	15	50

customer and the load number. While reverse picking sometimes slows receiving, it usually saves a substantial amount of time in the total cross-docking process.

Planning for improvements

Because order selection is usually the most labor-intensive aspect of warehousing, it deserves an appropriate amount of management attention. As you consider ways to improve the function, a prime emphasis should be on reduction of travel time. Typically travel is the largest time element in this process. Also, consider how better cooperation between the parties who ship merchandise to your warehouse and those who receive product from it can improve the process. For example, what can your suppliers or customers do to improve unitization and segregation and thus make the cross-docking jobs you do both easier and faster?

Figure 23-4

Product code 17315

Order	Load	Case Quantity
Grocer #1	5	200
Grocer #4	9	400
Grocer #5	1	200
Grocer #7	3	10
Grocer #10	13	30
		840

Questions that solve problems

If order picking is your largest expense category, then it is also the area that deserves the most penetrating questions.

Q What are the turns per year of inventory in our warehouse, and how does the turnover compare with last year's?
C If your people can't answer this, they may not be aware of the changes in velocity that influence operating costs.

Q What percent of current outbound orders are broken-case picking, and what percent are case picking or unit-load picking?
C Understanding the order pattern is the first step in improving order selection. If your people don't know then they are not paying attention to a crucial item.

Q What percentage of total warehouse costs are represented by order picking and cross docking?
C Again, failure to measure this is a sign of misunderstanding of the importance of the function.

Q What percentage of orders selected were discrete picking, and what percentage were of other varieties of order picking?
C Once you get the answer to this, find out how the percentages have changed in the past few years. If your system was designed at a time when the order pattern was very different, you need to take a new look.

Q What percentage of tonnage (or cases or units) received last week were cross docked for immediate shipment?
C Again, compare the percentage calculated for today with the one from one, three, or five years ago.

Q What improvements in order picking are we contemplating?
C Failure to answer this one in a positive and creative way suggests that your people are not paying enough attention to this critical function of warehousing.

Chapter 24

Unitized loads

A proven method of raising materials-handling productivity is to increase the size of the unit handled. It is less costly to grab two cartons than just one, and still less costly to move a pallet full of cartons. The ultimate in cost reduction is to move a container full of pallets.

Unitized handling as we know it today started with the military during World War II. As the industrial truck was developed, its users quickly recognized that the best way to move product was to place forks on the front of the vehicle and then build a wooden platform or pallet that could be used to transport cartons or other types of cargo.

The first such platforms were skids, consisting of a wood deck nailed across two or more vertical boards. These runner boards raised the platform enough to allow the forks to slide underneath and raise the platform. As the need for stacking stability became evident, additional deck boards were nailed across the bottom, and the skid became a pallet. Pallets were and are made of wood because that is usually the cheapest and most plentiful construction material.

The earliest skids and pallets were built in a wide variety of sizes. Small ones were designed for low-volume grocery products. The largest stevedore pallets are four feet by eight feet and designed for crane handling in marine transportation. When each warehouse had a different storage rack system, pallet standardization seemed impossible.

The standard pallet

Pallet standardization was fostered by the U.S. military, which used a standard pallet to move wartime supplies. Huge quantities of them became surplus in 1945 as World War II ended.

Figure 24-1

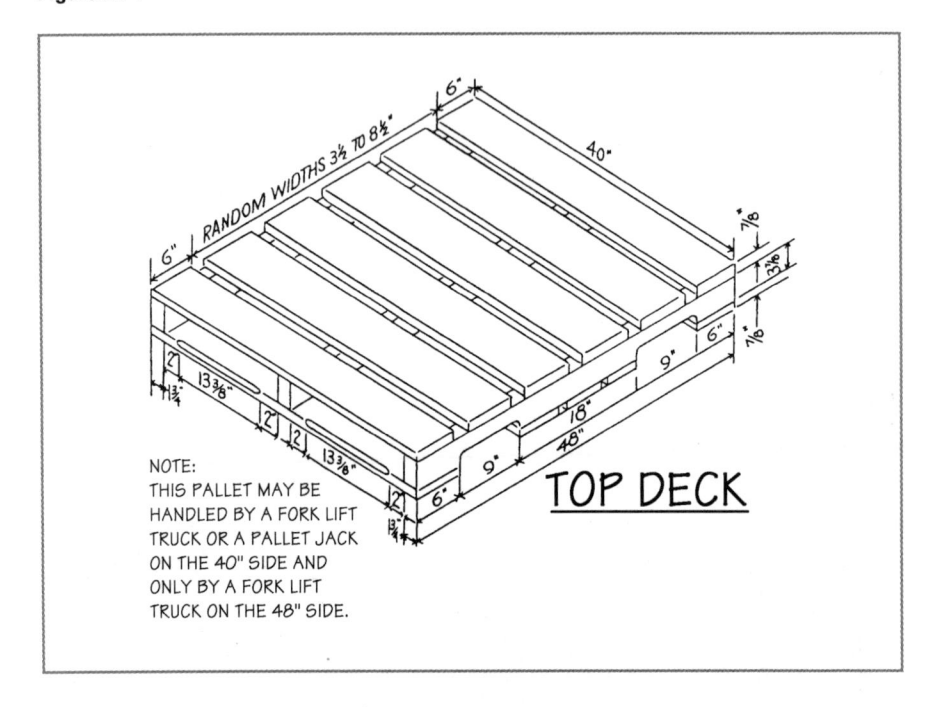

Figure showing a pallet top deck with dimensions: 48" × 40", 6" spacing, random widths 3½ to 8½", with notations including 13⅜", 2", 1¾", 9", 18", ⅞", 3¾⁶". Note: THIS PALLET MAY BE HANDLED BY A FORK LIFT TRUCK OR A PALLET JACK ON THE 40" SIDE AND ONLY BY A FORK LIFT TRUCK ON THE 48" SIDE.

The Australian government had a particularly large supply of materials-handling equipment left over after the war. It formed a Commonwealth Handling and Equipment Pool (CHEP); because the pool had a standard-size military pallet, Australia achieved standardization as a legacy of its war surplus.

Standardization came to the United States during the 1960s; General Foods deserves prime credit. Its standard (see Figure 24-1) specified the size and spacing of the boards on the top and bottom deck, as well as the size of the runner boards or stringers. Notches on the stringer boards allowed the forklift to lift the pallet from any of the four sides, although it is handled most easily from the forty-inch face because of its larger openings.

Because of its influence on both suppliers and customers, General Foods introduced and enforced a standard size for grocery pallets. The Grocery Manufacturers of America endorsed the concept and finished the job of establishing the original General Foods specifications as an industry standard.

Wholesalers and chains adapted their materials-handling and storage rack systems to use the new standard pallet.

A Grocery Pallet Council was established, but eventually efforts to maintain pallet standards disintegrated. As the hardwoods in the General Foods design became scarce and expensive, many pallet users switched to cheaper woods. Others changed the thickness and spacing of the deckboards, making a less durable pallet. Eventually the Grocery Pallet Council disbanded, and today the only remaining standard specification is the size: The 48-by-40-inch (1.0-by-1.2-meter) pallet remains the predominant size used in the grocery products industry,

Figure 24-2
Photo courtesy of Cascade Corporation

and most storage rack systems are designed to accommodate a unitized load of those dimensions.

Unitizing without pallets

One of the oldest devices to allow palletless handling is the carton clamp or grab truck. Figure 24-2 shows a clamp truck with a load. The arms or paddles lift the load by squeezing the sides. This technology was designed for bales of cotton and newsprint rolls. Some clamp trucks have curved arms designed to fit paper rolls or narrower arms designed for bales.

Because side pressure is required to lift the unitized load, weak packaging or excess clamp pressure creates a danger of product damage. In the early days of clamp truck use, considerable damage occurred when warehouse operators and lift truck manufacturers were ignorant about the need to properly adjust the equipment. The clamp device must be carefully maintained to provide damage-free performance. Some warehouse operators use clamp attachments to pick up everything from bicycles to baling wire, and the result is damage to both the clamp arms and the merchandise.

Because of the way it functions, the clamp truck eliminates the need for a loading platform. That means it can pick up a load from one pallet and drop it onto another. A disadvantage to the carton clamp is space lost in the warehouse or in trailers. A few inches of open space must be left for clearance of the clamp arms.

Another substitute for the pallet is a disposable shipping platform known as a slipsheet. This system was developed through cooperation between paper companies and materials-handling manufacturers. Made of laminated paper or plastic, the slipsheet is much thinner and cheaper than a pallet and usually cannot be handled with conventional forks. A special device known as a push/pull attachment grips a protruding tab of the slipsheet and pulls the load onto flat plates that support the load while it is being transported. The same device then pushes the loaded slipsheet off the plates at its destination. Figure 24-3 shows the slipsheet and push/pull attachment in use.

Mandated slipsheets

A large chain retailer astounded materials-handling professionals in the mid-1990s by issuing a "mandate" to require all suppliers to de-

Figure 24-3
Photo courtesy of Cascade Corporation

liver product on plastic slipsheets. A few years later, the mandate was relaxed. The retailer recognized three problems with slipsheets. First, not all product lends itself to stacking in a unit load. Some products, such as garden tools, are not shipped in rectangular boxes, and some do not have uniform carton sizes.

A second problem was discovered in LTL (less-than-truckload) quantities: most LTL carriers do not have the push/pull equipment needed to handle slipsheets.

A third difficulty is encountered with vendors who are too small to justify the $9,000 expense to add a push/pull attachment to a lift truck. The retailer also found that training in slipsheet handling is crucial. Lack of training has resulted in high damage and frustrated operators.

Although the mandate was relaxed, the retailer still works to maximize delivery on slipsheets.

The search for a better pallet

Frustration with the damage caused by substandard pallets caused an intensive search for alternatives during the 1990s.

Cleveland Consulting Associates developed two studies for the Joint Industry Shipping Container Committee, a new group sponsored by the Food Marketing Institute, the Grocery Manufacturers of America, and the National American Wholesale Grocers Association. The study concluded that pallet cost to the grocery industry alone is $1.9 billion per year, which translates to 16 cents per case of groceries, or $10 for a typical unit load. These costs include product damage caused by poor pallets, replacement and repair of damaged pallets, extra cost to motor carriers in transporting pallets, productivity loss as pallets are sorted and selected, workers' compensation costs from pallet-caused injuries, and administration of pallets. One wholesaler estimates that seven out of ten injuries in his warehouse are caused by pallets.

The joint industry committee announced a competition to develop a one-way disposable shipping platform.

At least four alternative pallets have been designed:
- Pressed-wood-fiber pallets have about the same durability as wood, and they save space because they are designed to be nested. They have no nails, so product damage is lessened.
- Corrugated fiberboard pallets are less durable than wood and are not repairable, but they could be suitable for single-use shipping applications.
- Plastic pallets are more durable than wood. Although they are not repairable, they can be made of a recyclable material and are often used in a closed-loop system where the pallet is always recovered for reuse.
- Metal pallets are similar to plastic pallets and have the same uses.

Both plastic and metal can be sanitized to meet FDA requirements for food processing. The U.S. Postal Service has experimented with both a nestable wood-fiber pallet and a nestable plastic pallet.

Some warehouse operations require that the stringer dimension face the aisle, and in high stacking it becomes nearly impossible for a lift driver to insert forks into a notched stringer without damaging the pallet. Some truck loading patterns also require rotation of the pallets, and an attempt to handle them through the notches creates similar damage opportunities.

The need for full four-way entry has created strong pressure to develop a practical block pallet that offers equal ease of entry from any side.

Perhaps the most significant design change for permanent pallets is a full four-way entry rather than the notched stringer board used in the earlier standard pallet. Figure 24-4 shows a full four-way-entry block pallet.

Figure 24-4

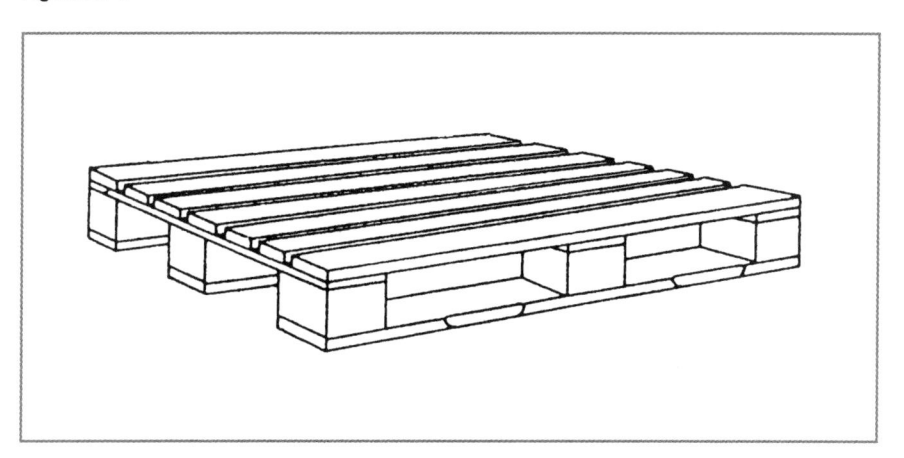

For both the one-way and the permanent pallet, there is also new emphasis on environmental features. About 63 million pallets are destroyed each year. Some are burned as boiler fuel, but others must be hauled to landfills at great expense. Environmentalists want a pallet that can be recycled or compressed and placed in conventional trash containers.

Plastic pallets grow in acceptance

When a food industry newsletter asked 15 executives about the best cost-cutting idea received during the past year, the one that received the most votes was the plastic pallet. Respondents indicated that they use these pallets in their warehouses for shipment to their own stores. Some plastic pallets are nestable, so they save space in the warehouse and on trucks. Respondents said that they can get more pallets on a truck. They also save on pallet repair and sortation of damaged pallets. One indicated that a plastic pallet can be used up to 70 times.

The initial cost of plastic pallets is higher than that of wood, but improved technology has narrowed the price difference.

Understanding pallet costs

Although pallets are recognized as a major challenge for most warehouse operators, few have tried to analyze the cost of maintaining a pallet supply. Once the pallet is purchased, it must be stored, repaired, sorted, and eventually sold or destroyed. Continuing costs are usually hidden as they are combined with other budget categories. If repairs are done internally, the cost of labor and materials must be isolated. Now that the option of leasing pallets from a third party exists, operators need to develop their true *total* pallet costs in order to compare those costs with pallet-leasing programs.

The search for a better permanent warehouse pallet continues. One of the goals for both the one-way and the permanent pallet is a weight of less than fifty pounds. No permanent pallet design has achieved the desired weight, but a few have come as low as fifty-five pounds.

Some designs use a mixture of hard woods and soft woods. The nonwood pallets continue to be expensive, but the cost is moving down.

Store-ready pallets for retailers

A strategy receiving increased attention is the use of a third-party warehouse to assemble and ship pallets ready for display in the retail store. These pallets may contain more than one SKU, and some are designed to move directly to the floor of a store.

One retailer reports that it costs more than thirty cents to handle each case of product at the warehouse. The store-ready pallets can bypass that warehouse and be delivered directly to stores, thus avoiding the retailer's distribution system. Sometimes the customers pay the bill for these custom-designed pallets, and at other times the fees are paid by retailers. Developing store-ready pallets moves the selection process from the retailer to a third-party distributor.

Questions that solve problems

As you re-evaluate the task of unitizing loads in your warehouse operation, use the questions below as points of discussion and review with your people.

Q Does our warehouse now use the standardized pallet dimensions of 48 by 40 inches (1.0 by 1.2 meters), or do we have some other size?

C Failure to standardize is a waste of money. You lose any opportunity to trade pallets with suppliers or customers. If your pallets are not standardized, be sure your people have very good reasons for their position.

Q Aside from conventional wooden pallets, have we considered any other materials-handling options?

C Be sure the people who answer are not reflecting a resistance to change. If they have not experimented with slipsheets, clamp handling, or both, they have missed a potential opportunity to gain new economies.

Q Do we know the cost of maintaining pallets in our operation? Have we reduced this to a cost per pallet and tracked that cost over time?

C The only way to justify considering a change is to know the cost of maintaining pallets in the current operation. A relatively high maintenance cost should stimulate exploration of improved pallet reconditioning operations, use of non-wood pallets, or use of other unitizing methods.

Q Do we exchange pallets with customers or suppliers?

C A negative answer could indicate resistance to change. However, even an affirmative answer requires further exploration of how well the exchange works. You need to learn whether you are accidentally donating pallets, or whether you are trading expensive permanent pallets for cheap and expendable ones.

Chapter 25

Specialized storage

Nearly all warehouses are equipped to handle packaged merchandise at ambient temperatures. A smaller number of facilities are properly equipped for specialized types of storage. Four special situations are considered in this chapter:

- Temperature-control storage (usually refrigerated).
- Hazardous materials (hazmat).
- Fulfillment.
- Household goods.

A growing number of packaged foods and fresh produce require some kind of temperature control for safe storage. At the same time, an increasing number of chemicals also require either temperature or humidity control.

Warehousing of hazardous products may not have grown in popularity, but it has certainly increased in complexity. As public awareness of chemical hazards is modified by experience, warehouses that specialize in storage of hazmat face growing risk-management and regulation challenges.

Fulfillment is undoubtedly the fastest growing type of specialized storage. The handling of catalog, mail-order, and e-commerce transactions to move products directly to the consumer is called fulfillment.

Household goods warehousing is a very old business, but the techniques used with household goods have been adapted to storage and distribution of office equipment and other commercial products.

Temperature-controlled warehousing*

There are four kinds of cold-storage warehouses. The standard food freezer operates at 0 to -10 degrees Fahrenheit; ice cream freezers operate at -20 to -25 degrees Fahrenheit; blast freezers combine extreme cold with rapid air circulation to freeze freshly packed products quickly; and chilled warehouses hold product at 35 to 45 degrees Fahrenheit. When you are designing a cold-storage building, consider potential future uses and the cost of conversion. For example, if you are building a chilled warehouse, you may design the building to allow for future conversion to a freezer warehouse. The lower the temperature one wants to maintain, the higher the cost of the building.

In the early decades of the 20th century, most temperature-controlled products were chilled rather than frozen. Consumer-sized packages of frozen foods were introduced in 1929 but did not become popular until the 1940s. By 1970, freezer space was more than 75 percent of the total public refrigerated warehouse space in the United States. *Cooler* space is used primarily for fresh fruits and vegetables, dairy products, and eggs. Chilled storage is increasingly used for nonfood products such as plastics, film, seeds, and adhesives.

One significant difference between temperature-controlled and dry warehousing is the cost of the facility. A freezer warehouse usually costs two to three times as much as a dry-storage warehouse of similar size. The cost difference in utilities is even more extreme, so the successful cold-storage operator depends on excellent energy conservation and building maintenance to control energy costs.

Temperature gauges should be placed throughout the freezer room, one at eye level near the entrance and others in the corners of the room. In addition, a temperature recorder with a weekly data storage medium should be used for a permanent record. A continuous monitoring system that warns of temperature fluctuations of three degrees or more should be installed. These reduce exposure to liability for temperature fluctuations and fire. Plastic curtains together with hydraulic doors help control energy costs.

---

* Much of this chapter was either written or revised by Jesse Westburgh of Florida's Natural Growers.

In a dry warehouse, walls may be thin steel panel with a modest amount of insulation. In contrast, the walls of a freezer are an important part of the insulation system, and a freezer may have six-inch foam insulation panels, clad by sheet steel, inside and out. The floor is an important insulator in a frozen warehouse. A typical specification would be six inches of concrete poured on top of six inches of foam insulation. To protect against heaving of the earth beneath the floor, heat is provided by piping warm ethylene glycol through a layer of sand beneath the insulation. The insulation layer thus serves a dual purpose: Keeping the cold in and the heat below out.

While the roof of a dry warehouse may consist of nothing more than a thin steel deck with a small amount of insulation, most temperature-controlled warehouse roofs start with a steel deck strong enough to hold refrigeration equipment mounted there. Above the deck is a layer of 3/4-inch fiberboard. Above that is an additional ten-to-twelve-inch layer of foam insulation and another layer of fiberboard. The weather seal is single-ply rubber roofing protected by a layer of stone ballast.

Lift trucks are affected by cold, especially the subzero temperature of a frozen-products warehouse. Tight insulation and limited air exchange prevent the use of internal combustion engines. Electric trucks need heaters for the electric contact points, as well as heavier-duty batteries. Because the harsh conditions produce additional wear and tear, preventive maintenance is even more important than in dry-storage warehousing.

The batteries on electric equipment used in a cold environment will last longer if they are charged every four to six hours rather than the eight hours recommended in normal temperatures. The manager who has both dry and cold space should rotate lift trucks so that each truck spends only part of the time in the freezer. Some trucks are specifically designed for this environment, with an enclosed cab to allow the worker relief from the cold.

Workers should have a break room where they can relax with coffee or soft drinks. A ten-minute break each hour will improve productivity for people working in the freezer. Rotate employees from all areas of the warehouse so that each worker spends only part of the time in the freezer. However, allow for those few employees who may request full-time work there.

Most warehouse operators provide protective clothing for employees, including insulated boots, gloves, and freezer suits. Working in a freezer produces greater fatigue since a significant portion of body energy is spent in keeping warm. In an ambient-temperature warehouse, a work crew can handle an overtime or emergency assignment of well over 12 hours without significant loss of productivity or accuracy. Fatigue takes its toll in a much shorter time in a frozen warehouse. Most operators experience more sick leave among workers in a frozen environment.

Supervision is more difficult in this environment. A supervisor in a dry warehouse can watch the loading dock and gain a good idea of what is going on throughout the warehouse. In a temperature-controlled warehouse, the dock is separated from storage areas by walls and doors, so a supervisor on the dock cannot see what is happening in the storage rooms. Effective supervision in the cold-storage area requires additional foremen in the cold rooms. Supervisors have even greater risk of health problems, because they may move in and out of cold rooms more often than workers and are less physically active.

The nature of cold storage changes the way work is scheduled. Because the cost of space is so high, operators tend to select outbound orders as close as possible to the time of shipment in order to minimize space committed to staging. The need to preserve cold product may prevent staging outside the freezer area. Performance of motor carriers is particularly important, so the cold-storage operator must run a scheduled truck dock.

Housekeeping is also affected by the harsh environment in a frozen warehouse. Spills that are not cleaned up will freeze, causing accidents and floor stains. Scrubbing a freezer floor is far more expensive than in dry warehouses, because it requires the use of a nonfreezing solution. Some cleaning solutions are banned by Food and Drug Administration rules, and sometimes the only way to clean a floor in a frozen environment is to scrape it.

Because the consequences of operations failure are so serious, the cold-storage warehouse requires an extra measure of management precision. Failure to maintain temperature control of the product can have very costly consequences for the owner of the merchandise. Therefore the warehouse operator must not only protect the product but also provide ample proof that such protection was continuous.

The use of chilled and frozen products seems to be growing faster than the economy as a whole. With today's lifestyle of working spouses and even working children, the convenience of prepared frozen meals is recognized by a growing percentage of the population. Therefore, temperature-controlled warehousing is likely to enjoy continued growth.

Hazardous materials warehousing*

Attitude is the key to successful storage and handling of hazardous materials. There can be no shortcuts, and a significant commitment is required in terms of capital and management involvement.

It is our responsibility to protect our employees and our habitat. Those choosing to warehouse hazardous materials must assume the responsibility to follow the appropriate rules and regulations. While recent laws have created new responsibilities, the moral responsibility is the same as it was: We must protect our employees, and we must not pollute or adulterate our environment.

What is a hazardous chemical?

Hazardous materials are grouped into the following categories: flammables, explosives, corrosives, poisons, radioactive materials, and oxidizers. In addition, as the Environmental Protection Agency's classification of materials continues to be expanded, the number of materials considered hazardous is likely to increase.

Since many agencies have responded to different regulatory needs, each has its own definition of hazardous commodities. OSHA excludes products packaged for retail sale. For example, swimming pool cleaners are excluded from OSHA's hazardous-commodity list, but such chemicals are closely regulated by the U.S. Department of Transportation (DOT) and local fire codes. At times, the local fire marshall may reach decisions that are in conflict with OSHA.

---

* Revised with help from Gary Fisher, Whiting Distribution Services, Inc.

Before you permit any unfamiliar material in your warehouse, you need to know its hazards. Determining the hazards and providing safe and lawful warehousing requires chemical knowledge, technical and regulatory references, and specialized facilities. Upon making a determination, you are responsible for any mistakes you might make once you have made the decision to store hazardous materials.

The problem is particularly difficult for third-party warehouse operators. The DOT has held that warehouse operators are *offerers* of material for transportation. In the past, the DOT considered third-party warehouse operators to be *agents* of the owners, and they could be held responsible only for failure to carry out the owner's instruction. In the eyes of hazardous-chemical regulators, the warehouse operator has a responsibility to protect the community.

Regulations and training

The regulation of hazardous materials storage and handling comes from several sources, three of them federal. The U.S. Department of Transportation publishes hazardous-material regulations that apply to anyone who ships such material in interstate and international commerce. A typical DOT regulation requires that every shipper and transporter provide training for all the people who could possibly affect a hazardous-material shipment.

OSHA has regulated warehousing activities for many years, and the agency is particularly concerned with hazardous chemicals. One OSHA regulation requires that every employee working with hazardous chemicals be trained on emergency spill procedures for each chemical. This may include training in proper use of respirators during an emergency.

A third federal regulator is the Environmental Protection Agency (EPA). Part of the EPA's concern is storm water regulations that restrict the storm water discharges from all warehouses, particularly those storing hazardous materials.

In addition to federal regulations, most of the states in the United States have their own regulations. Below the state level, there are usually city or county rules affecting warehousing of hazardous commodities. With so many regulators, it is a complex job to verify that warehouses in various jurisdictions remain in compliance with all of the local, state, and national regulations that could be applied.

The best hazardous-chemical warehousers view every warehouse worker as a skilled craftsman. To comply with regulations, one warehouse organization prepared a two-day weekend course on the handling of hazardous materials. It is necessary not only to provide such training but also to document the fact that everyone handling such materials has received and absorbed the training materials.

Reliable hazardous-materials information

It is not unusual for the warehouse operator to find that the person responsible for regulation knows less about the product than the operator does. In such situations, it is wise to influence selection of the authority having jurisdiction, since this can have a dramatic effect on cost. Sometimes the warehouse operator becomes the authority by default, simply because no other authority is willing to make a decision.

Unfortunately, it is not practical to provide a simple how-to that encompasses all the product variables and provides the storer with instructions on safe procedures. So where does the operator go to learn the best way?

Third-party warehouse operators might seek information from other companies that handle similar products. Private warehouses might share information with third-party warehouse operators and with other operators of private warehouses. Even makers of competing products are willing to share information about safe warehousing practices, simply because everyone is eager to learn from others in this field.

Some trade associations such as the International Warehouse Logistics Association (IWLA) and the Council of Chemical Logistics Providers offer advice and references regarding safe chemical storage.

Consultants who specialize in environmental safety assist both producers and distributors of hazardous chemicals. The names of reputable consultants in the field can be obtained from your local or state fire marshall or emergency planning office. *Hazmat World,* published by Tower Bornes Publishing Company, carries advertisements for experts in this field.

Finally, the National Fire Protection Agency is the leading authority on fire safety, and the cost of membership is nominal.

Because regulation in the field is changing rapidly, there is a danger that the information you have is now out of date. To be sure that your warehouse is in compliance with current standards, it is wise to employ an agency specializing in interpretation of the federal register.

Of all the information sources available, the best is the manufacturer of the product, since he is required to prepare information about the safekeeping of that product.

Becoming a competent warehouser of hazardous materials requires a serious commitment in organization, manpower, and capital resources. The hazmat warehouse operator is exposed to increased risks, uncertain requirements, greater costs, and a potential regulatory nightmare. Successful hazardous materials warehousing requires tight discipline throughout the organization, since the consequences of failure can be most severe.

Storers of hazardous materials must first be concerned with safety, then with service, and finally with cost. As the requirements become more stringent, only the most competent warehouse operators will remain in this line of business.

Fulfillment warehousing*

Seven special features make fulfillment warehousing different from most public and private warehousing:

- The warehouse operator has direct contact with consumers.
- Information requirements are instantaneous.
- Orders are much smaller than typical warehouse orders.
- The order-taking function at warehouse level is much more precise, particularly because it involves contact with the consumer.
- Customer service requirements are different and typically more demanding.
- The transportation function is more complex.
- Because of order volume, order complexity, and value-added services such as kit building, inventory management is much more complex and time consuming.

Storage and materials-handling functions are quite different because fulfillment warehousing involves more than simple storage. Fast turns and low volumes mean gravity-flow racks and high-security areas are almost always needed.

The handling function will also differ from the more conventional warehouse. Although there may be some less-than-truckload shipments, there will be a much higher concentration of parcel service, and handling operations will include the metering of parcel shipments. Thus the materials-handling equipment investment will have more emphasis on scales and meters to control outbound movements.

Receiving becomes especially critical because of the high volume of back orders, which are a fact of life in the fulfillment industry.

Paper flow for a fulfillment warehouse is more complex than for most other warehouses. Many orders are received by telephone, and a significant amount of time is spent in handling customer returns. Because a fulfillment operator deals directly with individual consumers, the customer service function is particularly important.

Some users want the fulfillment center to create invoices or even dunning notices. Accounts-receivable aging reports also can be a by-product of invoice handling.

Nearly every fulfillment center must handle the major credit cards easily, through either a local bank or an outside service agency. Many fulfillment centers handle banking for their customers, so a superior banking relationship is necessary.

The best of fulfillment centers offer a 24-hour turnaround on orders. Although a few take two or three days to process and ship, fast turnaround is becoming a standard.

This fast-turnaround requirement makes labor flexibility imperative to deal with seasonality and variance in workload. Superior fulfillment centers maintain a pool of part-time workers who are available if a second shift must be added or if extra people are needed quickly.

Staffing in a fulfillment center can be a continuous challenge. The nature of the jobs themselves is repetitive both in the warehouse itself

---

Revised with the help of Jim Dockter, PBD, Inc., Alpharetta, GA.

and in the call centers. Retention of experienced quality employees is a constant point of discussion for management and supervisors as well. The ability to staff a fulfillment center effectively, given the inherent seasonality of most operations, is an ongoing concern.

A fulfillment center has serious exposure to claims and theft. Because product shipped can be misdirected by a dishonest person running a postal machine, care should be taken in selecting the person for that job. Many fulfillment centers negotiate the inventory variance to be allowed, based on the customer's own experience with errors. Some users will allow a predetermined formula for shrinkage that is in line with their internal experience.

A fulfillment center must absorb the financial consequences of its mistakes; the public warehouseman's usual liability limitations do not apply in fulfillment. The fulfillment center normally needs more equipment for communications than for shipping, including equipment to handle credit cards and toll-free phone lines. Compared with the conventional warehouse, order volume is extremely high. The ability to automate many tasks by computer is far more important in the fulfillment center than in the conventional warehouse. Such an operation will also usually be responsible for a high number of stock-keeping units.

As companies constantly seek new ways to distribute their products, fulfillment warehousing is destined to increase in popularity.

Household goods storage

Although there are many similarities between the warehousing of household goods (HHG) and other merchandise, three essential differences define the activities and the way they are managed:
- Merchandise warehousing typically deals with *new* products. In contrast, the warehousing of household goods is usually *used* furniture.
- HHG storage is almost always a part of the transportation contract rather than a separately defined distribution activity.
- The ownership of the goods handled has passed to the end consumer, which personalizes the activity to a degree that does not exist in other warehousing.

In spite of these differences, warehousing of household goods has a great deal in common with merchandise warehousing. Both have accommodated the same changes in technology, from unit loads to computerization. Both require a high degree of cost control and information availability in order to meet the demands of their customers. Both are engaged in the growth of value-added services to ensure customer satisfaction and to produce increased revenues.

Third-party warehouse operators in both industries began much the same way: They were entrepreneurial businesses providing a localized service.

Because the HHG warehouse operator is required to provide transportation, trucking capability is mandatory. The transportation contract often calls for movement over a long distance, so the furniture warehouseman needs both state and federal authority.

In order to make a profit on a long-distance run, the HHG warehouseman also needs to find backhaul loads. To solve the backhaul problem, HHG warehouse operators banded together in agency relationships, and many of these evolved into national van lines. These associations provide the means of controlling equipment, and they also offer a division of revenue for services performed. HHG van lines have established a closer bond and a more formalized sharing of information than any of the voluntary merchandise warehouse groups.

Mechanization and unitization have changed household goods storage much as they have changed merchandise warehousing. With general merchandise, materials handling evolved from case handling to the movement of palletized unit loads. With household goods, containers called vaults are used to eliminate the piece-by-piece handling of furniture and personal effects.

Because of the specialized storage requirements of household goods, multistory buildings have retained their economic viability. Some operators developed creative programs to produce revenue, including customer self-storage and records storage. There is a significant liability problem in handling used furniture, so self-storage is particularly attractive to the HHG company.

Preparation of HHG for storage is labor intensive. Because the weight and configuration of many items requires more than one person to perform the service, handling costs are a larger part of the total expense than they are for merchandise storage.

Household goods are more vulnerable to damage than general merchandise. Furthermore, because the products are not new, the question of where the damage occurred is a potential problem. Frequency and cost of claims is greater for HHG than for general merchandise. HHG warehouse operators usually offer a supplemental cargo insurance, and they provide a claim service to provide expeditious repair or adjustment for damage.

The diversification of services offered by HHG operators has been driven by two forces, seasonality (most moves take place during the summer months) and diversification.

Seasonality forces HHG companies to seek low-season sources of revenue. Diversification requires a search for products other than used household goods. These additional commodities fall into two categories:

- **High-value products:** Computers, office products, medical diagnostic equipment, trade-show exhibits.
- **New products:** Furniture, fixtures, and appliances.

One of the fastest growing HHG segments is the temporary warehousing, consolidation, delivery, and installation of inbound shipments of furniture and furnishings for hotels, offices, and hospitals. Large hotel chains contract directly with moving companies to receive and store their products, including everything from furnishings and carpeting to wall hangings, drapes, kitchen equipment, silverware, and china. This requires coordination among builders, decorators, and warehouse operators. The period between the completion and the grand opening is usually *just in time*.

Van line service has long been recognized as an important third-party supplier for makers of mainframe computers and other large office machines. Van lines offer a service different from that of a common carrier in that they can store and transport an office machine unpackaged. The padded-van approach to distribution can eliminate the cost of packaging.

A reverse logistics service is performed as office machines are returned for refurbishing, leasing, or resale. In this case, the machines move from the office to a consolidation center. They may be refurbished or redistributed from there or returned to the manufacturer.

Trade shows have become increasingly popular as a marketing tool, and the crating or handling of materials into exhibit halls is a major growth area. Serving this market takes considerable mechanical skill as well as JIT capability.

Another growth area is the handling of oversized items, such as telephone switching equipment, which requires the use of a rigger to move it into buildings. Some HHG operators have created specialized divisions to provide these services.

HHG operations place a special demand on management, as the operations deal with consumers rather than managers. Although the arrangements may be made by a corporate manager, the goods are usually moved under the watchful eye of the owner. Both the beginning and the end of the transaction take place away from the premises of the HHG company. Add to that the usual stressful nature of a family being uprooted and it is easy to visualize the communications problems that can complicate the moving of household goods. In each HHG transaction, managing the exception seems to be the rule.*

---

* This section is adapted from writing by Frederick S. Schorr, *Warehousing Forum*, Volume 7, Number 11 © The Ackerman Company.

Questions that solve problems

The questions you ask regarding specialized storage will vary depending on whether you are a user or provider.

Q Are we absolutely certain that we can identify every hazardous material now stored in our warehouse and that we can verify that no hazards have escaped our attention?
C Consider an independent audit if you have any doubt. Training and auditing of hazardous materials operations is an emerging industry.

Q Are one or more of the specialized types of storage described here found in our organization but controlled by a different management group?
C Although we do not advocate empire building, you may wish to question why specialized storage is managed separately from the primary warehousing activity in your company. You should look at the potential management advantages if you consolidate the specialized functions with the general warehousing now performed.

Q Do we know as much as we should about specialized types of storage?
C Discuss whether you should do these jobs yourself or subcontract them. Consider whether some specialties represent a neglected opportunity.

Chapter 26

Warehouse technology

All warehouses have certain features in common: a floor, four walls, a roof, and loading docks. However, additional tools are always necessary to effectively utilize the building.

These tools are designed to improve space utilization, productivity, and effective movement of materials. Proper tools must be installed, because, as Henry Ford said, "If you need something and don't buy it, in effect you pay for it without ever having it."

Six factors typically influence the choice of storage and handling equipment:

- Degree of flexibility desired.
- The warehouse structure.
- The nature of the handling job.
- Volume.
- Reliability.
- Total system cost.

There is an inverse relationship between the sophistication of equipment and its degree of flexibility. In many warehouses, the perfectly flexible equipment item is a counterbalance forklift truck. This unit is capable of loading and unloading pallets from vehicles, moving those unitized loads to a storage area, and placing them in stacks or pallet rack. In effect, one industrial truck does the whole job. However, if you move to more specialized trucks designed to operate in a narrow aisle, typically you lose the ability to use one truck to do everything in the warehouse. Most narrow-aisle vehicles cannot be used for loading or unloading because they have very small wheels, so at least one other truck is necessary to perform the entire materials movement.

The warehouse building itself may limit the kinds of equipment that can be used within it. A multistory building typically has floor-load limits. A building with lower ceilings will limit the use of high stacking equipment.

The nature of the handling job will also define the kinds of equipment to be used. Unit loads require one kind of system, handling of individual cases requires another, and broken-case handling still another. Dry bulk or liquid bulk operations require very specialized storage and handling equipment.

Some tools can be justified only when there is substantial volume. When volumes are quite low, maximum flexibility is usually a priority.

Reliability is crucial with all tools, but the buyer should always consider the options available when equipment breaks down.

Cost is also a constant factor in purchasing equipment, and any consideration of new tools must be accompanied by a justification for the acquisition. It is important to always recognize total system cost and to compare costs and benefits of various equipment options.

Tools or toys?*

Many warehouse tools are easy to justify. For example, in a modern high-bay warehouse, if you try to store a large number of SKUs in small quantities without storage rack or shelving, the value of the space you waste will be more than the storage equipment.

But when does a tool degenerate into a toy? Sometimes it is a good tool that has been misapplied. Other times it is a tool that once was state-of-the-art but has become obsolete because better tools have become available. In other cases, it is a toy that was bought with no analysis or justification whatsoever, perhaps because a manager saw it in use with a competitor or just fell in love with new technology.

A floor-mounted tow line is a good example of a tool that was considered state-of-the-art several decades ago but has been made obsolete by improved technology. High-rise storage (see Figure 26-1)

---

* Adapted from an article by James M. Apple, The Progress Group, *Warehousing Forum*, Volume 12, Number 12, ©The Ackerman Company, Columbus, Ohio.

Figure 26-1

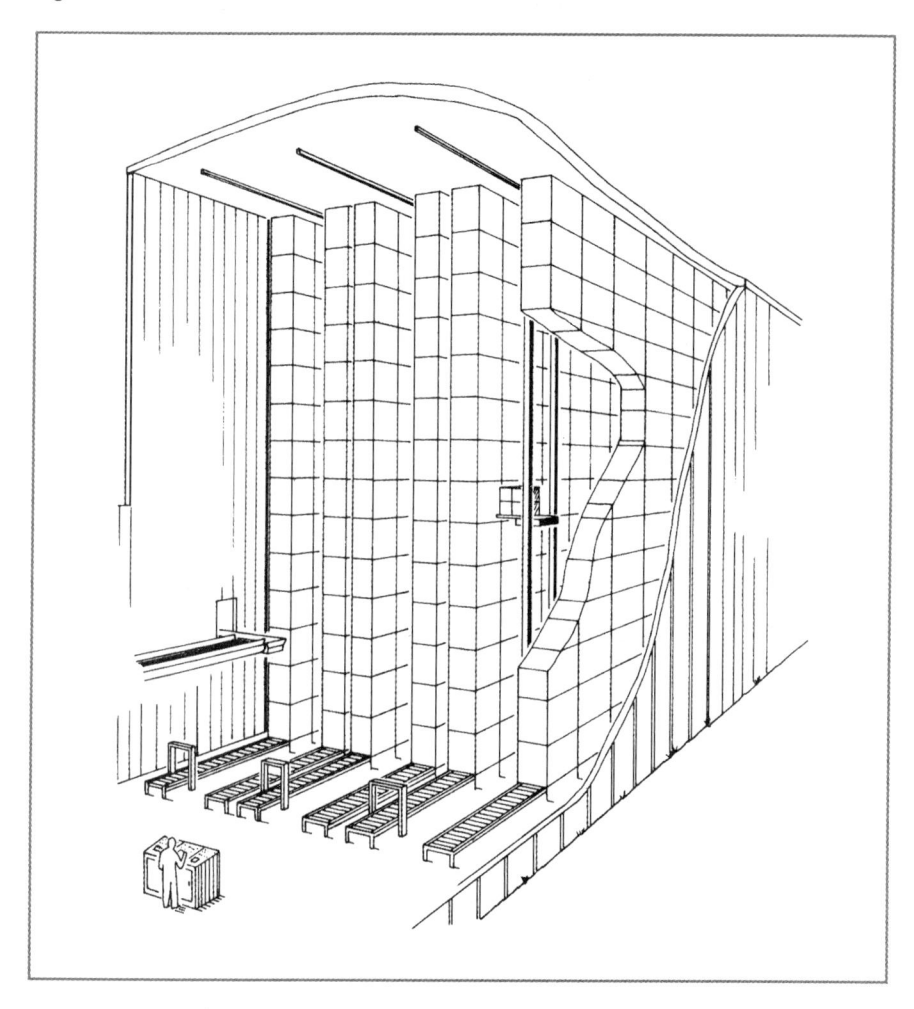

systems in rack-supported buildings are in the same position, at least in the United States. Such systems are better at storage than they are at throughput, and today the emphasis is on faster turns rather than more efficient storage. In other countries where land costs are much higher than in the U.S., the high-rise system is not considered a toy. Mini-load storage systems are useful tools for slow-moving spare parts, but for high-turnover items they are handicapped by their slow speed.

To ensure that you are buying a tool and not a toy, first analyze the equipment to decide whether you really need it. Consider these questions as you look at tools for order picking:

- How many lines per order?
- What is your average order size?
- Is your typical order one line or multiple lines?
- Is batch picking practical?
- How frequently are orders picked?
- How important is the cycle time?
- How steady is the demand?
- Will this tool improve ergonomics?

The various tools we use can be classed from three perspectives:

- Tools to save time vs. those to save space or both.
- Mobile equipment vs. static equipment.
- Order picking tools that move picker to product vs. those that move product to picker.

The ideal warehouse tool would save both space and time, but unfortunately some tools that save space do so at the expense of time. There is a constant trade-off in warehousing between space and time, and the buyer should always question whether one is acquired at the expense of the other.

Equipment with wheels is mobile, including wheeled conveyors. Pallet racks and shelving are static equipment.

Most order-picking operations move the order picker to the location where each SKU is stored. However, in a few the picker moves little or not all, and the parts move to the picker.

For virtually every materials handling problem there is a proper definition (sometimes very narrow) for which there is exactly the right tool. But remember these facts:

- Too many technologies in a single system may make it overly complex.
- The real difference between any two technologies may be small.
- The right technology for many situations may be surprisingly low-tech.

Understanding space economies

The lowest-cost space in any warehouse is the area closest to the ceiling. Because the incremental cost of adding interior overhead space is relatively small, failure to use the space you already have will create the need to acquire additional warehousing at a far higher cost. To check your space utilization, calculate the highest practical stack height in the building, and then determine how much of the available space is actually in use.

Saving space may also reduce travel time, since storage will be in a more compact area. You can justify the purchase of storage equipment by eliminating or at least delaying the acquisition of additional warehousing space.

How pallet racks improve space utilization

The most common pallet rack system, selective rack installed back to back and three high, might allow 7,000 pallets to be stored in 100,000 square feet. However, the three-high configuration may not use all of the available overhead space. In that situation, the purchase of rack extensions or new uprights could change the system from three-high to four-high, thus adding more pallet positions to storage capacity. Capacity can be further increased by bridging the rack over cross aisles.

Some pallet rack systems are designed for double-deep storage (see Figure 26-2). They require the use of a forklift truck equipped to reach into the rack to retrieve the inside pallet. The double-deep system would be used only when storage capacities can be increased without the need to increase the number of SKU facings. This system will nearly double the storage capacity available with selective rack.

Other storage rack options

Portable rack is one of the oldest and best available methods for achieving high stacking with products such as tires, which are stored without packaging and also lack structural strength. Some portable racks are designed to be nested when not in use. Others are easy to dismantle for storage.

Drive-in or drive-through racks allow even greater storage density than the double-deep rack. Each pallet is supported by flanges that grip the edge of the unit load. Drive-through rack is open at each end,

Figure 26-2

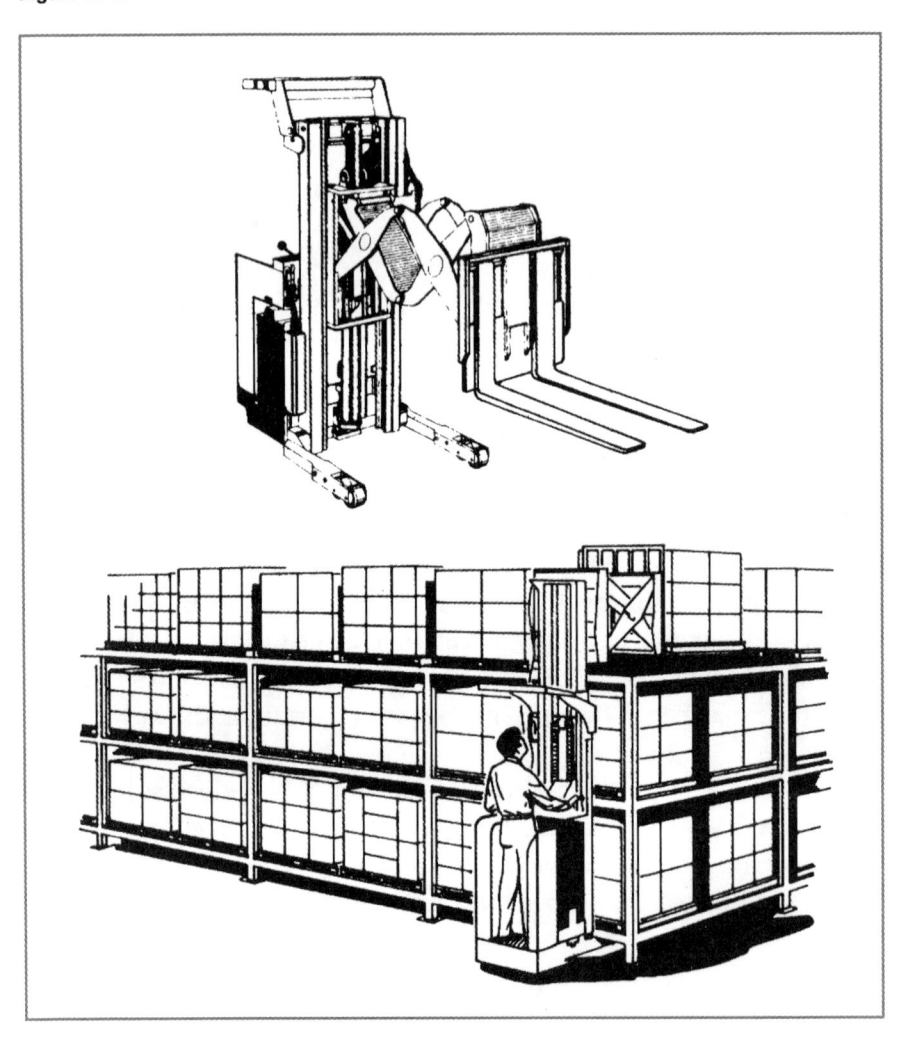

and drive-in rack is approached only from one side. Where first-in, first-out stock rotation is essential, the drive-through rack design is the only practical option. While this deeper rack system will improve density, handling efficiency is sacrificed because the lift truck operator must move slowly and carefully through the narrow alley between the uprights.

Some buildings use storage rack as the structural support for the walls and roof. The rack-supported building with an automatic storage and retrieval system (AS/RS) is designed to move pallet loads. Because these systems use a stacker crane rather than a mobile lift truck, storage heights can be substantially higher than in a conventional warehouse building. (See Figure 26-1.)

Live storage

Some equipment is designed to allow stored goods to move from the back to the face of the rack. A common type of live storage is gravity flow rack, which allows either pallets or cases to move on a roller conveyor to the front of the rack installation (see Figure 26-3). The flow rack will vary in depth (front to back) from as little as four feet to as much as twenty feet.*

Figure 26-3

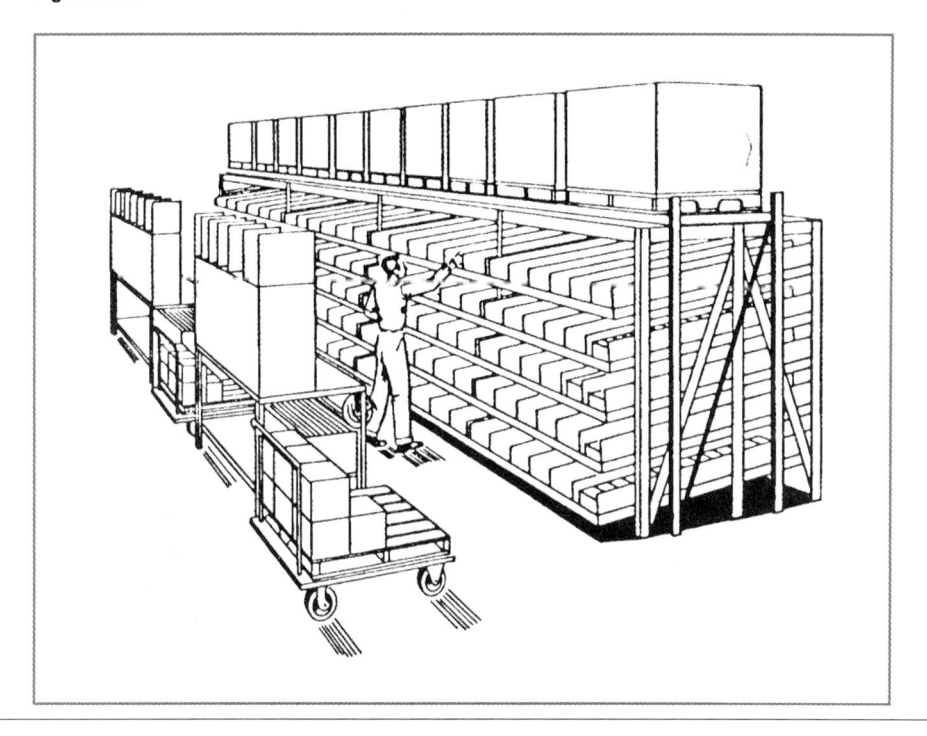

---

* From *Warehousing and Physical Distribution Productivity Report*, Volume 17, Number 8, by the late W. B. Semco, Semco, Sweet & Mayers, Los Angeles, CA ©Alexander Communications, Inc., New York, NY.

Two factors allow case gravity flow racks to improve order filling rates:

- Reduced pick surface allows the picker to reach a greater number of items without walking.
- Reserve stock storage above the flow rack allows the pick surface to be minimized.

A properly designed flow rack system will substantially increase order picking speed by reducing travel.

Since order picking speed depends not only on the number of lines (or hits) but also on the space between lines, speed is improved by reducing the facing of each line. Therefore, the short side rather than the wide side of each carton can face the aisle. Vertical space is also important. To waste as little space as possible, cartons of similar height are placed on the same shelf. It is best to put tall cartons on lower shelves and shorter packages on the upper ones.

Order size is also a factor. Small orders that require substantial travel between lines reduce the effectiveness of the gravity flow system. A badly designed flow rack installation will not increase order filling speed.

Flow racks containing slow-moving items are often ineffective. Items picked fewer than twenty times a month should not be in gravity flow rack. Similarly, a flow rack system with only one hit every four or five feet will probably be picked at about the same speed as static shelving. The benefits of flow rack depend on your ability to minimize space between hits and to have enough lines to establish a fast pick rate. You must also consider the cost of replenishing the rack, since flow rack takes more time to load than shelves.

Any operator who installs a flow rack system to hold 100 percent of the items in the warehouse is likely to have a cosmetically attractive pick line with marginal utility. The best picking system is a hybrid, using flow racks for high-activity items and shelving or bins for items with low activity or uncommon sizes.

Full pallets can also be handled in gravity flow rack. A variation is called push-back rack, because the lift truck operator places the inbound unit load against the existing pallets and pushes them back into the storage lane. Because the newest pallet is on the aisle, this system has no value when first-in, first-out stock rotation is necessary.

Other order-picking tools

Light-directed picking (also known as a pick-to-light system) combines gravity flow rack and computer technology. A display at the end of each flow rack lane will be illuminated at the appropriate time with a number. When the picker sees the number 2 at a given lane, he or she knows that two cases must be pulled to complete the order. When the merchandise is removed, the picker presses the button on the display rack to signal that the task is complete. The light goes out, and the picker moves on from light to light until the entire order is picked. The main advantage of this system is that it allows an unskilled worker to become a productive order picker in a short time. No paper is required. As long as the picker can read numbers and knows how to count, high accuracy and productivity can be achieved.

Weigh counting uses scale technology to ensure that the proper amount of material is picked for an order. Capturing weight by carton can be used as a partial check on picking accuracy.

High-speed sortation combines bar-code scanning with physical separation of products or cases into orders (see Figure 26-4). Order values and SKU range must be sizable to consider this tool.

Carousel systems*

The carousel is a prime example of equipment that moves the product to the picker. The warehouse carousel works like the merry-go-round at a carnival. A horizontal carousel moves a series of bins at sixty to eighty feet per minute in a horizontal loop. A vertical carousel rotates perpendicular to the floor and thus uses available space in a high-bay building. Carousels offer these advantages:

- ◆ Better space utilization. No aisles are needed; product moves to the picker.
- ◆ Improved accuracy. This system may use computer control to reduce the chance to select the wrong item.
- ◆ Increased productivity. Productivity is maximized when one operator uses two or three units. While one

---

* Adapted from an article by Bill Thomas, Consultant, *Warehousing Forum*, Volume 9, Number 10, ©The Ackerman Company, Columbus, Ohio.

Figure 26-4

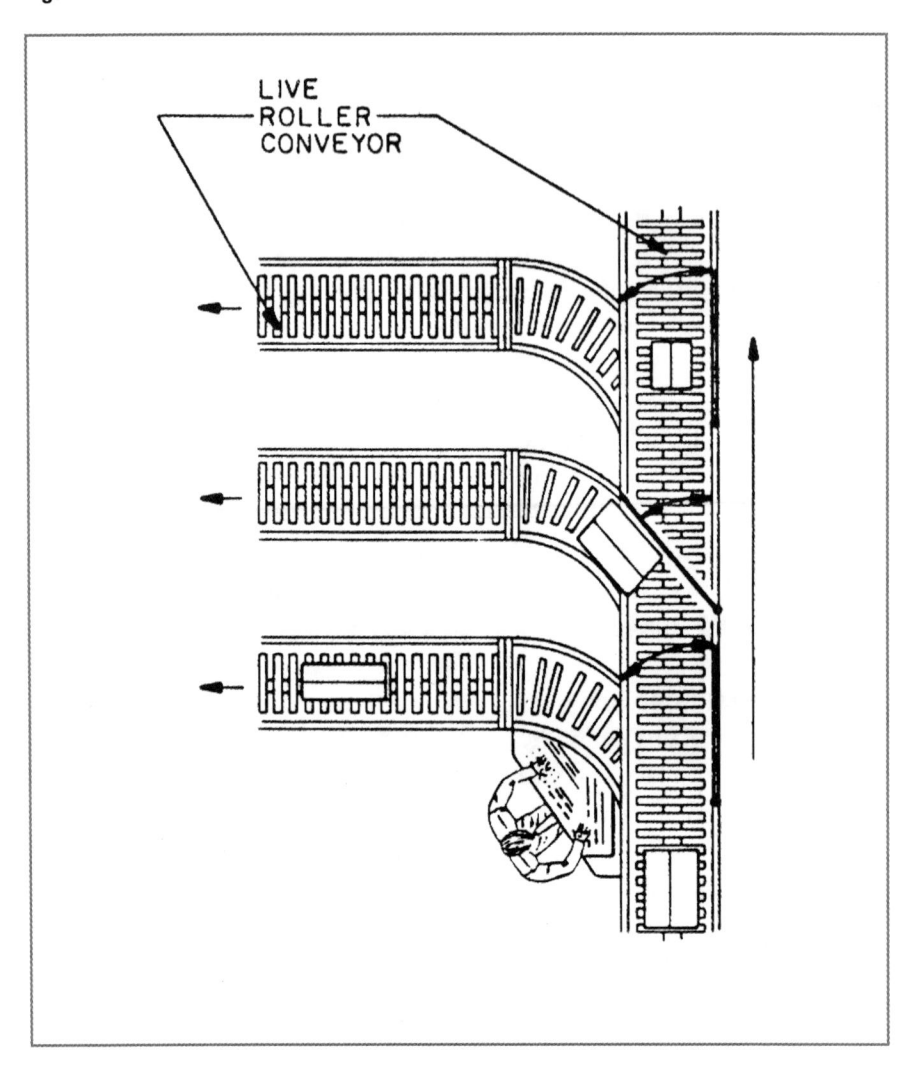

carousel is spinning, the operator pulls material from another.
- Improved security. The system can only be accessed by authorized personnel.
- Better inventory control. Both picking and restocking can be controlled by computer.

- Better management. Each order picker has a static workstation and job functions that are easily measured.

Carousel equipment is most efficient when there are many SKUs and the boxes to be picked are small. Items such as spare parts, catalog pages and pharmaceuticals are well suited for carousels. The carousel is particularly effective for picking of less than case quantities and of items that are either too small or too large for gravity flow racks.

Conveyor systems

Five factors must be considered when you analyze the acquisition of a conveyor system:

- Product or material to be handled.
- Weight and dimensions of packages.
- Number of items and flow rates.
- Fragility of the product.
- Restricting factors such as available space or allowable noise.

Some conveyors are powered by gravity, and some use mechanical power. Skate-wheel conveyors are the most common gravity devices. They are typically used to move cartons or tote bins. A roller conveyor has a more solid conveying surface and therefore can move a wider range of materials, including drums and bags. Power conveyors may have either a roller or a belt-on-roller surface. Accumulation conveyors are used to temporarily stop, hold, or release material. The slat conveyor has steel or wood slats and is used to handle heavier loads where the product could cause damage to a belt. Installing tilting slats makes it possible to sort while the product is moving. The slats tilt on command, dumping the load into specific slides or chutes.

Automatic guided-vehicle systems

Guided vehicles can mechanize a materials handling operation even if throughput does not warrant the use of conveyors. When the moves are long distance or the material must move into tight areas and share aisles with people and lift trucks, the guided vehicle is a versatile materials handling option. The heart of the guided vehicle is an onboard microcomputer that monitors vehicle functions and allows it to travel independently to a programmed destination. If the warehouse layout changes, the travel path can be altered. The earliest AGVs used wire guidance systems, but newer ones are guided by laser beams or gyroscopic navigation systems. Some AGVs are towing vehicles, and others are unit load carriers.

In operating the system, a worker might take a load from the home area, place it on the AGV, and direct that vehicle to a destination address. Then the computer takes over. The vehicle moves to the designated location, deposits the load, and then may return to the home area for a new assignment.

A big advantage of AGV systems is their flexibility. Older buildings available at bargain prices can sometimes be operated economically by using AGVs. In some cases, these buildings have docks that are not convenient to storage areas. Others may be multistory buildings that cannot be operated economically with conventional equipment. Automatic vehicles, in combination with vertical conveyors, can transport loads from docks to storage areas without intervention by people.

Choosing a lift truck

When you count all the options for power source, operator location, lift attachments, vehicle characteristics, and brands, there are thousands of choices to make in selecting a lift truck. Yet it is possible to develop a systematic decision procedure to select the truck that works best in your warehouse.

The most basic source of power is the human body, and some low-lift pallet trucks supplement body strength by using a hydraulic pump providing vertical lift.

The two sources of external power are internal combustion (IC) engines or electric motors. There are five sources of fuel, two of which are limited to outdoor use. Diesel and gasoline engines are used for equipment that operates outdoors where pollution is not a major problem. Electricity is the cleanest fuel source, but refueling can be a problem. For maximum battery life, the electric battery can be changed only when it is 80 percent empty. To change it earlier or later shortens the life of the battery. Therefore, the refueling process for most electric trucks is dictated by a warning light. When the light goes on, the operator must interrupt other tasks to change batteries. A few manufacturers claim that their maintenance-free batteries can be recharged on an opportunity basis. In contrast, fuel for IC engines can be replenished at the convenience of the operator. Refueling can therefore take place at lunch breaks, coffee breaks, or shift changes.

The two fuels used for indoor IC engines are propane (LP) or compressed natural gas (CNG). CNG is superior in cleanliness, safety, and cost. CNG produces less carbon monoxide per unit of fuel consumed. Propane is heavier than air, and if it leaks it will migrate to the floor of the warehouse, where it could burn or explode. Propane has more energy per cubic foot than CNG, so more operating capacity can be carried in each fuel tank. Some suppliers of CNG offer a system of tapping and compressing gas from the same gas lines that supply fuel to the warehouse heaters. This option makes CNG as easily delivered as electricity.

Operator location

There are three options in locating the operator, as shown in Figure 26-5. The walkie truck is the most economical but also the slowest. The rider vehicle provides greater speed and comfort. The man-up truck has operating controls on a platform behind the fork carriage, allowing the operator to ride next to the forks. Most man-up trucks have a guidance system that allows the operator to eliminate the need for steering. This vehicle saves time in selecting small orders because the operator can pull a few cases from a pallet without removing the entire pallet from its storage location. Furthermore, because order pickers can see significantly better, this method is usually faster. Some man-up trucks have two sets of controls to allow operation from either the truck chassis or the loading platform.

Lift attachments

While forks are the fastest and simplest tool to move unitized loads, there is a wide range of other attachments that can be mounted on the fork carriage. Most are designed to eliminate the use of pallets.

The push/pull device is designed to handle slipsheets. It grasps a unit load by clamping a lip on the slipsheets and pulling the load onto a set of wide and thin forks. A push device reverses the procedure to remove the unit load from the forks.

Carton or roll clamps are also designed to handle a unit load without pallets; they are designed with vertical arms that grasp the sides

Figure 26-5

Operator Location

	Advantages	**Disadvantages**
Operator Walkie	Facilitates horizontal travel. Good for order-picking tasks. May add power source to reduce operator fatigue. Reduces task time because operator need not mount and dismount frequently.	Not suited to long-distance travel. Fixed fork width, thus pallet size must be standardized. Low lift capability. Slow travel speed.
Rider	Operator may sit or stand. Greater speed than walkie truck. Reduces operator fatigue. Good lift capacity.	More costly than walkie. Increases task time when operator must mount and dismount truck.
Man-Up	Operator may move up and down with platform. Task time saver for order picking jobs. Better visibility in selecting loads.	Requires automated guidance system to steer. Most expensive. Less flexible for various tasks.

of the unit load to lift it. Chapter 24 provides more information about push/pull and clamp attachments.

Other attachments are designed to grab and lift cargo with a top-lift device, a vacuum cup, a magnet, a boom, or a rotating carriage. Each of these attachments is more costly and complex than forks, but for certain applications the specialized attachments are safer or more versatile.

As you consider alternatives to forks, it is important to learn whether the attachment has been successfully applied by other warehouse operators handling the same product. Significant product damage has sometimes occurred because the specialized attachment was misused.

Narrow-aisle vehicles

The conventional counterbalance lift truck usually requires a twelve-foot aisle. At the other extreme, the very-narrow-aisle truck will operate in a space just a few inches wider than the truck itself. These trucks eliminate the need to turn the entire vehicle to place merchandise in a storage slot. Figure 26-6 illustrates the advantages and disadvantages of narrow-aisle vehicles and conventional trucks. Ven-

Figure 26-6

Aisle Width Capacity

	Advantages	Disadvantages
Conventional	Industry standard truck. Easily transferrable to various tasks. Greater load stability. Greater load capability.	Requires 12-foot aisle. Decreases available storage space.
Narrow	Reduces need for counterbalance trucks. Decreases required aisle width. Increases available storage space.	Less flexible for various tasks. Lower load capabilities. Less load stability. May require "super flat" floor.

dors of narrow-aisle lift trucks justify the substantial extra cost by demonstrating the substantial increase in storage productivity that occurs when aisles are narrowed. Against this, you must balance the probable increase in handling time and cost.

Most of the increase in handling time occurs because very-narrow-aisle trucks have small wheels that are not equipped for loading or unloading of trucks. However, two manufacturers, Bendi and Drexel, have created an articulated lift truck with conventional wheels. These vehicles can do all of the tasks performed by a standard sit-down lift truck, and they still will operate in a narrow aisle.

Brand selection

Because most patents have expired and manufacturing is globalized, the lift truck has become a commodity. As in the automotive industry, many vehicles have lost nationality or brand distinction, with one manufacturer building units for another and many of them assembling a variety of parts produced all over the world. The result is that national origin and brand name become almost meaningless.

When you choose among brands of lift truck, consider these five priorities:

Priority one is the quality of the local dealer. Check on the financial stability, service reputation, and parts inventory of the dealer being considered. Truck buyers usually plan to use the equipment for a long time, so replacement parts and service are of prime importance. Talk to the dealer's other customers to learn whether the service record is as good as advertised. Find out whether the key people in the dealership are truly dedicated to service excellence. Attitude can be detected without making a customer survey: visit the dealer's service department and appraise the performance of the people who work there.

A second priority is standardization and the ability to substitute vehicles. When you use many different kinds of trucks, each vehicle may operate differently from the others. An operator who gets used to one brand may be accident-prone when using a vehicle with different controls. Furthermore, OSHA training standards require that every operator be specifically trained for each type of truck. It usually makes sense to standardize on one or two vehicle designs.

Reliability is the third priority. The cost of downtime is far more significant than the price differences between competitive lift trucks. A cheaper vehicle with poor reliability is always a bad bargain. Consider these reliability measures:

- Your own experience with the same brand or dealer.
- The availability of replacement parts.
- The experience of other warehouse operators using the same kind of truck.

The fourth priority is ease of training and operator satisfaction. This does not mean that management should let the workers decide which lift trucks to buy. However, if experience shows that most workers have tried to avoid using one particular machine, there may be quality considerations that cannot be ignored.

The last priority is price. The initial cost of the lift truck is always minor compared with the costs connected with maintaining it during its useful life. Choosing on the basis of initial price is probably the worst way to make a decision between brands.

Lift truck technology changes slowly, but technology changes will create new options in the selection decision. Fundamentally, the warehouse manager is buying a tool. The design and value of that tool must be related to the job for which it will be used.

Questions that solve problems

When anyone in your organization starts to talk about new technology for your warehouse, it is important to determine the real reasons for requesting new equipment.

Q **What justification has been given for the new equipment?**
C Watch for the difference between tools and toys. Be sure that the rationale for the purchase is well prepared and fully documented and that it includes an updated operations profile..

Q **Will the proposed new technology save space, time, or both?**
C Be sure the answer provides the proper level of detail and includes a rational justification. Sometimes your operations people may need your help in working up a persuasive capital request.

Q **Have your people investigated and considered the potential disadvantages or pitfalls in using the proposed technology?**
C Without trying to kill creative ideas, you need to isolate and modify impulsive decisions.

Q **Has every option related to the new technology been considered?**
C This chapter may be the basis of an options checklist, but still newer alternatives may be available. Review and comparison of every available option is a good way to avoid a poor decision.

PART 6

Information Systems

Chapter 27

Computers and customer service

Computer technology has influenced warehousing as much as any other business. Although information technology has changed every aspect of work done in warehouses, we prefer to think of the computer as primarily a customer-service tool.

Hardware vs. software

In the early days of computer applications in the warehouse, the few major vendors of hardware sold proprietary software systems along with the computers. Operating systems and even the programming languages were unique to each manufacturer. Application software written for one computer system would not run on another brand without conversion. There were even incompatibilities among computer models made by a single manufacturer. A programmer with particular skills on one system might not easily transfer those skills to another system.

In those days, a computer system was a major investment. Today perhaps the most pervasive fact about computers is that the purchase cost goes down each year.

In the early days of computer technology, companies bought computers first and then searched for compatible software. The choices in software were limited. Users who did not have application software and could not find a suitable package were forced to choose from what the hardware vendors offered.

Today, the hardware has become generic, almost a commodity. Brand has become nearly meaningless among the personal computer products used for many warehouse management systems. In contrast, the real competition in information technology today is the software, commonly referred to as warehouse management systems or WMS.

Choosing warehousing software

The first choice in software is whether to procure an off-the-shelf system or build it yourself. Some information technology people consider warehousing to be a relatively simple corporate function that can be readily controlled with a software program constructed in-house. Others recognize the peculiar complexities of warehousing and feel that it is both uneconomical and unsafe to consider anything other than a packaged system.

Finding a warehouse management system

There are several sources of information about packaged systems. The most complete catalog of logistics software is one published each October by Andersen Consulting and the Council of Logistics Management. Since 1998, this information has been published only on a CD-ROM. This format allows search by keyword, hardware type and function, package, or vendor. More than 1,000 different logistics packages are surveyed.

Some trade associations, including the International Warehouse Logistics Association (IWLA), have information about specific software vendors.

The first step in evaluating software is to define the functions you need to perform. Then you should evaluate all available packages based on their ability to deliver the capabilities you need. This process should reduce the number of software packages you will consider.

The next step is to check references. Talk to current users, at least some of whom should have a warehouse operation similar to yours. Include on-site visits to observe the package in a real-world environment. Meet the people who use it, and learn firsthand what experience they have had in applying the system.

In checking references, a key point is the quality and availability of support. No matter how well the system works on the day it is installed, changing conditions in your warehouse will require modifications in the information system. How well you will adapt to those changes depends on the quality of help you can get from the software vendor.

Consider the effect on your company if the software supplier should go out of business. Do you have access to the source code to protect yourself if the supplier is not available at some future date? A number of otherwise successful warehouse management systems have met disaster because of lack of support after they were installed.

Choosing a WMS*

A statement of requirements is the central reference point for any software source. Writing this statement can be a difficult project for any task force whose members are working less than full time at the effort. Allow ample time to complete the statement. The time spent will be well worth the effort if the end result covers all of your requirements and details the specifics of each necessary area. The components of the statement of requirements must include every aspect of your warehousing needs.

Figure 27-1 illustrates a systems requirements outline for a model warehouse management system.

Once the requirements are complete, you must then identify those software companies capable of meeting all the requirements on the list. This is a good way to compare packaged systems with custom systems. Another option is to have a semi-custom system, a package system with extensive modifications by your own information people.

A WMS meltdown

The most widely publicized system failure of the 1990s was described in *Information Week* for March 11, 1996. It described a distribution center in Spartanburg, South Carolina, operated by Adidas America. The center had earned a "warehouse of the month" recognition from a materials handling magazine when it opened in 1993. The *Information Week* article described the system failure in detail. One observer blamed the problem on the fact that management had not emphasized warehousing in planning its information systems.

---

* Adapted from *Warehousing Forum* Volume 10, Number 2, by Morton T. Yeomans.

Figure 27-1

The Xyz Company
A model warehouse management system — system requirements outline

1.0 General requirements
1.1 Support multiple geographic locations, warehouses, and sections within each warehouse
1.2 Support item definitions as well as single-item and mixed-item quantity location
1.3 Support definitions of equipment, storage, and human resources
1.4 Support work measurement criteria and track performance against those criteria
1.5 Support random location of inventory, FIFO processing, and multiple items per location
1.6 Provide management reporting capability
1.7 Provide ability to track orders by status
1.8 Provide inquiry capability
1.9 Handle exceptions and unusual situations
1.10 Support interfaces to materials handling equipment and radio-frequency devices
1.11 Support use of bar-code labels

2.0 Inventory location and management requirements
2.1 Item identification and tracking
2.2 Physical inventories
2.3 Support cycle counting
2.4 Inventory accuracy
2.5 Item history
2.6 Product profile analysis (ABC analysis)
2.7 Allocated and available inventory
2.8 Quarantine or "on hold" inventory
2.9 Storage locations
2.10 Storage location definitions
2.11 Storage location control
2.12 Storage fill rate
2.13 FIFO control
2.14 Support container sizes and equipment
2.15 Reporting capability

3.0 Inventory location / management requirements assumptions

4.0 Receiving requirements
4.1 Advanced notice of delivery
4.2 Various types of receipts
4.3 Availability of items
4.4 Exception status, handling, and reporting
4.5 Bar code labels
4.6 Multiple receipts
4.7 Purchase order reconciliation
4.8 Receipt inspections

5.0 Put-away requirements
5.1 Directed put-away
5.2 Exception handling
5.3 Inventory updating

Figure 27-1 (continued)

5.4	Confirmation of put-away	**9.0**	**Labor management requirements**
5.5	Cross docking		
5.6	Combined processing	9.1	Identify source requirements
6.0	**Order management requirements**	9.2	Work flow monitoring
		9.3	Operating levels
6.1	Order groupings	9.4	Management reports
6.2	Order statistics	**10.0**	**Shipping requirements**
6.3	Reporting	10.1	Fluid loading
6.4	Tracking	10.2	Order staging
7.0	**Replenishment requirements**	10.3	Confirm complete orders and trailers
7.1	Replenishment on FIFO basis	10.4	Identify exceptions and shortages
7.2	Replenishment based on current demand	10.5	Print manifests and other required documents for a trailer load
7.3	Replenishment confirmation	10.6	Interface with inventory and invoice systems
8.0	**Picking requirements**		
8.1	Sequential picking	10.7	EDI to intended destinations
8.2	Other than wave picking	10.8	Transfer of loads
8.3	Segregation of picks	10.9	De-assign products or orders
8.4	Confirmation of picking	10.10	Picking status
8.5	Use of radio-frequency equipment	10.11	Verification or orders and items
8.6	Plan warehouseman work	**11.0**	**Work flow management**
8.7	Order integrity	11.1	Daily and shift workload
8.8	Exceptions	11.2	Exceptions
8.9	Efficient picking	11.3	Work in progress
		11.4	Future workload

Other WMS pitfalls

Most of what is published about warehouse management systems is a celebration of successes. Less is reported about the systems that crash and burn. Those systems that crashed have things in common. Here are characteristics that could create a disaster:

- A system designed by information specialists with minimal knowledge of warehousing.
- Minimal interchange between systems people and warehouse managers.
- A system whose primary purpose is locating stock.
- A system designed primarily for inventory control.
- A system designed primarily for productivity measurement.
- A system not implemented gradually but put into operation all at once.
- A system installed simultaneously with the move to a new warehouse.

Implementing a WMS*

Warehouses functioned well before computers were invented, and they can operate without computers today. Software and hardware are not cheap, although relative to the price of everything else they cost less today than ever before. At the same time, the risk of failure is a real one that can be avoided by keeping things as they are today.

Therefore, it is essential to consider how the expense of a WMS will be justified. If today's shipping error rate is 1 in 5,000 and a new system will change it to 1 in 20,000, what is the value of this fourfold increase in shipping accuracy? If walk time for order picking is now 65 percent of the overall time, what is it worth to achieve a 50 percent reduction in walking through an improved WMS? If shipping capacity today is three million units per week, and the new WMS can increase capacity to eight million without adding any employees, then what is the system worth?

Claims are easy to make, but realization of them depends on establishing benchmarks in each of the areas before a new system is appraised. If you do not know how you are doing now, it is obviously impossible to know how much you might improve.

---

* Adapted from an article in *Warehousing Forum*, Volume 13, Number 6, ©The Ackerman Company, Columbus, Ohio.

Some of the gains expected from a WMS are quantifiable, and others are qualitative. The following quantifiable benefits should occur in most warehouse management systems:
- Elimination of order checking — the scanner replaces the checker.
- Reduction of clerical duties — the system should reduce paper.
- Improve lift truck productivity — put-away and picking are directed.
- Improve shipping productivity — accuracy is assured.
- Reduction in claims — error rate is drastically reduced.
- Monitoring of engineered labor standards.
- Improved inventory accuracy.

The following nonquantifiable benefits will improve quality:
- Happier customers.
- Reduction of internal manual errors.
- Consolidation of shipments to the same destination.
- Reporting of performance and exceptions.
- Improved cube utilization of warehouse space.
- Improved operations planning.
- Providing a platform for future advancements.

One large system was designed to be installed in three phases. This allowed people to become accustomed to the new system gradually rather than to experience the shock of doing every operation differently all at once.

The first phase involved using the WMS only for receiving and directed put-away. Picking and shipping were done as before.

Phase two was introduced 14 months later and included replenishment, order planning, order selection, loading, and cycle counting.

Two more years passed before phase three was implemented. It included engineered labor standards and installation of an operational decision support system (ODSS). The ODSS uses a personal computer to extract data needed to monitor workloads, warns of potential shortages, and maintain a transaction history. It also allows management to simulate "what if" conditions. The ODSS can assist supervisors in balancing resources to meet changing workloads.

Training

A key step in the successful implementation of a WMS is training people to use it. This training must be supported by software vendors, but the most successful installations reduce dependence on outside trainers as much as possible. As the system matures, modifications will be made to adapt to changes within your warehouse, so training must be a continuous process. The best training program is one that is eventually handled by your own people.

One excellent approach is to allow the software vendor to train the trainers. A key tool is the vendor's reference manual. Keep in mind that both workers and management need training in using the system, and training detail may differ depending on who is being trained. From the reference manual, specific employee training manuals can be developed. Part of the training process must be demonstrations of the equipment to be used, particularly the scanners. As training progresses, tip sheets are developed to provide practical approaches to stamp out the bugs. These tip sheets will probably be revised on the basis of field experience. Training reaches its most critical level at the time when the system first goes live, but follow-up training is needed for new workers or for changes in the system. Some users develop in-house training videos. Others combine training with WMS certification for users within the warehouse. Employees are motivated to complete the training program and become certified for higher-rated warehouse jobs.

Lack of training may be the most common pitfall in unsuccessful WMS applications. A new system is a culture shock. Change is difficult for many people, and ample training is the best way to cushion the shock and make people feel good about the new procedures for running the warehouse.

The warehouse information system is a dynamic product in a constant state of change and growth. Success depends on training your people to initiate the system and gradually improve it to meet future changes in your warehouse.

If the hourly people in your organization are involved in the WMS from the start, they will take ownership in the system and take pride in making it work. No system will function well without support from your people, and selling them on its virtues is vital to the success of any warehouse management system.

Systems and service

Reduction of total cycle time is a goal for nearly every warehouse operator. A key factor in shortening that time is the delay between entry of a sales order and availability of shipping documents. Sometimes the clerical time lag is greater than the materials handling timeline.

What is acceptable depends on the customer. Allowable time varies substantially from one industry to another as well as from customer to customer in the same industry.

For the private warehouse operator, the key customer is the receiver of the merchandise shipped from the warehouse. In some operations, other corporate departments are viewed as customers.

The third-party warehouse operator has three customers to serve: the client, the client's customer, and the shipper of inbound materials. The client is the party who hires and pays for warehousing services. The consignees who receive deliveries from the warehouse are the client's customers. The shipper of inbound material may be an independent supplier or a part of the client's company.

Both consignees and shippers are crucial elements in measurement of customer service. Their satisfaction with the warehouse or lack of it can be critical to the success or failure of any warehousing program.

Today, the responsibility of the warehouse operator should not end with the active shipping. Shipping does not solve a customer's problem; only delivery does that. Therefore the shipper should be held responsible for selecting and controlling delivery services that adhere to a dependable standard that places merchandise in the customer's hands on time and in good condition. Your warehouse service standard should trace the elapsed time from the minute you are aware of the need to make a shipment until the shipment has been signed for at the customer's dock.

Questions that solve problems

Because information systems have become the centerpiece of warehousing excellence, it is impossible to be too careful in questioning the processes involved in developing computer technology for your warehouse.

Q Are you fully satisfied with the present information system? If not, what should be changed?
C Ask many people in your organization. The last people to be asked are those closest to the information systems effort.

Q Do you know of bottlenecks caused by the WMS?
C Ask this many times in many different ways. If bottlenecks are described, be sure to get ideas for corrective steps.

Q Has your warehouse ever been at a competitive disadvantage because of information technology?
C If you get an affirmative response, it is essential to get ample detail.

Q Describe the best and worst single features of the information system used in our warehouse.
C It is essential to be sure that the answers are free of unreasonable biases or the classic resistance to change.

Q How has our information system changed within the past year?
C You may wish to ask about the last month, depending on the pace of change. If nothing has changed, this is the signal of a problem.

Q How has our information system enhanced customer service?
C A parallel question is how we measure customer service, and it is most important to avoid generalities and get down to specifics in this crucial area.

Chapter 28

Electronic identification

Electronic identification may have caused more changes in the technology of warehousing than any development since the introduction of the lift truck. Elimination of the need to manually read part numbers has allowed us to increase the speed of order picking while reducing errors to practically zero.

Several methods exist to "machine read" information from a package, but the most common is bar coding. Although the technology for bar coding has existed for several decades, its application in the warehouse was not recognized until the 1980s.

Bar code scanning improves warehouse operations by increasing both speed and accuracy. Scanning a bar code is 75 percent faster than entering the information on the keyboard and 33 percent faster than entering it on a ten-key data board, according to a government study. Furthermore, keypunchers had an accuracy of 98.2 percent; bar code scanning accuracy was recorded at 99.9997 percent.

Bar codes

Because they are used so extensively at retail, nearly everyone has seen a bar code on a package. The code itself is a group of bars and spaces in a pattern that can be interpreted by a scanning machine and converted to letters or numbers. A bar code is on the back cover of this book. The code is typically applied when the carton or package is manufactured and printed; at that stage, the extra cost of applying the bar code is virtually nil since the package must be printed anyway. In the warehouse, codes can be added to the inbound product by a code-printing machine at the receiving dock.

Once the code is on the carton, it can be scanned or "captured" by one of several kinds of scanners or readers. A demonstration of the process can be found at the checkout counter of nearly every supermarket and many other stores. When used in the warehouse, electronic identification offers many advantages, and new applications are constantly under development.

At the receiving dock, bar codes are read and the information is compared with data on the advanced shipping notice (ASN). Once discrepancies are reconciled, the scanned information is used to update the inventory. This method eliminates many of the errors that can take place in receiving product. Once product identification is verified at receiving, instructions are given as to the proper storage location for the inbound merchandise.

Bar-code scanning greatly increases the speed and accuracy of a physical inventory or a location check. When it is time to ship, automatic identification drastically reduces the possibility of shipping error through misidentification. Scanning every piece as it is loaded also verifies the item count.

A user's view of bar coding

A trip to your supermarket is the best way to see how bar coding can work in your warehouse. Take a close look at the procedure at the checkout counter. When the last item has been scanned, the clerk presses a button to create your grocery bill. Watch the scanning process. Occasionally the clerk must override the system to key in an item that could not be scanned. Sometimes the clerk keys in a quantity number rather than scan each of several identical items. You leave the market with a paper record and confidence that your purchases were accurately calculated. Errors are rare. The paper record at the supermarket is the equivalent of the shipping or receiving document in the warehouse.

Bar coding will not eliminate confusion in a poorly run warehouse. The purchase of scanning equipment to achieve discipline in that warehouse will likely result in a new kind of chaos. Scanning works best where systems are already documented, good warehouse discipline is present, and workers understand their responsibilities.

The myth of bar coding expense

The basic tools for bar code scanning should not cost more than a new lift truck. If you already own a personal computer and printer, packages that include software can be purchased for less than $10,000 and intelligent scanners for less than $2,000 each.

Management often delays the decision to acquire bar coding by trying to justify an overly sophisticated system with capabilities beyond the needs of the warehouse. It may be better to consider a more modest system that fits your needs and budget. Some companies spend more money studying bar coding than it costs to adopt it.

What will bar coding do for you?

Scanning of bar codes reduces the time required to process information. Consider, for example, the receiving process. Without bar coding, the receiver first writes a report while unloading each inbound shipment; she then carries the report to the office for entry into the inventory system. A clerk compares the documents to resolve any discrepancies and then enters the information on a receiving document. Then the clerk obtains appropriate storage locations and writes the locations on that document. Finally the report goes back to the receiver for put-away.

With bar coding, the clerk's job can be eliminated. The receiver scans a label on each item and compares it with the ASN. The information is uploaded to the computer system. A screen then displays the appropriate storage location for each SKU that was scanned. The entire process takes a few seconds.

In one case, bar coding and electronic data interchange (EDI) improved accounts receivable by two days and reduced the need for one clerk. Scanning equipment can send electronic messages confirming current inventory levels within minutes after a shipment is made, while a traditional warehouse would need far more time.

Scanning can be used to record each worker's productivity because transactions can be associated with the worker's time clock number. By recording the time spent on each activity, the system generates a daily report that shows productivity levels by employee, by customer, by function, or any other measurement received during the scanning process. This productivity information is available in real time, enabling a supervisor to monitor individual productivity and spot potential bottlenecks as they are happening.

The radio frequency epidemic

The conventional wisdom tells us that every scanner needs a radio. In fact, adding radio increases expense without necessarily increasing accuracy. Radio frequency terminals work best in areas where high mobility is required and cabling is not practical.

There are actually two substitutes for radio in scanning technology. One is a scanner that can store data and transmit it later through a hard-wired workstation. Another is a scanner with an internal logic that allows it to recognize bar codeal bar codes or to signal if one of the codes does not match the other. This technology allows a picker to compare the code on the product with the code printed on the pick list. When the two do not match, a picking error has obviously taken place.

A scanner with radio frequency is sometimes the most efficient way to transmit and receive information, but never install it without considering the alternatives.

Bar coding and Luddites

In 19th-century England, there was a revolt by people who were called Luddites. In an effort to turn back the Industrial Revolution, these marauding groups smashed textile machinery in an attempt to save jobs. The Luddite movement didn't get very far in England, but unfortunately similar things have been observed in warehouses. Some people may want scanning technology to disappear.

Consider the example of two major appliance warehouses. At the first, a lift operator scans the code on each serial-number ticket, and the scanned information is used to create a loading manifest. At the second warehouse, one worker has the job of detaching each serial ticket in a procedure originally developed several decades ago. After the tickets are detached, they are carried into an office where a clerk scans each of them to create the load manifest. Because a job classification was created for pulling tickets, two people perform tasks that could be eliminated by sensible use of scanning.

Pitfalls of automatic identification

The most dangerous pitfall is resistance to change, as shown in the Luddite examples. Many people feel threatened by change, and introduction of scanning can be unsettling if it is not done properly.

The best way to introduce scanning is to always involve hourly employees in the process. What works well on paper may not work well in the warehouse. When hourly workers are part of an evaluation team that plans implementation of scanning, the process is more likely to be done effectively and accepted by the workforce. Workers should feel that their input is valuable and that they are involved in the planning process.

Another potential pitfall is the bar code itself. When printing quality is inadequate, the receiver may need to replace the code label at the receiving dock to avoid interrupting the receiving process.

When a pallet consists of many pieces with a single SKU number, it should not be necessary to scan every carton. A popular alternative is to apply a pallet code that displays the SKU and perhaps a unique lot or serial number. The receiver then enters the number of pieces on the pallet by using the keyboard on the scanner.

What do you do with product that is not bar coded? One manufacturer produces a product in very small cartons. The product is stored in locations identified by bar codes. When picking, workers obtain a master picking label with information that displays the ship-to address. As they scan the bar coded label, the system displays the first location to pick from and the number of units to be pulled. The worker goes there and scans the master pallet label. Scanning the pallet label will confirm that the correct location is identified and the proper item is picked. As the picking process proceeds, the computer program follows five rules to improve picking:

- Minimize travel distance.
- Obey selection priorities (FIFO, LIFO, or lot number).
- Pick similar cases for pallet stackability.
- Reduce inventory by the number of pieces picked.
- Compare the location bar code with the code on the picking label.

The presence of multiple standards is another potential pitfall. There are several different bar code methodologies used in automotive, paper, chemical, and grocery manufacturing. A third-party warehouse serving several of those industries may need to adapt to different coding systems.

2-D bar codes

The two-dimensional bar code is no longer new, but the number of logistics applications remains small. UPS has been the leader in this new type of bar code, which puts far more information in the same space. One company has used the 2-D bar code as a substitute for a bill of lading. It contains nearly all of the information shown on a conventional bill of lading and saves paper as well as time. The equivalent of two pages of text can be put into a bar code symbol about the size of a postage stamp.

As the technology grows in sophistication, we can anticipate that the 2-D bar code will be found in warehouse operations as well as other logistics applications.

To check or not to check?

A recurring debate among warehousing professionals concerns the desirability of checking the accuracy of outbound shipments. Checking originated because of the presumption that the typical warehouse worker was semiliterate and that a more educated person was needed to verify picking accuracy.

For example, at one warehouse, the operation is divided into departments. The receiving department unloads a truck, signs a tally, and delivers the freight to the warehousing department. The warehousing group then counts the material a second time before moving it to storage locations. The process is repeated when goods are picked and shipped, resulting in constant rechecking by one department to verify the accuracy of the work performed by another. The result is a warehouse operation with at least twice as many people as necessary.

Scanning of bar codes is an electronic substitute for checking. As scanning technology improves, the cost of checking is lower than ever.

If manual checking still takes place in your warehouse, compare the cost of errors with the cost of checking. When error frequency is low or the error consequence is minimal, the cost of checking is greater than the benefit received. For example, if the warehouse is part of a closed-loop system shipping to retail stores, what are the consequences if a pink sweater is shipped instead of a blue one? The store can probably still sell the blue sweater and replace the pink on the next shipment.

Again, as you look at the checking process, ask two questions:
- ◆ Have you applied state-of-the-art scanning technology?
- ◆ Is the catch worth the chase?

Questions that solve problems

If your warehouse is one of the declining number that have not started using bar code scanning, the major thrust of questions would be to determine why. Resistance to change is likely to be behind the slowness to adapt bar coding. Be sure you are able to identify causes of resistance to change, as well as any legitimate reasons why bar coding technology is not appropriate for your operation.

Q Is there any feature of our existing information system that might impede the use of bar code scanning?
C Look for impediments that may have arisen from unusual sources. Be sure to be sensitive to the differences between true problems and resistance to change.

Q If bar coding is not in use, when was its implementation last studied? What were the results of that study?
C Watch for negative feedback to this question, and be sure that the response is based on fact rather than emotion. Consider a benchmarking approach to explore bar code scanning.

Q Have our competitors implemented bar code scanning and gained any advantage by doing so?
C In most industries, it is not easy to interchange ideas with competitors. However, in this area you probably can discover whether your company has lost competitive advantage by failure to use scanning when competitors have done so.

Q How is the checking function performed in our warehouse today?
C If scanning is not mentioned, probe for the reasons why.

Chapter 29

Approaching warehouse automation

Some say that the fully automated warehouse is a practical impossibility that exists only in the imaginations of technical theorists. Yet for many years we have seen ample writings and seminars dealing with the subject of warehouse automation.

The driving forces have been shortages of either space or people. Where land is scarce or extremely expensive, machines such as the AS/RS (automatic storage/retrieval system) allow the user to have a high-rise storage system that retrieves pallets with a stacker crane. When labor is scarce, machines replace people in manual handling tasks, such as building or stripping a pallet-load of cartons.*

Mechanizing a warehouse is a major investment, and making a profit from this investment involves taking risks. Your experience allows you to evaluate those risks and the benefits assessed. The main problem with investing in warehouse mechanization is that this decision is not frequently made, so it is easy to make a mistake. The secret of success is meticulous planning and the use of appropriate technology that takes into account the difficulty of predicting what various operations within the warehouse may need to do in the future.

Two mistakes are sometimes made in considering automation. The first is not taking into account probable changes in throughput. Higher technology in materials handling requires a larger initial cost and a smaller variable cost than lower-technology alternatives. When the planned volume is high, the unit throughput cost projection may

---

* Most of this chapter is adapted from an article by the late John Williams, former director of the National Materials Handling Centre in England.

seem favorable. However, as actual throughput volume starts to fall below the plan, the cost per unit will rise rapidly. Therefore, you must have confidence that planned volume levels will be maintained or exceeded before investing the money in advanced technology.

A second frequent mistake is to compare the costs of a high-technology operation with existing methods, without considering other options that will improve existing methods by implementing simpler techniques. A project advocate may overzealously pursue automation without exploring alternatives.

Making radical changes in warehousing methods as a response to an immediate problem is a recipe for disaster. Technology changes should be included in the corporate strategy plan and should be part of your program to achieve company objectives. Technology has its part to play in modern warehouse operation, but it requires proper planning and implementation, with methods chosen to match your company's strategy.

How technology fits in

Consider the example of a conventional warehouse that receives and stores goods on pallets, selects orders in carton or broken-case quantities, and ships to a wide variety of locations. Primary functions are receiving, reserve storage, order selection, and shipping.

In receiving, the vehicle is typically unloaded by lift truck. Primary uncertainties are volume fluctuation and the degree of control you can achieve over inbound deliveries. If you consider placing unit loads into an automatic storage system, then you must consider the extent of standardization of pallet type, unit load size and extent of overhang, and risk of pallet damage.

Depending on volume and distance to be moved, it may be feasible to convey unit loads from the receiving dock to storage zones. The more flexible automated guided vehicle (AGV) system may be a better solution for some applications.

Identifying each pallet by bar-coded label is common to all methods. The greatest flexibility is achieved by using bar-coded labels in conjunction with scanners that communicate with a warehouse management system. This proven method might be used as the benchmark against which you can compare costs and benefits of more advanced technology options.

Reserve storage is relatively easy to mechanize reliably because it is normally a pallet-in, pallet-out operation. Because 80 percent of the construction cost of a warehouse is in the floor slab and roof, taller buildings reduce the cost of each cubic foot of storage. Therefore, the reserve storage area should be high with narrow aisles.

Rack-supported buildings may be considered as an alternative to the conventional structure. The rack-supported warehouse must be built with some care, because if construction stress distorts the racking, operation of stacker cranes may be impossible.

Computer-controlled reserve storage may reduce the number of storage locations. For example, quarantined items may be locked by the computer so their removal is barred to those who do not have the necessary password to release the material. In a similar manner, other merchandise held in reserve can be secured until management releases it.

There is a safety challenge if manual order-picking operations take place in an area where industrial trucks and stacker cranes are also in use. One solution is to handle manned order picking on the day shift and allow mechanized operation only at night.

Order selection is the most expensive part of many warehouse operations. Today nearly all of it is handled by people rather than machines. However, labor shortages and ergonomic initiatives are likely to stimulate redesign of many traditional order-picking methods. Changes stimulated by ergonomics may include reduction of the weight of cartons or presenting cartons to the picker in a manner that eliminates bending, stretching or twisting. This might involve mechanized carton lifting devices or more use of parts-to-picker systems rather than conventional order-selection methods.

In a parts-to-picker system, product is moved to and from a stationary workstation. In the more common picker-to-parts system, the picker moves from one location to another, selecting cartons as each correct address is reached.

Automatic picking systems such as the one shown in Figure 29-1 are used for very high-throughput picking. In these, cartons are loaded into gravity lanes and fed into tote bins by computer-controlled gate mechanisms, similar to product delivery found in automatic vending machines.

Shipping is usually preceded by movement of goods to a staging area. Cartons are moved from the order pick area and then sorted into outbound loads in various ways. Sometimes the order picker moves the merchandise in a bin or on a pallet that is deposited at a staging area. At a higher level of technology, conveying equipment is used to make that move. In some operations, order pickers accumulate a batch of orders. Simultaneously, other pickers in different zones are collecting from the same batch, all using labels that specify the staging location.

Figure 29-1
Photograph provided by SI Handling Systems, Inc.

The challenge is to balance workload between zone pickers and to correct imbalances when they arise. You may need computer simulation to find the balance among volume, product mix, order size variations, and variations in the picking zones. Figure 29-2 shows the results of one simulation study. A typical simulation might reveal the following problems:

- Cases belonging to later waves start accumulating in the recirculation loop of the conveyor until the system comes to a halt.
- Because pickers move ahead of palletizers, cases in large orders from earlier waves end up behind cases for newer waves. This keeps the early orders from being completed.

Figure 29-2

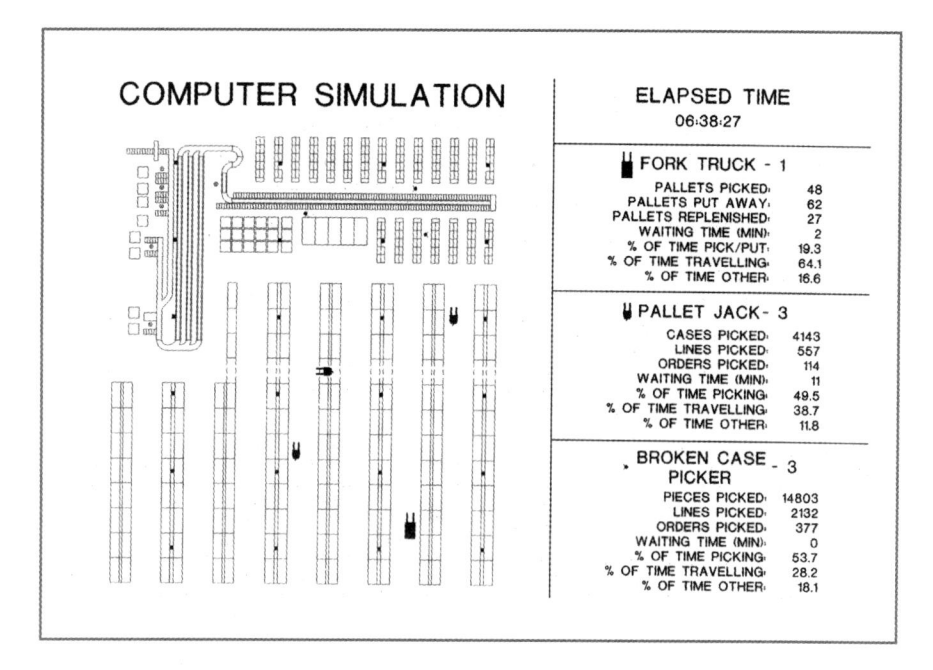

```
COMPUTER SIMULATION          ELAPSED TIME
                               06:38:27

                             ▼ FORK TRUCK - 1
                               PALLETS PICKED:       48
                               PALLETS PUT AWAY:     62
                               PALLETS REPLENISHED:  27
                               WAITING TIME (MIN):    2
                               % OF TIME PICK/PUT:  19.3
                               % OF TIME TRAVELLING: 64.1
                               % OF TIME OTHER:     16.6

                             ▼ PALLET JACK - 3
                               CASES PICKED:       4143
                               LINES PICKED:        557
                               ORDERS PICKED:       114
                               WAITING TIME (MIN):   11
                               % OF TIME PICKING:  49.5
                               % OF TIME TRAVELLING: 38.7
                               % OF TIME OTHER:    11.8

                               BROKEN CASE - 3
                                 PICKER
                               PIECES PICKED:     14803
                               LINES PICKED:       2132
                               ORDERS PICKED:       377
                               WAITING TIME (MIN):    0
                               % OF TIME PICKING:  53.7
                               % OF TIME TRAVELLING: 28.2
                               % OF TIME OTHER:    18.1
```

♦ Although pickers are effectively utilized, palletizers are idle as they wait for the system to finish sortation.*

The benefits of mechanization

If you expect to justify warehouse automation by immediate reductions in handling and storage costs, you are likely to be disappointed. The justification for advanced technology usually lies elsewhere.

The most frequent justification for using a high-rise building and the AS/RS system is the ability to achieve a higher storage volume on a restricted but strategically located site. It may be possible to justify the technology investment when the costs of site change or increased transportation costs are considered.

---

* Adapted from an article by Maida Napolitano, Gross & Associates, *Warehousing Forum*, Volume 12, Number 1, ©The Ackerman Company, Columbus, Ohio.

Another benefit of mechanization can be better resource utilization. When people are scarce, machines are attractive. The machines work at a steady tempo without fatigue. Multishift operations become more feasible, and that can be a key element in cost justification.

Human-resource issues are frequently used in justifying mechanization. When fewer hourly workers are employed, and those who are hired have engineering and process-control skills, the recruitment policy becomes more selective. Hiring costs may be greater per person, but the number of people needed is reduced.

As the size and complexity of the warehouse operation increases, density of people may become an issue. Put quite simply, workers get in each other's way. When order pickers are working in zones, there is the problem of work balance and load scheduling. Automation may significantly reduce the number of pickers and lift trucks.

People cause errors. One of the benefits of automation is improved data capture, resulting in improved inventory control, greater customer satisfaction, and reduced inventories.

People sometimes cause fires. The fewer people there are in an area, the less risk of loss or injury through fire. However, high-rise buildings also present a fire risk. Underwriters are concerned about the "chimney" effect of high stacks and narrow aisles.

Some argue that a major benefit from using advanced technology is an improved corporate image. The creation of a high-tech image may be attractive to employees, investors, or managers who enjoy association with a progressive organization.

The risks

The biggest risk is that the new system will not do what you want it to do. That usually happens because you have failed to predict what you will require the system to do in the near future.

The business of warehousing has a great many variables. Throughput will vary by season or even by the hour. Order size has a similar variation. Number of SKUs and size of packages will change from time to time. Omission of any factor from performance specifications is likely to cause failure. There is a clear inverse correlation between technology and flexibility. When the design is wrong, you cannot adjust for errors or omissions by adding people.

This risk is controlled by being very sure that you get your specifications right. People within your own operation should be responsible for planning, since no one understands your business better than they do. There can be no hiding behind the excuse "Don't blame us because it doesn't work, we had nothing to do with it."

Planning takes time. Failed systems are usually accompanied by regrets that people did not allocate more time to the planning stage. Systems suppliers complain that they are pushed into contracts with earlier completion dates than they consider desirable.

Failing to contract successfully is a frequent cause of system failure. There is considerable opportunity for misunderstanding in the complicated exchange of information in major mechanization projects.

Choose a prime contractor with a clear responsibility to fill all of your specifications, including coordination of specialist subcontractors. Resist the temptation to coordinate these yourself. Check all references and investigate the prospective contractors' financial status to be sure that each contractor can complete the project.

Be sure the contract stipulates the maximum system downtime that you will accept over a period of time. Reliability must be defined, including a rated throughput per hour, per shift, and per week. It is at this stage that additional time spent on specification and preplanning will pay dividends. To prevent misunderstanding, all communication links should be formalized and detailed records must be maintained.

A sometimes overlooked risk is overestimating your employees' ability to cope with change. Mechanized systems require the acquisition of new skills. They also demand that managers understand the process and make rational decisions for controlling the system.

Your workers may feel apprehensive and stressed by the changes resulting from mechanization. Some will be unable to make the transition and meet the challenge of using new techniques. Managers may also be disturbed by change. The importance of training programs cannot be overemphasized. A system can only be as effective as the skills and attitudes of your people allow it to be.

Mechanization in the 21st century

The National Association of Wholesaler-Distributors (NAW) completed a study to predict mechanization progress. Bar coding was the area where greatest growth was predicted. Next was automated inventory control terminals. The least popular mechanization idea for wholesalers was robotics.

A wide range of technology is available for both information handling and cargo handling at the warehouse. There is no shortage of product, nor is there any lack of ability to design systems. The real challenge is that future requirements in warehousing are not always predictable. Warehousing is a flexibility business, and some systems are not very flexible. Therefore, automation must be approached with considerable caution.

Questions that solve problems

Because automation of warehouse operations involves substantial risk, managers cannot ask too many questions before authorizing a capital expenditure for automation equipment. Such questions should be asked at all levels of the organization, including hourly workers as well as supervisors, information managers, and financial people. It is important to fight an emotional urge to install warehouse automation. Here are a few of the questions that might be asked:

Q What is the likelihood that the size and shape of the products we handle in our warehouse will be substantially different in three years? What is the ability of the proposed equipment to accommodate changes in size and shape?
C Because of the inverse correlation between automation and flexibility, consideration of adaptability is of paramount importance.

Q What variations from today's volume can be expected in the next three years?
C Because cost of automation climbs rapidly when volume drops below planned levels, a severe downward fluctuation is a substantial deterrent. On the other hand, be sure that the planned system is able to handle substantial growth if such change is anticipated.

Q Have simulation techniques been used to demonstrate how the automation equipment will work under a variety of predictable conditions?
C Since computer simulation is more common and less costly than ever, not using simulations is difficult to justify.

Q What are the risks and the disadvantages associated with the proposed purchase of automation equipment?
C This is a good question to ask many people all over the organization. It may reveal legitimate risks, and it will also reveal resistance to change.

Q How will the proposed automation influence activities of other departments in our company, and what changes will they need to make to adapt to the changes in the warehouse?
C The answers to this question tell you how much detailed planning has gone into the automation proposal.

Q How much resistance to change can be anticipated by our people, and how will this resistance be controlled?
C Comments on this question will tell you how much the human-resources aspect of automation has been considered by those who advocate the new program.

PART 7

Starting A New Warehouse Operation

Chapter 30

Finding the right location

The question of where to locate your next warehouse is closely related to the reasons you are considering a new warehouse site. In other words, *why* you want to move has a great deal to do with *where* you are likely to move.

Consider the four most common reasons for seeking a new warehouse site:

- Your warehouse is not big enough — more storage or dock space is needed to accommodate growth.
- Your company is expanding into a new market, and a new warehouse is needed to serve it.
- You have to relocate an existing warehouse operation that has operating problems.
- Contingency planning requires decentralization — there are too many eggs in one warehouse basket.

Depending on which reason motivates your search for another warehouse, the site search will take different forms.

Site selection involves art as well as science. The decisions usually involve a weighting of priorities, determining which factors are most important, and then using a process of elimination. Since every location has both advantages and disadvantages, the final selection of a site invariably requires compromises.

Press reports frequently offer listings of sites that provide the best network to cover the nation's population. These computer-driven analyses fail to account for many important factors in site selection. Such analyses are prime examples of using science without considering art.

Developing a requirements definition

A starting point for your location search should be a list of your company's specific requirements in order of importance. You should define and list those requirements before doing anything else. For example, if you are moving an existing operation because of labor troubles, measuring the quality of the labor market at potential new locations would be high on your requirements list.

Warehousing has always had a "ham and eggs" relationship to transportation. In most industries, transportation represents a larger portion of total logistics cost than warehousing. Thus an uneconomical transportation situation at a proposed new site could easily destroy the value of an otherwise desirable warehouse.

Consider all four primary modes of transportation — highway, rail, water, and air — even if you do not use all of them today. Although truck transportation has become the primary mode for most warehouses, there have been significant changes in the recent past and there could be more in the future. For example, one large cluster of distribution centers uses air as its primary transport mode and therefore is located next to a large airport. The location of the distribution center, both its general geographical position and its specific site within a community, may be decided by the transport modes selected. The mode will also influence operating methods, labor, equipment, and plant layout. Although the warehouse layout will probably be designed to handle the primary transport mode, it should be flexible enough to adjust to changes in transportation. Special conditions could influence transportation decisions today and in the future, including transit time, costs, and local service conditions. Traffic management decisions will include the selection of transport modes as well as the selection of specific carriers within each mode.

Because of its cost and its crucial role in service, transportation should have the greatest influence of all the variables when you locate a new warehouse. The availability, speed, and reliability of transport must be considered when you determine how many distribution centers will be needed. The type and quality of transportation should have prime consideration in comparing different communities that might serve as a distribution point.

When air freight has a high priority, accessibility to airports becomes crucial. Waterfront sites will be sought if the user plans to use water transport. When rail is considered, there are two options: If TOFC (trailer-on-flat-car, or piggyback) is planned, a location close to a piggyback ramp is desirable; if boxcar service is necessary, the availability of a rail siding becomes crucial.

As rail is considered, many shippers look for a site that allows service by more than one carrier. With the trend toward merger in the rail industry, that has become increasingly difficult. Some sites allow reciprocal switching, which allows the user to switch cars to any railroad in the community at no extra cost. Deregulation of rail tariffs has made this privilege less easy to negotiate today than in the past. Some communities have terminal railroads that exist to connect to each of the carriers serving the city. When rail volume is high, proximity to a switching yard and availability of switching service become important in site selection.

Speed limits and warehousing

One of the trends in warehouse locations during the past half-century was a reduction in the number of warehouses. At midcentury, it was not unusual to find consumer goods distributors using more than 100 locations to serve the continental U.S. Today, they offer comparable service with four or five.

Several developments encouraged reduction in the number of warehousing points. Emphasis on inventory management and electronic order transmission have allowed distributors to provide good service with a smaller number of warehouses. At the end of the century, legal speeds for vehicles on interstate highways were increased in most of the United States. Higher speed for trucks means that the territory available for overnight or second-day delivery was larger than before. This change may further reduce the number of warehouse locations needed to provide a given level of service.

Access

Ease of access is a sometimes overlooked factor in site selection. Your proposed warehouse site may be along the border of an expressway with great visibility to motorists. But that means little if trucks must make a long detour to the nearest highway interchange. Furthermore, if the access roads serving the site do not have the load-bearing capacity to accommodate the heaviest trucks you might consider in the future, the site may become unusable. The question of how easily a distribution center can be reached is very important. A warehouse in the right place becomes invisible to the customer. The customer is not buying a warehouse but rather the timely service that results from an effective operation located in the right place.

In the past, labor was less important for warehouse operators than for manufacturers. In today's relatively tight labor market, quality and availability of workers have become an important selection factor in warehousing as well as manufacturing. Today's warehouse offers an increasing number of services besides storage and handling. While some operations may be mechanized, others may require significant increases in labor to handle packaging or assembly. Many users place a high priority on a union-free operation, particularly in warehousing and distribution. In these cases, the quality and orientation of the workforce can be a key factor in site selection.

Attitudes

Community attitudes toward new warehouses should be evaluated by every site seeker. These are sometimes expressed in tax policy. There can be wide variations in taxes, particularly inventory taxes, within a single metropolitan area. When the warehouse inventory has high value, the rate of taxation may be a crucial competitive factor. Taxes are usually negotiable, and willingness to negotiate is a reflection of community and government attitudes.

Most development authorities prefer a clean and quiet warehouse development to a manufacturing plant that may pollute the air and require a large number of workers that add to road congestion. But some community authorities oppose any new industrial development, including warehouses. When such opposition exists, it is best to look elsewhere for your warehouse site.

Utilities

Water is the most important utility in warehousing because it is needed to power a sprinkler system. Furthermore, state-of-the-art systems today require more water than the older sprinkler systems did.

As you look at the other utilities, consider whether the state you are considering is moving toward energy deregulation. Utility costs are less of a factor for warehouses than for manufacturing, but the relative costs still need to be measured and compared.

Reliability is also a major consideration when utility services are appraised. Dependable telephone and electrical services are absolutely essential to the operation of every warehouse, and evidence of disruptions should be carefully investigated.

Climate

The conventional wisdom says that warmer is better. However, it may be more important to look at a community's history in handling weather disruptions. A northern city with a fine record of snow removal may be preferable to a southern city that has been frequently paralyzed by ice storms. Furthermore, windstorm and flood risks may be greater in a warm climate than a cold one.

Flexibility and financing

Part of the requirements definition mentioned earlier is the question of whether a new building is necessary or whether an older warehouse could be adapted. Rehabilitating older buildings is an option described in the next chapter.

When your need for space varies by season, the availability of overflow space may be an important requirement. Either short-term lease space or public warehousing may satisfy this requirement. When flexibility is needed, your site search should consider the current availability of empty space and public warehousing services. Because it is seldom possible to construct or purchase a building that is always the right size, many warehouse users plan to find overflow space for seasonal requirements.

Financial questions are always a key part of the requirements definition. The question of whether to own or lease the new warehouse must be considered, as well as consideration of various ownership and lease options.

The selection process

After the requirements definition is complete, the best selection process is one in which the decisions start broad and get narrower and narrower. For example, the first determination might be that the new site must be within the continental United States. The second is that the location should be in the southwest. Next, we determine that it should be in Texas, and then we decide that it should be in the Dallas–Fort Worth metropolitan area. As that region is studied, the decision then moves to the southwest quadrant of the city of Dallas, and finally to a specific site on Duncanville Road. By following the process in exactly this order, you can avoid the confusion of considering offers for specific sites that ultimately do not fit your requirements.

As you check sources of information in this process, the most important warning is to always be skeptical. If you are told that there is no history of floods, get a second opinion from another party who cannot possibly be influenced by the earlier informant. When multisource checking produces the same answers to critical questions, only then should you have confidence in the information.

As you zero in on a specific site, it is essential to have a contingency plan. Once you start negotiating for the best site, be sure you have an alternate location that is almost as good and equally available. When you let the seller of the first site know that you have a secondary one in the event that bargaining breaks down, your ability to gain the best price is greatly improved. At the same time, remember that land price is seldom the most important criterion in site selection. A cheap piece of land may have development costs that will ultimately make it far more expensive than a competing site.

A location theory dating from the 19th century is still useful in considering warehouse sites. J. H. Von Thunen wrote about the advantages of producing the bulkiest and cheapest farm crops on the land closest to the community that buys these commodities. The same theory applies to manufactured products. The lower the value added, the more important it is to locate the product close to the market. An inventory of gold or diamonds might be kept in one place and moved by air to customers all over the world. In contrast, a producer of bagged sand finds it necessary to keep the product close to the customers.

Outside advice

Seeking a site for a new warehouse nearly always involves a search for advice from people outside your organization. For this reason, it is essential to consider and evaluate the most commonly used advisory sources.

Real estate brokers are usually involved in any search for property. Remember that the traditional broker compensation is based on a successful transaction, and this motivates the broker to complete a commissionable sale. When the value of the broker's invested time begins to approach the value of the commission, the broker may lose motivation to continue the search. Today, some brokers prefer to serve as management consultants when site seeking is involved. They do this to be sure that they are adequately compensated when substantial time and effort is required.

Not all brokers have multiple listing services. Furthermore, commission restrictions not known to the buyer could make it difficult for the broker to remain objective in providing advice. The user must recognize that the commission system for brokerage tends to create pressures that influence the results.

Once you have established the general area for the sites, the development departments of electric and gas utilities offer excellent sources of advice. Since most communities are served by just one electric company and one gas utility, the representatives of those companies should be unbiased in recommending sites throughout the entire community. These utility departments usually cooperate with all local brokers and therefore become a clearinghouse of information on available buildings and land.

Chambers of commerce and other government development agencies are also sources of information. Since those people are motivated to attract new industry into their area, they will also serve as a clearinghouse for information from brokers. Government development representatives usually serve only one community, so make sure you have decided upon that area before using this source of advice.

If you plan to use third-party warehouse services, sales representatives could be useful. Several national marketing chains represent public warehouses. The chain sales agent normally does not represent competing warehouses, but he or she will provide comparative services in most big cities. The large multicity warehouse providers also have marketing people who may help in developing alternate proposals for third-party services.

A management consultant may be a useful outside source of advice. When confidentiality regarding the search is a necessity, the consultant can conduct a search without revealing the name of the potential buyer. In selecting a consultant, be certain that the individual is really independent and objective in approaching the site search. Some people who call themselves consultants may be involved in other activities that influence their objectivity in handling a site search.

There are three reasons to bring in an outside consultant. The most important is the need for an objective view. A consultant with extensive site-seeking experience will probably save time. Finally, the consultant represents a source of management skill with no long-term commitments. A detailed site search may take many hours, but hiring a new manager to handle it will not make sense if the job will end once the site is selected.

A checklist to locate your next warehouse

Because this list is designed for both new construction and acquisition of existing warehouses, each user will find some parts of it more useful than others. It is essential to double-check the accuracy of information received in considering the answers to each of the questions on this checklist.

Governmental restrictions
1. Is the property zoned for warehousing and related uses?
2. Will the zoning description impede conversion to other uses?
3. Are there any variances or special exceptions in the zoning?
4. What are the limits or restrictions on employee parking?
5. What is the maximum expansion capability of the facility?
6. Are there any easements or protective covenants on the property?
7. Are there any restrictive load limits on roads leading to this facility?

Geographic restrictions
1. Are there grade problems on the land?
2. Are there any problems with drainage?
3. Are there streams, lakes, or wetlands near this site?
4. If so, what is the 100-year flood plain?
5. What is the level of the groundwater table?
6. Is there any history of earthquake in the area?
7. If so, have we received the U.S. Geodetic Survey of fault lines?

8. Does the site have any fill?
9. If so, what material was used?
10. What is the load-bearing capacity of nearby soil?
11. Is any part of the site wooded?
12. Are there any restrictions on tree removal?

Transportation
1. What is best access to the nearest freeway interchange?
2. What is the distance from primary motor freight terminals?
3. Have you interviewed motor freight managers?
4. Is the facility inside the commercial delivery zone of the city?
5. If not, what is the extra delivery cost compared with deliveries within the commercial zone?
6. What is cartage cost to a TOFC (piggyback) terminal?
7. What is cartage cost to the nearest marine terminal?
8. What is cartage cost to the nearest air freight terminal?
9. Will customers who pick up at your warehouse have any transportation problem with this facility?

Utilities
1. What is the size of the water main serving the site?
2. What is the water pressure, and when was it last tested?
3. Are there water meters on hydrants and sprinkler systems?
4. What is the source of the water supply?
5. What is the electric power capacity?
6. Is submetering of electricity permitted?
7. Have we received copies of recent utility bills?
8. Are incentives available for reducing peak electric demand or installing HID lighting?
9. Is submetering of gas permitted?
10. Are there limitations on capacity or demand?
11. If fuel oil is used for heat, what is the source of supply?

Security considerations
1. Does the sprinkler system meet preferred risk standards?
2. If not, what is the cost of upgrading the system?
3. Is the sprinkler capable of conversion to ESFR?
4. If so, what is conversion cost?

5. Is there a secondary water source for the sprinkler system?
6. Have we seen insurance inspection reports?
7. Have we interviewed law enforcement officials?
8. Have we interviewed neighboring managers?

Labor market
1. Are neighboring businesses unionized?
2. Have we measured community attitudes toward unions?
3. Is there a labor shortage or high unemployment?
4. How are nearby schools rated in comparison to other sites?

Community attitudes
1. Do community leaders welcome industrial expansion?
2. Is there any discernable opposition to warehouse operations?
3. Is there any history of difficulty in rezoning?

Taxation
1. What is the date of the most recent property appraisal?
2. What is real estate tax history over the past ten years?
3. Have there been any recent tax assessments?
4. Are there any tax abatement programs in effect or available?
5. Is the facility in a duty-free or enterprise zone?
6. Are there planned public improvements?
7. How do inventory tax levels compare with other sites?
8. Is this a free port state?
9. What are recent trends in taxation?
10. Are industrial revenue bonds available, and can we qualify?
11. What are tax rates for:
    - Corporate income tax?
    - Payroll tax?
    - Unemployment compensation?
    - Sales tax?
    - Workers' compensation?
    - Franchise tax?
    - Other taxes?

New construction considerations
1. Have soil tests been made at all key points on the site?

2. Are there landscaping or buffer zone requirements?
3. How will roof drainage be discharged?
4. What are estimated costs and time requirements for all construction and occupancy permits?

Questions that solve problems

Because the search for a new location is a short-term process with long-term implications, the questions shown below must be asked at a midpoint in the search process, early enough to correct potential errors but late enough to discover where the search is headed.

Q Which people took part in creating the requirements definition?
C The quality of this document will be strongly influenced by the number of people involved in creating it, and particularly the involvement of people from a diverse group of departments within the enterprise. If one person did it alone, the results are unlikely to be satisfactory.

Q Which modes of transportation will be available at the proposed new site? What contingency plans are in place to change modes if necessary?
C Because of the key role of transportation, it is important to appraise efforts to gain flexibility through use of alternate modes and alternate carriers.

Q Have any sources of outside advice been retained, and if so, which were chosen and why?
C The response to this one will indicate your manager's ability and willingness to seek unbiased advice to help with the site selection process.

Chapter 31

Warehousing is real estate

For most of the time since World War II, industrial real estate has been a profitable and reliable investment in nearly every part of the United States. The exception was a brief but severe real estate recession during the 1980s. There has always been a close relationship between the functions of warehousing and real estate development.

Of all the tools used in warehousing, the most expensive and least flexible is the real estate that houses the operation. If or when it becomes obsolete, it may be the most difficult tool to dispose of. If the wrong tool is purchased, correcting the error will be slow and expensive. Unlike lift trucks, computers, and people, real estate cannot be transferred from one place to another. Real estate is frequently misunderstood, despite its intimate relationship to warehousing.

Wall Street has never understood real estate, and as a result publicly held companies usually avoid real estate investments. Stock analysts treat real estate the same way they treat other capital assets such as machinery — just one of the tools of the trade.

The traditional treatment of capital assets calls for value of these tools to be established at time of acquisition, and that value is reduced each year as they age. Accountants call this depreciation; it is based on the theory that every asset wears out and loses value over time. Real estate, however, often defies this rule by appreciating rather than depreciating. Because real estate is the only corporate asset that behaves this way, most stock analysts are not inclined to handle it differently from other capital assets. For that reason, publicly held companies are reluctant to invest in real estate.

Changes in ways of measuring corporate performance have also complicated the role of real estate in a public company. A growing number of financial officers measure performance on the basis of return on assets (ROA) or economic value added. Under a return-on-asset measurement, the company's progress is judged not by profit as a percent of sales but rather as a percentage return on assets.

If your company measures progress by return on assets, acquisition of warehouses or any other kind of real estate creates a problem.*

A case example

The Smith Co. is an importer and wholesale distributor. The company earned nearly $20 million on sales of $489 million, or a modest profit of 4 percent. However, it accomplished this with total assets of only $106 million, which means it achieved a healthy capital turnover of 4.6 and a return on assets of 18.4 percent. Figure 31-1 shows how the ROA calculation works for this company.

A newly hired logistics vice president recommended that Smith Co. invest $75 million to build new distribution centers. If this program is carried out, and if all other conditions stay the same, the ROA will fall from 18.4 percent to less than 11 percent. This happens because the total assets employed have been drastically increased, thus re-

Figure 31-1

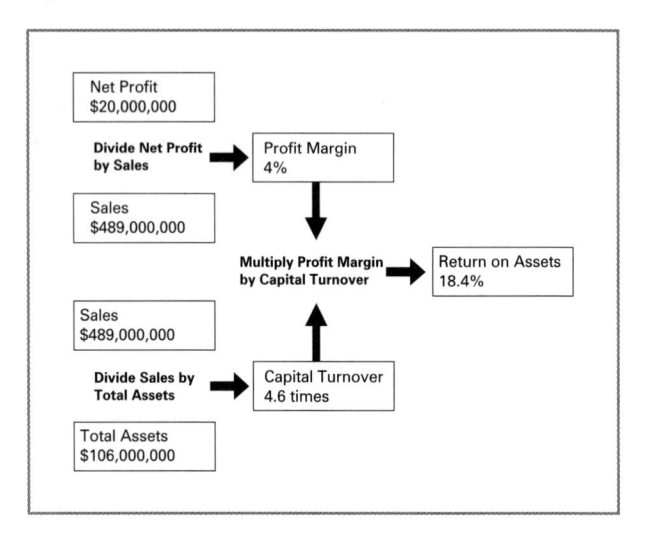

Net Profit $20,000,000		
Divide Net Profit by Sales →	Profit Margin 4%	
Sales $489,000,000	↓	
	Multiply Profit Margin by Capital Turnover →	Return on Assets 18.4%
Sales $489,000,000	↑	
Divide Sales by Total Assets →	Capital Turnover 4.6 times	
Total Assets $106,000,000		

---

* The first seven subchapters are adapted from Volume 14, Number 7 of *Warehousing Forum* ©The Ackerman Company, Columbus, Ohio. This text was prepared with substantial help from Dane Brooksher and Tom O'Donohoe of ProLogis Trust, Phil Maynard of ASW Services, Perry Ozburn of Ozburn-Hessey, and John Porter, Jr. Of CB Richard Ellis.

ducing capital turnover and, consequently, return on assets.

This case shows why those who keep score by measuring ROA recognize that the easiest way to raise that return is to reduce the value of assets. Short-term leases and third-party warehousing allow a buyer to gain the use of warehouses without showing the real estate on the books as a capital asset.

Getting around accounting standards

For the publicly held company, real estate must have a depreciation schedule even though it is likely to grow in value. Public companies are governed by regulations from the Financial Accounting Standards Board (FASB), which sets the rules on the treatment of capital equipment, including capital leases.

Synthetic leasing is a vehicle to finance buildings without violating FASB rules. The lessee has a three- to five-year contract to rent the warehouse with an option to buy it. At the end of the contract, the lessee has three choices:
- Renew the lease.
- Buy the building.
- Sell the building on behalf of the lessor.

One developer uses a similar program to finance both existing and new real estate.

If real estate is considered a poor investment, then why are so many new warehouses under construction? One reason is that logistics is one of the biggest growth industries in the world. Within the field of logistics, warehouse buildings are an attractive investment because the spread between cost and sales price is usually greater than for buildings constructed for retail or residential purposes. Even if public companies avoid real estate, specialist developers fill the gap.

Flexibility vs. control

The ultimate control is to own your warehouse. The second-tightest control is a long-term lease (five years or more). Short-term leasing and third-party warehousing are both more flexible, but shorter-term agreements are subject to modification by either party on short notice. The most flexible option is public warehousing, which involves a commitment of only 30 days.

Compared with other kinds of real estate, warehousing has better prospects as a long-term investment. There is minimal "retrofit" cost when one tenant leaves and another takes over the space. Maintenance is lower than with other kinds of real estate, and vacancy rates are usually lower as well. This means that there is a steady return with fewer headaches. While control of property may be emotionally satisfying, real estate may become an anchor for a distributor such as Smith Co. when current space has been outgrown and expansion is necessary.

Real estate as a corporate investment

If investments in real estate could generate steady profits, then property management could be treated as a profit center. However, the history of property management in large corporations is not good. In the oil, railroad, and utility industries, some companies had internal real estate departments. In theory, this is a reasonable strategy for a business that holds large amounts of land. In practice, many such departments were later abandoned. Real estate as a side activity had proved to be a distraction from the core business and an unsound strategy.

The decline of cookie cutters

Some of the early developers of warehouses created standardized buildings in a variety of locations. A simple construction plan was used, and the developer looked for land that would accommodate the standard building rather than adapting the building to available land. Just as Henry Ford changed auto manufacturing by cloning millions of black cars, cookie-cutter developers dotted the landscape with identical warehouse buildings.

Computer-aided architectural techniques have lowered the value of the cookie-cutter approach. One large owner of warehouse real estate uses extensive research to construct buildings that are specifically designed to meet the specialized needs of customers.

Third-party operators as investors

There are a few third-party warehouse owners and managers who have leveraged their knowledge of the warehousing business to create a real estate profit center. Some of these operators develop buildings and rarely sell one. Others make it a practice to harvest and replant their warehouse real estate. One operator has found an excellent market in selling buildings to real estate investment trusts under a short term leaseback. This lease allows the operator to either stay in the building or vacate it after the lease has expired.

One of the windfall profits which can come out of this activity is in leasehold improvements. When a tenant puts in substantial improvements and then abandons them with the building, the owner may end up with a facility which is substantially more valuable than the one that he originally constructed.

When a third-party operator acts as both developer and warehouseman, there is a potential conflict of interest. That conflict exists between the highly competitive business of third-party warehousing and the relatively stable activity of renting space to another user. Compared to third-party warehousing, space rentals represent a relatively low risk. The second conflict occurs in pricing. Should the third-party warehouse operation pay the same prices that prevail for leasing of space in the marketplace? Some third-party warehouse operators use the "opportunity cost" approach in establishing rental rates for the warehousing subsidiary. Under opportunity cost theory, the rent to a subsidiary should be no different from the rent charged to an outside user of similar space. In other words, the public warehouse should pay the market rate for space. However, some operators feel that they must subsidize third-party warehousing to retain that portion of their business, and therefore they discount the opportunity cost in order to ensure that the public warehousing operation will be profitable. One operator provides a 5 to 7 percent discount to his public warehousing subsidiary.

The warehouse owner may want to convert lease space to public warehousing when a tenant vacates a building and a new renter is not readily found. However, there are times when it is easier to sell public warehousing services than it is to find a lease customer for a building. The third-party operator/investor is able to maximize opportunities by readily switching from one kind of warehousing business to the other.

The make-or-buy question

Whether you choose to invest in real estate or use other people's property is a classic make-or-buy decision. If you believe you can build at a cost below market, and if you are confident of your ability to sell buildings when you no longer want to own them, then real estate investment may be a sound move for your company. Always consider total costs, the time involved, and the relationship between cost, time, and risk. Always consider the opportunity cost of real estate — its value to a third party on the open market. Buildings, like fruits and vegetables, will reach a point of ripeness when they should be harvested and replaced.

Understanding real estate costs

The ownership of property has both visible and hidden costs. The five visible costs are:

- Rent.
- Taxes.
- Insurance.
- Utilities.
- Maintenance.

If you own the property, you calculate depreciation instead of rent. Because these costs will change, it is important to revise budgets to show these changes.

In addition to the five visible costs, there are seven hidden costs:

- Cost of vacancy.
- Professional costs (legal, engineering, etc.)
- Corporate staff support.
- Losses of insurance deductibles.
- Relocation.
- Travel.
- Opportunity costs.

No warehouse is full all the time, yet many budgets fail to calculate the cost of vacancy. Opportunity cost is listed to be sure that you consider the difference between the book value of your real estate and the true market value for that property.

When should you build?

The decision to build will be influenced by location, supply and demand for existing buildings, construction costs and capabilities, and the ability to obtain financing.

If you have determined that there is only one suitable location for your next warehouse, and there are no available buildings there, you will logically conclude that a new building should be constructed. For example, a manufacturer may need a finished-goods warehouse within conveyor distance of the production plant. The project may be justified by reduction of transportation to remote warehouses. If no existing warehouses are available close to the plant, a new one will be built.

Supply and demand will influence the decision. You may find that existing buildings are available but that the scarcity of space has driven prices so high that they exceed the occupancy cost of a new building. In that situation, construction is more economical than leasing or buying.

Financing will influence the decision because financing for a new building may be easier to obtain and cheaper than financing for purchase of an old one. There may be significant tax incentives for construction of a new building in a city that is trying to attract new industry. At other times, an existing building can be purchased by assuming a mortgage with an interest rate below market. Attractive financing is often a prime reason for buying an existing property.

Obsolescence is also a consideration. All used buildings have one thing in common: their original owners no longer want them. The buyer should carefully examine an existing property to determine whether its location, design, or construction will become obsolete in the foreseeable future.

The rehabilitation alternative

The adaptive re-use of older buildings gained attention when federal tax law provided credits for rehabilitating historic structures and other buildings more than fifty years old.

Sometimes rehabilitation has economic incentives other than taxation. It may be more economical to rehabilitate a well-built older structure than to build a new one at the same location. A city with an older building is likely to offer tax abatement, favorable financing, or other incentives to attract a new user. These incentives must be balanced against the cost of rejuvenating the building. Then compare operating costs in that building with costs in alternate facilities.

Repairing warehouse roofs

The two most important construction components in warehouses are the floor and the roof. Walls are comparatively easy to modify or repair. A roof or floor with a serious problem can be difficult to correct.

Most roofs in older warehouse buildings consist of layers of felt material, bonded and saturated with hot asphalt. These are called *built-up roofs*. Sometimes gravel is applied to add additional insulation and protection. Built-up roofs will deteriorate from heat, moisture, and sunlight. The process may be accelerated by windstorms, ice, or ponding water. Deterioration will be aggravated when people walk or move equipment on the roof.

Built-up roofs are repaired in a variety of ways. Coatings of hot or cold material can be used to seal leaks. New felt plies can be installed over the old ones, or old roofing can be removed and replaced.

One alternative in replacement is the single-ply roof, similar to a giant rubber sheet. The single ply can be installed with or without a gravel ballast.

Rejuvenating warehouse floors*

The true function of a warehouse floor is to support materials handling operations. A smooth floor will allow trucks to operate at maximum productivity and will reduce wear and tear on the vehicles. The condition of the floor should always be a prime consideration in buying or leasing a facility or in considering improvements to your present warehouse. Conditions of warehouse floors will vary because of construction methods and previous maintenance practices.

The two most important criteria in evaluating floors are stability under load and wear-surface quality. Cracks and deteriorated joints

---

* Adapted from material written by Steven Metzger, Metzger/McGuire Co., Concord, NH.

can almost always be repaired. But instability of the floor slabs (rocking at joints) and surface delamination are expensive and sometimes impossible to fix.

Slab rocking at joints is fairly common in warehouses. The primary cause is curl. As slabs dry and moisture evaporates, the slab ends curl up off the ground. You can detect curl by standing with one foot on each side of the joint and feeling the slab deflect as lift trucks cross. In severe cases you can see the slabs move, but if the curl is minor you will only hear a thump. The cure for rocking slabs generally requires pressure grouting to fill the void beneath the slab, followed by joint filling and repair.

Surface defects such as delamination will expose the concrete aggregate. This happens because corrosive materials were spilled on the floor or because the wear surface is deficient. Sometimes this is corrected with application of an epoxy or polyurethane seal. In severe cases, it is necessary to place a new concrete slab over the existing one.

Floor cracks always create an appearance problem. Where sanitation is important, they may allow entry of insects or rodents. Cracks will be a serious concern if they are so wide that the structural integrity of the floor has been compromised. Hairline cracks are usually left unrepaired with no significant consequences. Cracks wider than the thickness of a credit card with can be repaired by using a concrete saw and filling with a semirigid filler.

Deteriorated (spalled) joint edges should always be repaired. Spalling is the dislodging of pieces of floor at the edges of the joints, and it happens through the normal wear and tear of warehouse work. Minor spalls will expand to cause rapid wear of lift truck tires. In the extreme, they will also damage the transmission and axle and could even tip a load. Spalls are repaired by making deep cut at the outer ends of the spall, removing the concrete between the cuts, and re-filling with a semirigid epoxy or polyurethane.

Some floor deficiencies cannot be repaired. Where the slab is too thin to adequately support vehicles or rack loads, replacement may be required. Sometimes a new floor can be placed over the original, but this may create elevation problems at the doorways and docks.

Questions that solve problems.

The opinions of your people can be helpful in developing or changing your strategy regarding real estate. The following questions will help to display those opinions.

Q Are you comfortable with our company's strategy regarding owning (or leasing or outsourcing) of warehouses?
C The quality of the answer will depend on how well it is defended. You need to determine whether your organization has a well-developed strategy or just a habit of doing things as they were done before.

Q If we build a new warehouse next year, how would you like to see construction and ownership handled?
C Answers to this one will provide further insight on attitudes toward real estate.

Q What is the most serious maintenance challenge in our warehouses?
C Once the question is answered, you need to find out what people are doing about it.

Q Do we have opportunities for major rehabilitation of any of our warehouses?
C Be sure the answer is enlarged with details about methods and how the cost is justified.

Chapter 32

Warehouse construction

The process of constructing a new warehouse is deceptively complex. Some inexperienced developers have referred to warehouse buildings as "bricks and sticks." The development of a new building is an opportunity to correct the mistakes that occurred in your existing facility and at the same time to create a more attractive and productive workplace. This job is far too important to be left to construction specialists; it deserves the input of those people who will have to live with the new building. The tales about warehouse design errors are generally traceable to poor communication between the people who construct the building and those who will operate it. Here are three examples:

- A builder from Ohio started construction on a warehouse in an Indiana town famous for its limestone. No soil tests were made. After much of the main steel was erected, the flooring contractor hit the limestone. They were forced to dynamite the limestone after the steel frame had been erected.
- A warehouse in Texas was built on unstable soil. The developer poured a floor without doing anything to stabilize the ground beneath it. The floor quickly developed a rough surface, and ultimately the building was torn down because it could be neither used or repaired.
- A warehouse was built with high-intensity lighting. After the building was finished, the operator found that the lights were not over the aisles. An additional $20,000 was spent moving the lights before the building could be opened.

Everyone who will have anything to do with a new warehouse should be consulted on any construction details that cannot be easily changed once the building is started.

Understanding total development costs

Before construction ever begins, it is essential to analyze the development costs of the selected site. Cost of land acquisition is only one element of the total development expense. That cost will vary significantly depending on the condition of the land, the cost of providing access, and zoning restrictions.

If the soil is unstable or rocky, site preparation costs may exceed the cost of the land itself. Access costs include not only roadways but also the cost of providing water, sewer, natural gas, or railroad sidings. Most communities have zoning laws that restrict the amount of land to be covered by buildings. One common limitation is 45 percent building coverage, but another community may set the limit at 30 percent. The cheaper site with 30 percent coverage may well be more expensive to develop than the alternate site that allows 45 percent.

Part of the development cost is the time you will spend getting the job done. If the city you have selected has a reputation for bureaucratic delay, excessive construction time becomes part of the total development cost. Therefore, when you compare sites, be sure that the total cost and development time for the selected site will not destroy either your budget or your timetable. An apparently inexpensive site may end up being more costly than one with a higher land price.

Better ideas for construction*

During the past two decades, there has been a quiet revolution in the construction of warehouse buildings. While the price of most other products and services has escalated, the cost of construction has remained fairly static, and in some cases it has even gone down.

As you consider new construction, look at the priorities for controlling quality. First priority must go to the floor. The floor is your

---

* Substantial help in this writing was received from F. Douglas Reardon, Exxcel Contract Management, Inc., and from Stephen N. Metzger, Metzger/McGuire.

work surface, and its quality will have a lasting effect on your operational productivity. As previous examples demonstrated, a defective floor can destroy the utility of the building. Next in importance are docks and dock doors, which are the key points for the flow of materials into and out of the building. If doors are poorly placed, the material flow will be degraded. The third priority is the framing and roof system. These can be repaired if they are done badly, but the repairs will be difficult and expensive.

The lowest priority is the part of the building that gets the most attention from the uninitiated: the walls. Most warehouse walls are not load-bearing, so it matters little from a construction standpoint whether they are made of granite or cardboard. From an operation standpoint, they probably need to be accompanied by a perimeter alarm system and insulation to provide protection from temperature extremes. However, one distribution center designed for building materials has no walls at all.

Because financing is provided by people with little knowledge of warehouse construction, perhaps the prime purpose of walls is to impress the lenders.

Parking lots

Construction of a parking lot is frequently neglected in construction planning. If the sub-base is not properly prepared, the parking lot will deteriorate rapidly. Furthermore, if it does not have sufficient slope with drainage, water will pond after a rain, and motor traffic will turn the pond into a pothole.

Foundations and floors

No warehouse floor will be any stronger than the earth beneath it. If the soil beneath the floor is not properly prepared and compacted, voids under the concrete will inevitably cause the floor to fail. The quality of foundations and floors depends on the quality of the soil beneath them, and that can be determined only with tests. Soil tests will measure the risk of underground problems. Such problems include aquifers, peat bogs, old foundations, mines, rock, or other hidden underground structures. Soil tests will also determine the load-bearing capacity of the site. These tests may also pinpoint the best location on the property for the warehouse building.

Load-bearing capacities on the same land may vary from 1,000 pounds per square foot to more than 10,000 pounds. In such situations, the building would be placed on the most stable soil available.

The ideal warehouse floor is reasonably flat, has durable wear surfaces, and requires a minimum of maintenance. To reduce maintenance, the floor must be poured in a manner that minimizes curling. Curling is the development of concave patterns in the floor as the cement cures. Large floors have joints, and the joints must be made in a way that minimizes spalling, or failure of the surface at the joint. It is important that the concrete material be dense and nonporous to create the strongest wear surface.

In one warehouse, the floor was poured with a series of strips. One strip was poured, with an adjacent area of similar size left vacant, then another strip poured. The voids between strips were poured after the initial strips had cured. This builder believes that this method develops a higher-quality floor.

Another builder controls floor quality by emphasizing the installation environment. The floor is not poured until the walls and roof are nearly complete in order to reduce temperature variance or weather damage to the curing floor. Exposure to the sun may cause concrete to cure too rapidly. When the curing process is slower, a higher-quality floor is developed. The curing process should take four weeks to achieve maximum strength.

The strength of the concrete is controlled by reducing the amount of water mixed with the cement, and each load of cement is tested as it is delivered to measure water content. Dowel joints in the concrete are used in high-traffic areas. A surface hardener is always installed. When budget permits, a plasticizer may also be added to produce a mirror finish on the floor.

Laser technology is a key to quality in floors and dock areas. Because the sub-base is of critical importance, a laser-guided bulldozer and vibrator roller are used to create a solid, level foundation. A laser screed (Figure 32-1) serves as a giant trowel. The machine creates a flat floor and eliminates one of the slowest and dirtiest jobs in construction, the manual finishing of concrete. The laser screed reduces flatness variance to 0.25 inch over a length of 50 feet, about one-third of the variance for manually finished floors. The speed of the machine allows a larger pour of concrete and fewer joints.

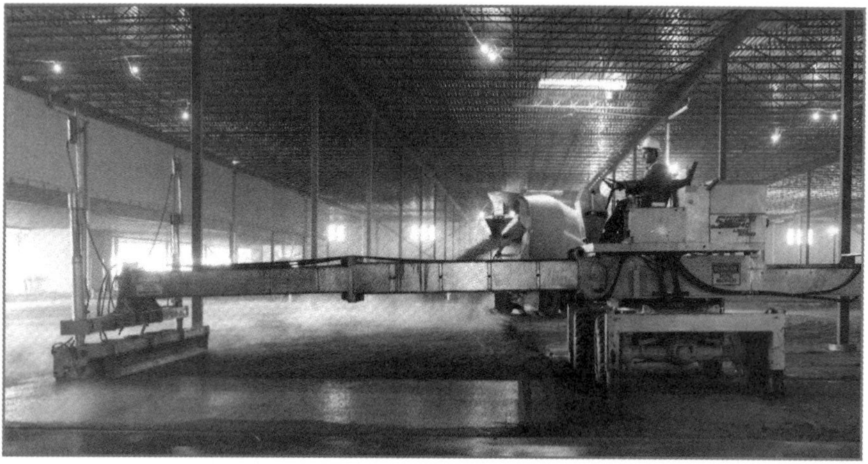

there is greater risk of accidents and often a need for more land because the maneuvering is more difficult.

The dock apron should be prepared to specifications exceeding those of the warehouse floor. That apron should extend at least fifty feet from the face of the dock doors. It should be of eight-inch-thick concrete with reinforcing steel mesh to handle the stress of highway trailers.

The dock doors should be designed to minimize maintenance. Docks should be placed on the leeward side of any warehouse wherever possible. Prevailing winds in much of the world come from the southwest. However, in Southern California the Santa Ana windstorms typically come from the northeast. Check on prevailing winds for the place where the warehouse will be built and be sure that the dock doors are on the opposite wall.

Metal and plastic have replaced wood for many of the overhead doors. Dock doors should have a channel that brings the door straight up rather than making a 90-degree turn like residential garage doors. This allows space for racking over the doors and eliminates maintenance problems. Mechanical dock levelers are an investment that pays back in reduced operating costs for any busy truck dock. Dock lights will enhance productivity and safety.

Structural system and roof

The steel structure and the roofs should be designed to provide the longest possible life with minimal maintenance and leakage. Outside the Sunbelt, the roof must also be capable of absorbing significant temperature changes and weather hazards during its installation and useful life.

The best option in roof structures for most regions of the United States is a pre-engineered metal roofing system. On the Pacific Coast, some structural support systems use wood rather than steel beams, because wood has a more favorable cost.

The metal roof is built with expansion and contraction capabilities in the design. Roof slope is essential to provide drainage and prevent ponding. The earliest pre-engineered metal roof had a slope of 1 in 12, but technology now allows a slope as gentle as 1 in 48. The gentle slope makes it safer to walk on the roof for maintenance and cleaning. The fastener holes in the roof system are pre-punched to assure that the roof is properly aligned and to minimize the stress of expansion and contraction. The length of each metal sheet is staggered to control the transfer of thermal stresses from one sheet to the other. An important feature is the sealing system of the metal sheets, which is a double-rolled seam similar to that seen in the caps of soft-drink cans. Adhesive and nylon spacer chips are used to splice seals between the laps of the roof.

In contrast to the heavier and more complex roof systems that use layers of felt and asphalt, the metal roof is simpler, lighter, and easier to maintain. Furthermore, there is less risk of settlement as the building ages because the entire structural system is significantly lighter than a conventional roof.

Illumination and heating

Like other aspects of warehousing, lighting has changed greatly in the past few decades. Fluorescent lights have proved relatively ineffective and uneconomical in any space where temperature falls below 60 degrees. Even where the space is heated to higher temperatures, the lighting is less effective than the newer high-intensity discharge (HID) lighting.

Many warehouses have relied on skylights and translucent wall panels to provide sunlight, the cheapest and best form of light available. However, skylights do nothing for the night shift, and in a cold climate the cost of heat loss through skylights is more than the savings in power for illumination. As more warehouses move to second- and third-shift schedules, the importance of sunlight is reduced.

The best way to heat a large warehouse is with an air rotation system. This type of heating allows a single unit to cover more than 100,000 square feet of space. However, if your warehouse is to be partitioned into several smaller areas, then smaller air rotation units are installed to provide heat in each area. The fans in these heating units are frequently run in hot weather to prevent heat buildups inside the building. Where internal-combustion lift trucks are used, maintenance of air circulation is crucial, but it also raises the heating costs. Temperature sensors are equipped with carbon monoxide sensors, which activate the fans when exhaust fumes build up.

Fire protection systems

Your insurance underwriter should always be involved in fire protection system design. Protection standards usually specify fire lanes around a building to allow access by firefighting equipment.

Nearly all warehouses in North America use sprinkler systems to fight fires. Some systems require booster pumps to provide additional water pressure. The state of the art in sprinkler systems today, the ESFR (early-suppression, fast-response) system, will often eliminate the need for sprinklers mounted in storage racks, but it also requires more water and more pressure than conventional systems. Present specifications for ESFR call for a minimum clear height of twenty-eight feet and a maximum of thirty-three feet. These specifications must be considered in designing the building.

Walls and interior finish

A pre-engineered metal wall is usually the least expensive partition available. However, some builders prefer a hollow-core pre-stressed concrete wall with foam insulation inside the cores. They argue that the concrete wall is more durable and resistant to abuse. Furthermore, it has more eye appeal to the bankers who finance the building and the brokers who will lease it.

Wall panels should be designed to allow for future installation of additional dock doors. Changing uses of the building will probably require new doors during the life of the structure.

Bright white paint is the best way to enhance interior finish. Color coding may be used to indicate certain features of the warehouse, such as red paint on columns with fire extinguishers. Use of a maximum amount of white finish improves light levels and general appearance.

Exterior finish

Although the exterior has little to do with operating efficiency, it has a great deal to do with the impressions left with visitors, including your customers. Landscaping is one of the most cost-effective ways to improve the appearance of any warehouse. Just as good housekeeping is a sign of good warehouse management, attention to the exterior and grounds will greatly influence the impression of those who see your warehouse from the street. A poorly kept exterior may not necessarily signify a bad warehouse operation, but many observers will immediately downgrade management if the building exterior is an eyesore.

Layout design

No building can be constructed without the advice of architects or engineers, but the best source of layout advice comes from your own operating people. Good warehouses are designed from the inside out.

Start the project with your own layout based on necessary stack heights, aisles, staging areas, order picking lines, and reserve storage. Then have your architect fit the structure to your layout. Consider construction cost options as you look at bay sizes, but the prime consideration is to design storage bays that will accommodate your layout plan.

Remember that construction cost is a one-time expense, but the cost of operating the building will probably increase each year. Consider the trade-offs between layout and building costs. The least expensive building to construct is square, because that provides the most square feet of space per linear foot of wall. Yet a square building might be less efficient to operate than a long and narrow one.

Economies of scale

The square-foot cost of large buildings is always lower than that of small ones. One cost study indicated that a 60,000-square-foot building will cost 16 percent more per square foot than a 100,000-square-foot building. As the size moves above 100,000 square feet, the savings are lower.

Wear and tear

Carelessness on the part of the operator is a frequent cause for building deterioration. The most vulnerable area is the walls, particularly those made of fragile materials. The lift operator who keeps moving until he hits something can seriously damage building walls. Similar abuse comes from outside the building by those who park cars too close to the walls or hit the building with trucks. Warehouse walls should be protected from damage by barriers on both sides.

Materials handling practices can also cause damage to floors. Among the worst practices is "freight training," which occurs when a lift operator pushes several pallets across the floor in a train. This can damage the concrete, but it also damages the lift truck and the pallets. Furthermore, it is unsafe because the operator does not get a clear view ahead of the front pallets.

Given reasonable care, a good warehouse building should last for many years. If abused, the building will start to deteriorate early in its life. With flexible design and proper maintenance, your new warehouse should have a useful life of many decades.

Questions that solve problems

The most important questions regarding any new construction project relate to whether the operating people have been truly involved in specifying the building or whether the whole job was left to construction professionals with minimal knowledge of your operation. These questions should be directed to your operating people:

Q Who checked the specifications for this building, and when were these checks last made?
C Inadequate or vague answers to these questions indicate that operations people are not sufficiently involved, and you have the potential for a dangerously incomplete project.

Q Have you verified that roadways and truck dock areas are properly sized for the largest vehicles we are likely to handle?
C Be sure your planners anticipate equipment that might be allowed on the highways in the future as well as that used today.

Q Do you have a written report from fire underwriters on the building design?
C If the underwriters were consulted, they should be asked to put their opinions in writing. Obviously failure to produce writing creates the suspicion that they have not approved the design.

Q Have we verified that dock designs as well as heating and illumination are the current state-of-the-art?
C Not every builder or engineer knows about all the latest developments in these areas. It is important to get more than one opinion.

Q Have the designers anticipated the wear and tear that would take place if we operated around the clock?
C Consider the fact that many warehouse operations operate with two, three, and even four shifts and that many are extending their hours to meet new customer demand. If your people have not allowed for this kind of wear and tear, the specifications should be revised.

Chapter 33

Warehouse start-ups

Planning is by far the most important activity in starting up a new warehouse. Early in the planning stages, consider communications, packaging, transportation, security, and perishability of stored products. Communications include the method and frequency of data transmission. Consider package sizes, unitization, bulk storage, and any other materials-handling options. Measure the best mode for both inbound and outbound transportation. Make a final audit of security preparations to protect against fire, storm damage, and theft. Measure all available means of protecting the product going into the new warehouse.

The importance of a smooth start*

The first days and weeks are absolutely critical in any new warehousing operation. A flawless startup creates a competitive advantage. A weak opening can create bad first impressions and may hobble operations for weeks or months. Every third-party logistics provider faces this problem when a new customer is acquired and a new operation begins. Start-up planners typically emphasize the technical details of a fully functioning facility. However, by concentrating on the logistics aspects of the project, they may lose sight of what matters most: customer focus.

Customer focus is a matter of priorities. The emphasis is not on technical elegance but on the warehouse team's ability to effectively

---

* Adapted from an article by Marilee Tatalias, DSC Logistics, Inc., *Warehousing Forum*, Volume 13, Number 5, ©The Ackerman Company, Columbus, Ohio.

serve the needs of both your customer and your customer's customers. Because those needs change, building customer focus into the startup process is a task that cannot be standardized.

Even without standards, it can be done. The warehouse operator must take the leadership role in a start-up. The emphasis should be on flexibility and responsiveness to customer needs. The goal is a new facility that not only serves the customer well on opening day but also continues to perform in the months and years ahead. There are four key elements in that process:

- A diverse project team.
- Flexible programming.
- Communication with all parties.
- Allocation of the resources to do the job properly.

Building the project team

An effective startup needs people who can quarterback the effort through its inevitable ups and downs. Some companies use a dedicated team that roves from startup to startup. This approach guarantees experience and ability to work as a team. It promises a cookie-cutter approach to every startup, no matter what features are unique about the new facility and its mission.

Another approach is to draw widely from available company personnel for each startup. An experienced startup manager spearheads the effort. However, this person builds a team from company personnel, some of whom may not have been involved in such an effort before. Typically, the selected staff spend one to several weeks away from regular assignments to complete the startup operation and get the new facility on its feet. This team supports the startup program in three ways:

- Filling in for permanent staff not yet hired.
- Training new people as they arrive.
- Supporting new hires as they move through the orientation process.

This approach provides flexibility and responsiveness. Pulling in new talent for each project brings freshness to the startup process. Furthermore, this method develops a broad group of employees who develop startup competency and experience. This training process increases your ability to handle unforeseen demands for startup support

Charting the process

Even before the team is in place, the startup manager creates a master planning chart. This chart has more than 1,000 line items listing every possible activity associated with the startup. The tasks are categorized by the type of startup event. Each line on the chart has a task number, task description, percentage of completion, time duration, and start and finish dates. The name of every outside resource is listed here. This master chart gives every task an owner and a target completion date. Controlling each task is an important part of any successful startup.

But beyond control, it is essential to examine the process. Figure 33-1 is a process flowchart for a typical startup. The chart is easily correctable, and it becomes a living document that reflects present and future changes in the startup effort. To maintain flexibility, this process flowchart is adjusted to conform to the requirements of each new startup.

Ongoing communication

The quality and quantity of communication are absolutely critical as the startup moves forward. The startup manager is responsible for initiating most of this communication. That manager's tools include updates to the master chart, weekly conference calls with the startup team, and daily onsite status briefings once the startup is physically underway. A procedure called "pulse points" is used to measure important activities. Three examples of pulse points are damage, case fill ratios, and on-time shipping. During start-ups, these pulse points are measured daily to create a report card and a benchmarking system.

There are really two important factors in this communication. The first is what is communicated, and the second is *with whom*. When a third-party provider is immersed in technical decisions, it is possible to overlook the need to check in with the customer. Yet frequent customer coordination is absolutely necessary. While the customer may not need to be present for every meeting, a checkup at least once a week is essential. Use conference calls to share the week's pulse points with the customer. Ask the customer to appraise progress and provide feedback and suggestions. This kind of communication accomplishes

Figure 33-1

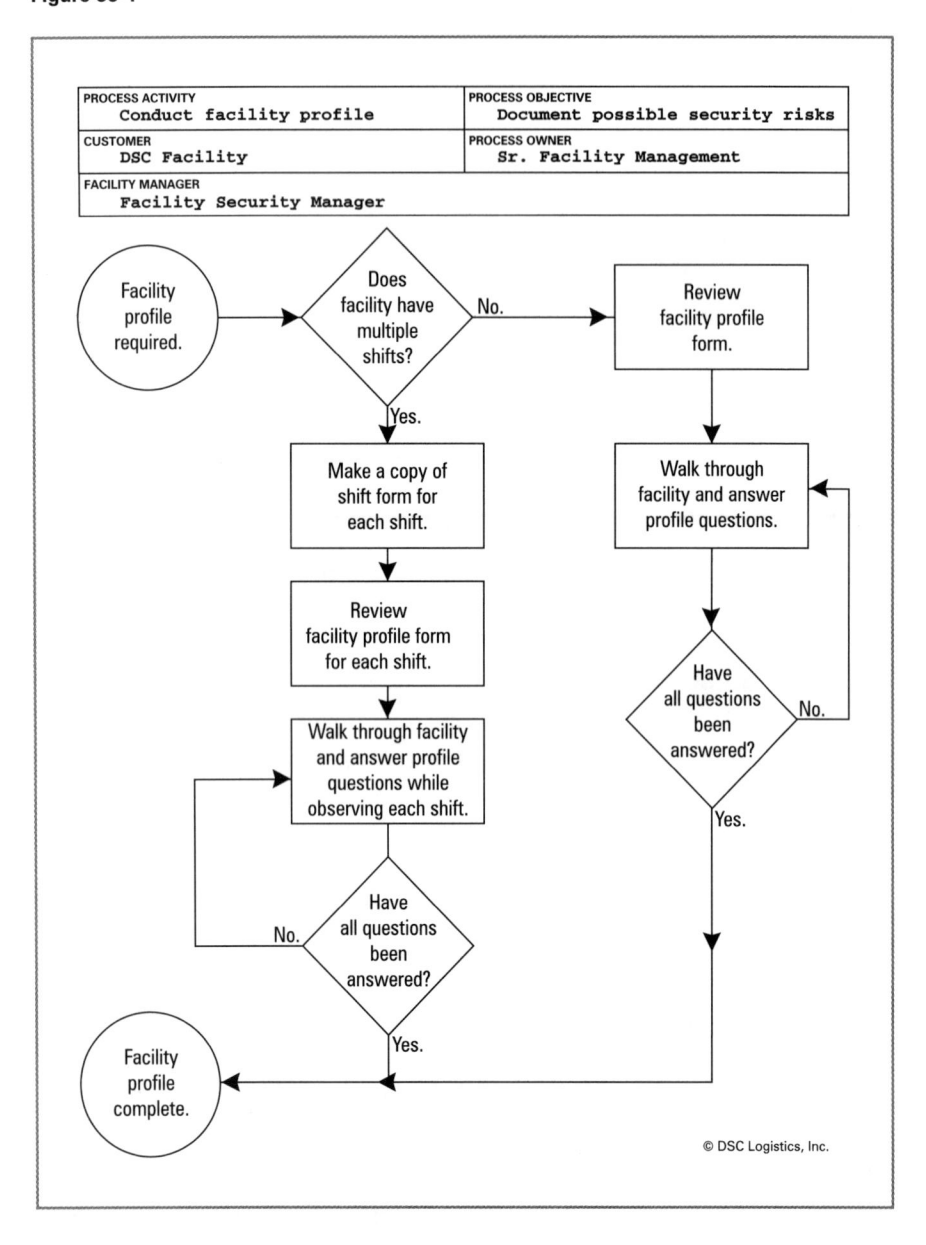

PROCESS ACTIVITY Conduct facility profile	PROCESS OBJECTIVE Document possible security risks
CUSTOMER DSC Facility	PROCESS OWNER Sr. Facility Management
FACILITY MANAGER Facility Security Manager	

```
Facility profile required.
    ↓
Does facility have multiple shifts? ──No.──→ Review facility profile form.
    │Yes.                                         ↓
    ↓                                         Walk through facility and answer profile questions.
Make a copy of shift form for each shift.         ↓
    ↓                                         Have all questions been answered? ──No.──↑
Review facility profile form for each shift.      │Yes.
    ↓                                             ↓
Walk through facility and answer profile questions while observing each shift. ←──┐
    ↓                                                                              │
Have all questions been answered? ──No.──────────────────────────────────────────┘
    │Yes.
    ↓
Facility profile complete.
```

© DSC Logistics, Inc.

at least two purposes: first, it sustains the customer's confidence in you; second, it keeps you informed of the customer's needs, concerns, and goals. Some of these may change as the project moves forward, and they may be somewhat different from those expressed in the original plan. Working with the customer, the warehouse operator plans process improvements that will reduce total delivered costs while maintaining high service levels. During the startup, there is still time to adapt the operation to emerging conditions.

Resources

The most limited resource of all is time. Emergency start-ups are possible but difficult. There is a direct correlation between longer lead times and successful start-ups. Therefore, early in the planning stage, negotiate for a schedule that provides ample time to make plans, recruit the best talent, and move through the process in an orderly manner.

Management commitment may be the most important critical resource. If the startup does not get the attention it deserves at all levels of the organizations, then that the process could be neglected. When a third-party is involved, the logistics provider should take leadership on the startup, particularly when the customer has had very little experience in launching a warehouse operation. Leadership does not mean seizing control but rather guiding decisions in a responsible and responsive way.

The third resource is training. In a startup, we are typically dealing with a large quantity of untrained and inexperienced people. New hires in the startup may begin in a workshop setting, where they learn about the process for each specific function. Armed with that overview, they then learn the specifics of their jobs, including lift truck operation, use of scanners or other electronic tools, customer requirements, and safety.

How much can your warehouse hold?

In essence, the warehouse protects stored goods in a minimal amount of space. Minimizing space usage while protecting the inventory requires careful planning.

Assume that a warehouse operator needs to develop a total-space plan for toilet paper. A carton measures 20 by 24 by 10 inches and arrives in trailers containing 1,500 cases, with just one SKU per load. The product can be stacked 15 feet high. The operator determines that the product can be stacked in tiers measuring two units by two, five tiers high, on a 48-by-40-inch pallet. With a stacking limitation of 15 units, this converts to a height limitation of three pallets. A pallet load, allowing for normal overhang, will occupy 15 square feet.

Layout plans show that 40 percent of the building will be used for aisles, docks, and staging areas, leaving 60 percent available for storage. From this 60 percent net storage, an additional 20 percent is lost to honeycombing (the space lost in front of partial stacks).

After making the space calculation shown in Figure 33-2, we find that 31.25 square feet are needed for each stack, or 0.52 square feet per case of product. This information allows us to plan the total space requirement. Similar calculations should be made for each item planned in the inventory.

Figure 33-2

Storage Space Calculation
Assumptions
1. A portion of the gross space must be dedicated to aisles and staging, leaving 60% net space.
2. Honeycombing losses further reduce net space, leaving only 80% typically in use.

Calculations
A. Each pallet of a product contains 5 tiers with 4 cases per tier, or 20 cases total.
B. Each stack of 3 pallets contains 60 cases.
C. Each stack is the size of one pallet plus 1 inch overhand on each side (42"x50"), or 2,100 square inches. This is 14.6 square feet, which we round to 15 square feet.
D. Gross square feet needed per stack is 15 divided by 60% = 25 sq. ft.
E. Square feet per stack after honeycombing is 25 divided by 80% = 31.25 sq. ft.
F. Square feet per case is 31.25 divided by 60 cases = 0.521 sq. ft.

Developing a procedures manual

Regardless of the size of the operation, a procedures manual is important both during and after the startup. The smallest warehouse operation needs the best manual because the absence of one person in a small crew can be critical. The purpose of a procedure is to describe and document the way each job is done.

Procedures writing begins with input from people who are intimately familiar with the work. While they may not be great writers, the content can be edited by others who are. If the manual is to be truly useful, it must accurately describe each task done in the warehouse or the warehouse office. The procedures manual might be divided into six sections:

- Introduction and objectives.
- Definition of terms.
- Storage layout.
- Job descriptions.
- Work flow and staffing.
- Quality assurance.

The purpose of this manual is to provide a guideline for using space, labor, and equipment. If you have substantial seasonal variation in volume, a prime function of the manual is to describe ways to meet the seasonal peaks and to avoid undue waste of space and labor during the slow season. The manual must also deal with other anticipated changes in the operation.

The best procedures are those that address all of the questions that are asked or might be asked about your warehouse, and then provide some answers. Here are some sample questions, but every operator could add to this list:

- How should we handle damage discovered at receiving?
- How do we handle warehouse damage?
- What do we do if we cannot find an item shown on the inventory?
- What do we do when we cannot find a location to put away an inbound shipment?
- If there is a date coding system, how does it work?

Building on successful experience

The process of launching a warehouse operation can be tedious, but when it is neglected or mishandled it can be downright painful. The worst part about an unsuccessful startup is the loss of credibility when everything starts to go wrong. Confidence is an essential quality ingredient in warehousing, and a poor startup may cause everyone involved to lose confidence.

On the other hand, a successful startup builds a foundation for the next one. The planning, policies, and procedures that proved successful must be recorded so they can be used for future warehouse operations. So the process of writing procedures and recording details may be nearly as important as the planning that goes into the startup.

Opening the warehouse

In addition to the process flowchart shown in Figure 33-1, the opening of a new center will be greatly facilitated by the use of checklists that can be used to ensure that nothing has been overlooked. The pages that follow include a warehouse start-up checklist.

A warehouse start-up checklist

Using the checklist: This checklist is divided into five sections. It is designed to provide reminders to help ensure that nothing is overlooked during the busy time before you open a new facility. Never assume that this is a complete checklist. Each user should treat it as a starter, and each should add additional checkpoints to cover specific features of your own warehouse operation.

Receiving

1. Has a detailed procedure been prepared for receiving of freight?
2. Is a manifest or other form designed to cover receiving?
3. Will bar coding be used to identify received materials correctly?
4. What procedure will be used for shipments that arrive without manifests or without any advance notification of what is in the load?
5. What procedure is established to handle overages, shortage, and damage (OS&D)? Who will be responsible for checking

OS&D reports? Who will be responsible for checking the accuracy of each receipt?
6. What procedure will be followed to document the time each vehicle is held at the dock in order to approve or dispute carrier detention charges?
7. What procedure variations will be established for receipt of merchandise returned by customers?
8. How will receiving reports and other reports for the receiving dock be routed through the warehouse office?
9. If lot numbers are used, how will they be assigned at the receiving dock?
10. When product is palletized at the receiving dock, what pallet pattern will be used? What control will be exercised to ensure that all product is palletized according to the prescribed pattern?
11. How will storage location be determined when goods are received at the dock?
12. As merchandise is staged to be moved to storage, how will stacking limitations, stock rotation, and other storage specifications be communicated?
13. If a locator system is used, what checks will be made to be sure that the product is actually stored where ordered?
14. Has an appointment procedure for inbound carriers been established? How will it be enforced?
15. Do all inventory procedures go as far as they could to prevent fraud or dishonesty in receiving?

Shipping
1. Has a detailed shipping procedure been prepared?
2. Will there be a priority system for handling of outbound orders?
3. What checking procedure will be established to ensure accuracy in shipping?
4. Has an appointment procedure for outbound carriers been established? How will it be enforced?
5. Will we include a manifest or load plan with the outbound shipment?

6. Will special procedures be developed for shipping of hazardous products, freezable merchandise, or other goods requiring special treatment in transit?
7. Do all inventory procedures discourage fraud or dishonesty in shipping?

Materials handling operations

1. Will lift trucks or other mobile equipment be owned or leased?
2. Are the specifications for this equipment appropriate for the new warehouse operation?
3. Will aisle turning radiuses be adequate? Are lift heights adequate?
4. Is each piece of mobile equipment properly identified and equipped with an hour meter?
5. If used equipment will be acquired, is it in perfect operating condition?
6. Is there a training procedure to orient equipment operators?
7. Is storage equipment adequate to maximize cube utilization?
8. What mix of pallet rack, drive-in rack, drive-through rack, flow rack, self-supporting pallet rack, or other storage equipment will be used?
9. Has all rack been lag bolted to the warehouse floor?
10. Is there a training procedure to discourage abuse of storage rack?
11. In materials handling equipment, what will be used?
12. Have the safety hazards for each piece of mobile and storage equipment been determined and communicated?
13. Will records display the age and maintenance cost per year for each piece of equipment used in the warehouse?

Use of space

1. Will one person be designated as a space planner?
2. What space planning procedures will be followed?
3. Which merchandise is on a first-in, first-out basis?
4. Has a detailed layout for the warehouse been prepared?
5. Has the layout been reconciled with the types of storage and handling equipment that will be used?

6. Has the layout been checked against fire regulations and safety procedures?
7. What procedures will enforce proper storage procedures, including maintenance of aisles, housekeeping, and stacking limitations?
8. What procedures will minimize honeycombing space losses?
9. Is the location, width, and number of aisles adequate to allow effective movement of all materials?
10. Is there adequate space to stage inbound and outbound cargo?
11. Are storage pallets of uniform specification, in good repair, and in sufficient quantity to hold the planned inventory?
12. Is storage of surplus pallets in compliance with fire regulation?
13. Will storage locations be random, fixed, or a combination of the two?
14. Will a pick line be used for all or a portion of the inventory?
15. How many units of product can be stored in your new warehouse?
16. What percent of capacity is occupied at any given time?

Sanitation, security, and safety

1. Has a detailed housekeeping procedure been prepared?
2. Do you know which stock-keeping units, if any, are subject to inspection by the Food and Drug Administration?
3. If a portion of the product is FDA controlled, do you know FDA's requirements for safe storage of this product?
4. Is a member of the warehouse staff specifically assigned to sanitation maintenance? Is that individual also responsible for safety and security?
5. Has a professional sanitation service been retained?
6. Have training procedures for sanitation been established?
7. Is there a procedure for checking the ratio of lost-time accidents to total hours worked and comparing the safety record with other operations?
8. Have the safety hazards of all equipment been identified and made part of the training program?
9. Have any safety guards or other safety devices been deactivated for any reason?

10. Have you anticipated all the ways in which equipment or tools might be used unsafely?
11. Have refueling procedures been reviewed?
12. Have all warehouse operations procedures been reviewed by insurance underwriting inspectors to check on fire safety?
13. Is a no-smoking policy strictly enforced?
14. Are hazardous materials segregated from other materials?
15. Will random unloading and reloading of outbound shipments be performed? If so, how frequently will random checks be made?
16. Will check weighing procedures prevent deliberate overloading of outbound vehicles or underreceiving of inbounds?
17. How will physical counting procedures be used to improve security?
18. What procedures are used to control pilferage?
19. Do procedures warn employees of the consequences of pilferage or theft?
20. Will undercover procedures be used to detect dishonesty?
21. What procedures will be used to prevent unauthorized people from entering parking lots, grounds, or other outdoor property next to the warehouse?
22. How will lighting be used to discourage unauthorized entry?
23. What kinds of alarms, watch services, or other procedures will be used to detect unauthorized entry?

Questions that solve problems

The checklist at the end of this chapter is one means of reviewing the readiness of your people to handle a warehouse start-up. Just as in site selection, the important time to ask questions is early enough to cause some change in the activity but late enough to determine just what plans are in place.

Q Are there any points in the start-up checklist that are not included in our current start-up plan?
C Why?

Q Has anyone calculated those costs that should be identified as one-time start-up costs for the warehouse operation?
C Failure to identify start-up costs as a separate and nonrepetitive item could cause distortion in future cost accounting.

Q Describe the chain of command and responsibility for the warehouse start-up.
C The quality of this answer will show how much planning has gone into the start-up process.

Chapter 34

Moving a warehouse

A permanent element of warehousing is the need to adapt to change, and sometimes that involves changing warehouse locations. Changing warehouses is clearly more expensive and more difficult than changing motor carriers.

There are two kinds of warehouse moves:
* Changing from one third-party provider to another.
* Physically moving inventory from one warehouse building to another.

A change in third-party warehouse providers will be much simpler if the owner of the merchandise has separated the real estate agreement from an operating service arrangement. When the user controls the real estate, a new provider can be substituted for the old one without the need to move the inventory to another building. However, a change of providers typically involves the completion of a physical inventory and a clear cutoff date to pinpoint the responsibilities of each party.

When a change of warehouse providers also requires a physical move, the procedure outlined below will be followed. However, it is important to recognize that the provider who is losing the customer may lack motivation to handle the product transfer in the best possible manner. In those circumstances, close supervision of the move is particularly necessary.

Establishing a target move date

A target date is essential for planning purposes. Weather and seasonal inventory level variations should be considered. If you are moving into a newly constructed building, it is dangerous to base the target date on the contractor's estimate because builders are eternal optimists. Moving a warehouse operation into an incomplete building, particularly one with improperly cured floors, can have serious long-term consequences. To avoid that, add a comfortable cushion to the builder's estimated completion date.

Remember that it is desirable to pick a moving date that coincides with lower inventory levels or reduced shipping activity. Sometimes it is possible to begin receipts at the new building and continue to handle customer shipments from the old one, thus reducing the amount of product to be transferred.

Estimating moving costs

A first step in estimating costs is to calculate the amount of inventory that must be moved and the time and distance involved in the transfer.

After setting the target date, estimate the inventory to be on hand on that date. The simplest approach forecasts the future date's inventory levels as a percentage of today's inventory levels.

After estimating the level of on-hand inventory, determine the number of transfer loads. You can do this by counting the full and partial pallet loads and pallet equivalents and then dividing the number of pallets per load into the total.

For example, assume the current inventory consists of 3,500 full and partially loaded pallets and pallet equivalents. (Pallet equivalents are items, not palletized, that equal a pallet in cube requirements.) Anticipate 26 pallets per transfer load. The number of loads of inventory to be transferred may be calculated as:

3,500 pallets/26 pallets per load = 134.6 loads

That 134.6 loads adjusted by a 92 percent factor to compensate for reduced inventory levels on the move date yields 123.8 loads of inventory (round to 124) to be transferred on the targeted move date.

Experience has shown that, for a short-distance move, floor loads (goods stacked just one pallet high) allow for quicker turnaround of transfer vehicles and are more efficient. For longer moves, fully loaded vehicles are more economical. When the trucks used to move the inventory can be turned around quickly by using a floor load, you'll be able to reduce driver waiting time.

The cost of each load to be transferred can be calculated by summing the following costs:
- Transfer vehicle operating cost, or vehicle rental cost, plus driver labor and fuel, per round-trip.
- Outloading manpower and machine cost per load.
- Unloading and put-away cost per load.
- An allowance for damage, clerical labor, and contingencies.

The sum of these costs is the cost per load, which is multiplied by the number of loads to be transferred to yield the total cost of transferring the inventory.

An example

Truck cost: 20 miles/round trip @ $1.80/mile	36.00
Outloading cost: 0.3 hours/load @ $22.00/hr	6.60
Unloading cost: 0.25 hours @ $22.00/hr.	5.50
Overtime allowance @ 25% x labor cost	3.03
Damage/clerical/contingency allowance @	1.44
Total cost per transfer load	$52.57

In addition to relocating the inventory, the warehouse support functions must also be moved. So the following costs should be added:
- Cost of relocating the office operation.
- Cost of relocating the warehouse maintenance shop.
- Cost of transferring the materials handling equipment.
- Cost of moving value-added services (packaging, recoopering, assembly, and so forth).
- Cost of disassembling, transferring, reassembling, and lagging down storage racks.

These can be costed in the same way, then additional labor costs added for rack reassembly and lag-down labor.

How long will it take?

The following is an example of how to calculate the number of days that will be required to make the move:

Volume Assumptions:

Inventory loads to be transferred .... 124 loads
Additional loads to move the support services .... 5 loads
Total loads to be transferred .... 129 loads

Time Assumptions:

Truck travel time, one way loaded .... 25 minutes
Return trip time, one way not loaded .... 25 minutes
Outloading time, one lift operator .... 18 minutes
Unloading and time, one lift operator .... 15 minutes
Total round-trip cycle time .... 83 minutes
Time available, one shift operation
Available truck time, 7.5 hours .... 450 minutes
Minus allowance for delays/interruptions, 10% .. 45 minutes
Minutes available per truck per shift .... 405 minutes

Calculations

- 405 minutes per truck per shift divided by 83 minutes per round trip cycle = 4.9 loads/truck/shift.
- With moderate overtime or extra efficiency, five loads may be achieved per shift per truckload with one lift operator loading and another unloading.

The 129 total loads to be moved will require:
- 129 loads / 5 per day = 25.8 days with one truck, two lift operators on one shift.
- 129 / 10 = 12.9 days with two trucks.
- 129 / 15 = 8.6 days with three trucks.

Continue services or suspend operations?

A vital question is whether to continue services or suspend operations during the move. *Customer service considerations* should take priority.

The warehouse operating manager's preference will probably be to shut down because moving costs can be minimized and coordination of the move is much simpler. When operations are suspended, all that is required is thorough planning, having everything ready in advance, and a few hectic days of concentrated activity. Overtime costs may be significant, but the period of disruption can be kept to a minimum. Overtime days and weekends may be best for this type of move.

The customers should be the deciding factor in choosing whether to close during the move. Moving a warehouse without a break in normal customer service requires special coordination. First, and of critical importance, is communication. Each customer must be contacted during the early planning stages to discuss the move and to outline the tentative plan and timetable.

As the move date approaches, there must be frequent contacts on the administrative and clerical levels between the warehouse and its users to ensure that loads dispatched to the warehouse are routed to the new location on the proper dates and that carriers are sent to the proper location for pickup of outbound shipments. There may be a short-term requirement for carriers to pick up outbound shipments from both the old and new locations.

Communications

Customers need to be sold — tactfully — on the benefits of the proposed move. All customers must be informed well in advance of the move and then provided with frequent progress reports. An overinformed customer seldom complains.

Points that must be covered in communications with customers include:
- Out-of-service dates, if the warehouse is to suspend operations during the move. Also provide for the emergency service requirements that surely will arise.
- Date and time of transfer of each class of inventory. This is needed to coordinate delivery and pickup carriers. It requires daily, even hourly, contact.
- Phone number and address changes and their effective dates.
- Dates and times when data communications may be out of service.
- Directions to the new location.

- New hours of service, if they are to change.
- Changes in service charges or standards of service.

Common carriers, employees, suppliers, the phone company, and the postal service need to have timely notice of the move.

Employees should hear about the relocation well in advance; if you don't inform them, the grapevine will. Explain what is happening, why, and what to expect at the new site. Employees should be given regular information updates, and it is important that they tour the future facility. A complete walk-around, explanation of the location system, and any needed training in the use of new or different equipment will pay off in higher morale and a faster learning curve at the new site. Union organizers may take advantage of any uncertainty to play on employee concerns, and good communications will help you avoid this.

Carriers also need to be informed. This is a good time to look at any special arrangements with carriers. For example, for nighttime rail switching, the rail crew needs a key to the rail door and the security system.*

---

* From an article by Lee P. Thomas, logistics consusltant, Sugar Grove, OH.

Questions that solve problems

Because the physical move requires extremely precise planning and calculation, it is important to determine who has taken responsibility for it and how the calculations have been made.

Q Describe the personnel and chain of command involved in organizing the movement of the warehouse.
C A detailed answer to this question should indicate that the planning process is well under way.

Q What is the estimated cost of moving the warehouse?
C Just as in start-up costs, moving costs should be separated from normal operating costs because they are a one-time occurrence not related to normal operations.

Q How was the move date established?
C Discussion of this question will show whether your management has considered the best possible time to accomplish the warehouse move or whether the timing was dictated by external considerations.

PART 8

The Future

Chapter 35

Warehousing in a world economy

For most businesses in the U.S., global commerce is either a dream or a nightmare. Few expected it to be the reality it has become today. Overseas trading is no longer reserved for the giant multinational corporations; it is now practiced by medium-sized and small companies.

One measure of the globalization of logistics is the fact that the leading professional society, the Council of Logistics Management, has well over 10 percent of its members and attendees at its conferences from outside the United States.

Globalization has also come to the logistics industry. A significant number of logistics operations, both third-party and private, include international operations.

Meeting customer demands

In most cases, the push to expand overseas comes not from expansionist ideas but from requests of key customers. Years ago, Americans were surprised to find Japanese warehouse companies quietly operating in the United States. They did not belong to the trade associations or professional societies frequented by competitors. They did not have American customers, only Japanese clients. They made no effort to get involved in local community life.

All of this is more understandable today when we see U.S.-based third-party warehousing companies operating in a similar fashion. They move overseas to satisfy one or more American clients, they have neither the time nor the space to solicit local clients, and thus they have little motive to get involved in local marketing. Their mission is to take care of existing American customers.

Centralization is one stimulus for globalization. In earlier years, a director of logistics for a U.S. manufacturer had no authority outside the home country. When exports were involved, other managers took charge. Today, many logistics managers have global responsibilities, and when they need warehousing overseas it is comforting to deal with a company based in the United States that follows proven American practices. Therefore, as manufacturers move into a global arena, their warehouse suppliers inevitably do the same.

Globalization can sometimes create a turf war. When an international logistics firm started expanding into Mexico, the presumption was that the operations would be managed from its North American headquarters. However, its managers in Spain pointed out that Mexico was a former Spanish colony with Spanish language and culture. Why should the Yankees run it when the Spanish could do it better? The result was a compromise involving managers from both Spain and the U.S.

Re-engineering the warehouse

Re-engineering was a management concept originated by Michael Hammer and James Champee that reached a peak of popularity during the 1990s. Two hallmarks of re-engineering are a widening of the span of control and a reduction of bureaucracy.

Many corporate ideas about span of control date back to the writings of Julius Caesar, who ran the Roman army with multiples of ten, based on the theory that ten was the most people that one leader could control. In the warehouse, the question of how many warehouse workers can be effectively supervised by one leader is changing. The answer is fast approaching zero. The supervisor has changed from straw boss to coach. As a coach, a single leader can serve the needs of far more than Caesar's group of ten. One company changed its span of control from 1/8 to 1/27.

Bureaucracy is reduced by eliminating layers of management. How many reporting lines are crossed before a worker can talk to the chief executive? The re-engineered corporation is leaner and flatter than its predecessor.

Postponement

Postponement in distribution is the art of putting off to the last possible moment the final labeling, assembly, or formulation of a product. The theory of postponement is nothing new. It has been discussed in marketing and logistics textbooks for decades.

The concept's full potential for saving money in the warehouse, however, has not been reached. For example, an inventory of 20,000 units could replace an inventory of 100,000 simply by converting branded merchandise into products with no brand name. It's being done today in some industries.

Postponement was practiced long before marketing theorists started writing about it. Coca-Cola used the process early in the 20th century. Postponement was described by a marketing theorist as the opposite of speculation.

Postponement can take any of several forms:
- Postponement of commitment.
- Postponement of passage of title.
- Postponement of branding.
- Postponement of consumer packaging.

Figure 35-1

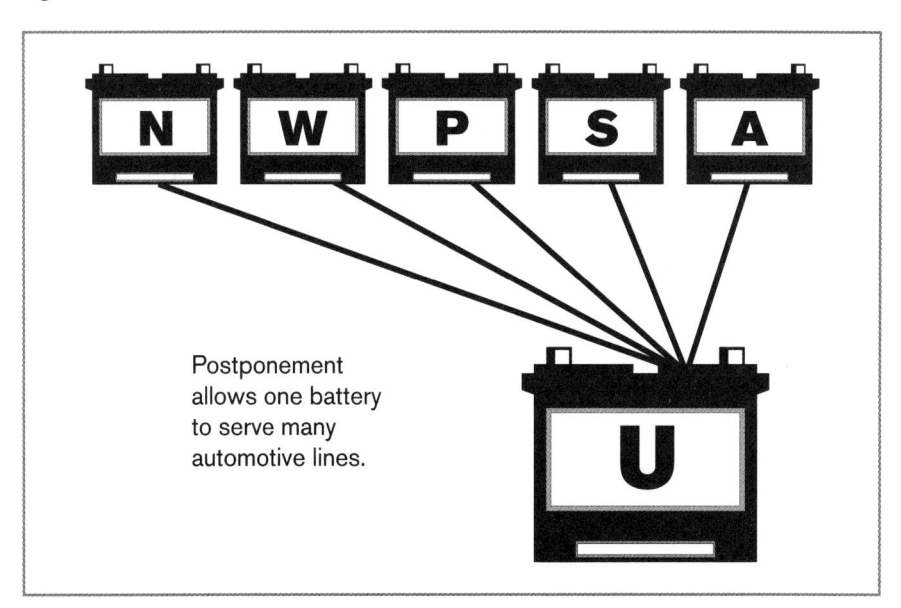

Postponement allows one battery to serve many automotive lines.

- Postponement of final assembly.
- Postponement of mixture or blending.

What does postponement do for warehousing efficiency? Basically, it enables one inventory to do the work of many. Where blending is postponed, the warehouse can have a single stock-keeping unit that is convertible to many different products as the final brand is applied. To illustrate, consider one line of automotive batteries: The only difference between brands is a decal applied to the top of the battery. Delaying the application of the decal and the final consumer package until the last moment dramatically reduces the number of line items in the warehouse.

Postponement can also reduce freight costs, which are usually the largest component of physical distribution costs. One example of postponement involves an Italian toy manufacturer producing a light-density item. The item is shipped in bulk boxes to a warehouse at the port of entry. Consumer packages purchased in the United States are shipped to the same warehouse, where workers package the bulk items for consumer sale. Not only are freight costs reduced, the consumer package is more attractive because it has not been subjected to the wear and tear of trans-Atlantic transportation.

Delaying final branding or packaging also reduces the risk of obsolescence. When moving to a multinational market, labels in the correct language are applied after the product is sold. Certain brands may decline in popularity, reducing warehouse turnover and increasing the risk that the product will become stale.

In the grocery industry, warehouses can create store-ready pallets that allow the retailer to move the unit load directly from the truck to the sales floor at a savings of up to sixty cents per case. Rehandling of goods on these pallets is postponed until they are removed by the ultimate consumer. Some discount retailers require customized packaging, and club packaging services offered by third-parties allow the retailer to display shrinkwrapped units without doing the wrapping at the store or at the original source.

Expanding into developing nations

In some parts of the world, logistical competency and infrastructure are not well developed. The concept of warehousing as practiced in the U.S. is virtually unknown. This provides both a challenge and an opportunity for the overseas warehouse operator expanding into a third world market.

One of the main challenges is the need to create redundancy in all utilities, particularly communications. Extensive power failures are rare in the United States, but in many parts of the world they are a common occurrence. Loss of power can mean loss of computers as well as lighting and electric lift trucks. Where the risk is prevalent, warehouse operators design emergency backup generators to provide power when the public source is out of service.

Communications are equally critical. In some parts of the world, a breakdown in telephone service may last for days, not hours. In such places, radio communication provides a necessary backup.

The future of world logistics technology

Mankind's progress in producing goods can be divided into three waves, or significant changes.*

The first wave was *agrarian,* marked by the abandonment of hunting and gathering and the development of agriculture. This period lasted for 4,000 years. Warehousing was crucial to distribution of agricultural products, since granaries and other storehouses enabled people to protect themselves from famine. They accomplished this by keeping a bank of surplus food to be used at times of food shortages.

The second wave is commonly called the *industrial revolution,* and it lasted less than 400 years. People moved from the farms into the cities to work in factories. Logistics systems were developed to handle the movement of raw materials from source to factory and the outbound movement of manufactured products from factory to customer.

The third wave is the *information age,* and we are still in the process of entering it. This wave is based on the computer and on communication among computers. The third wave will be characterized by eight major changes:
1. Shorter product life.
2. Increased product variety.

---

* Adapted from a presentation by the late J. M. Williams at the Eighth International Logistics Congress, Beijing, China.

3. Increased competition.
4. Increased cost of labor, space, and capital.
5. Increased concern for health and safety.
6. Increased use of computers.
7. Faster transport systems.
8. Lower inventories.

Warehousing practices will adjust to meet the third wave. Third-wave thinking is characterized by interdependence of suppliers and customers. The warehouse is frequently the buffer between them, which means that the warehouse must adapt to these changes.

Because the third wave is still new, it is difficult to describe how it will influence warehousing in the future. It is increasingly obvious, however, that the traditional role of warehousing in the information age is changing rapidly.

Change remains a driving force of the developing information age.

Questions that solve problems

Q Is our warehouse now involved in international shipping and receiving transactions? If not, are we prepared to handle such transactions in the future?
C As you consider this, measure the training needed to deal with customs documentation and other procedures found only in international transactions.

Q Have we explored every opportunity to use postponement as a means of meeting world markets or saving money in inventory management?
C When you explore this, be sure that imaginations can flow to consider the wildest ideas in postponement. The most aggressive kinds of postponement require a major restructuring in the traditional ways of building and distributing products.

Q Can we expand our warehousing operation to other parts of the world?
C Discussion will depend on whether you are in manufacturing, wholesale or retail distribution, or third-party warehousing. If a global vision seems too broad, perhaps you should start with a regional approach, such as all of North America rather than just the U.S.

Chapter 36

Staying current in the new century

The first thirty-five chapters of this book have illustrated the world of warehousing as it has existed up to the year 2000. As we have seen, the pace of change seems to be accelerating. There is no indication that the industry will be anything but even more dynamic in the foreseeable future. This chapter will explore the nature of present and future change and then will consider what you need to do to remain current.

The facets of change

The Ohio State University continuously explores change in logistics through its supply chain research. Figure 36-1 shows the results of

Figure 36-1

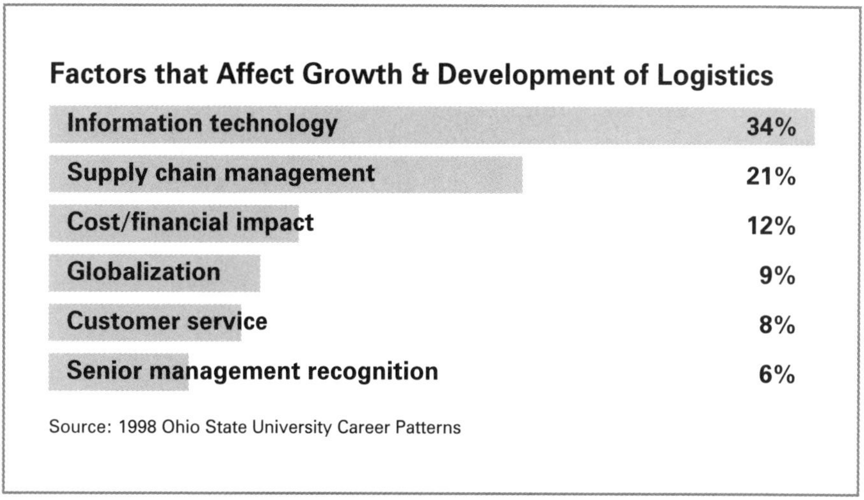

Factors that Affect Growth & Development of Logistics

Information technology	34%
Supply chain management	21%
Cost/financial impact	12%
Globalization	9%
Customer service	8%
Senior management recognition	6%

Source: 1998 Ohio State University Career Patterns

a 1998 study of factors that will affect development of logistics. It is not surprising that information technology is the leading factor.

Other research in 1999 by Professors Bernard La Londe and James Ginter traced a continued growth in third-party logistics. Driven by continuing shortages of warehouse labor, the research showed that the use of warehouse mechanization has continued to expand. The concept of vendor-managed inventory, a novelty in the early 1990s, is expected to become a common business strategy.

Mike Jenkins of International Warehouse Logistics Association has researched the major changes affecting third-party warehousing. The giant logistics companies existing at the turn of the century are primarily an outgrowth of common carriers. In some cases, they hire warehousing services from a traditional public warehouse, but they control the relationship with the consumer.

Another megatrend in warehousing is the emergence of real estate investment trusts (REITs) as owners of warehouse facilities. A significant percentage of warehouse space in the United States is owned by several major trusts.

A few years ago, common-carrier trucking and public warehousing were viewed as distinctly different industries. Today there is a convergence of transportation with warehousing in a new service called third-party logistics.

Electronic commerce

There was a time when neither the Internet nor electronic data interchange was in our business vocabulary. Today, the hopes and expectations of electronic commerce are driving a significant percentage of business decisions. Although there is little difference between the operating procedures for an e-commerce warehouse and a fulfillment warehouse (see Chapter 25), the reputed magic of e-commerce creates enormous interest in not only warehousing but all other aspects of getting the job done.

In the face of all these changes, how can today's warehouse manager keep up with the pace of change?

Information sources

In the United States, several professional and trade associations provide continuing sources of information about warehousing.

The only professional society that specializes in warehousing is the **Warehousing Education and Research Council** (WERC). Its international membership includes people from many occupations who share an interest in warehousing. Its publications include technical articles as well as research on legislative changes that could influence the field. Its university research center produces in-depth studies on a variety of projects.

The **Council of Logistics Management** (CLM) is older and larger than WERC. Its breadth of focus is larger, including every aspect of logistics. The council also produces continuing research in the field of logistics, including warehousing.

There are two trade associations for third-party companies. The International Warehouse Logistics Association (IWLA) is the group formerly known as the American Warehouse Association. Its members are companies rather than individuals. Formed in 1891, it is one of the oldest trade associations in the United States. The IWLA increasingly offers its seminars and publications to nonmembers as well as members.

A similar organization is the International Association of Refrigerated Warehouses (IARW); its activities are centered on the temperature-controlled warehousing business.

Many other societies and associations devote part of their agenda to warehousing.

Outside the United States there are similar counterpart organizations. Furthermore, many of the organizations listed above have expanded globally.

Publications and research

Each year, the Council of Logistics Management publishes a bibliography to list significant books and articles in the field of logistics. A section is reserved for warehousing.

Dozens of trade magazines deal in part with warehousing and are available to qualified subscribers at no charge. A number of other magazines, newsletters, and books are also available. Most of the magazines are designed primarily for domestic consumption, and comparable trade magazines exist in nearly every country that has a developed warehousing industry.

Seminars

Educational programs ranging from one day to a full week are offered by both trade associations and professional societies. Some management consultants also package their own seminars, as do professional seminar organizations. Seminars can be valuable for two reasons: the attendee should gain new information about warehousing, and he or she may make useful contacts with peers in other industries who have similar challenges. A seminar allows people to understand how warehousing functions in organizations besides their own. Things learned from other participants can be as valuable as the seminar material itself.

A developing professionalism

No warehouse is any better than the people who work in it. Although some people in your company may still think that the warehouse is a dumping ground for the marginal employee, your warehousing operation can and should earn the respect of other corporate departments. That respect comes only when you have demonstrated an excellence in performance through the development of talented and motivated people. Part of the process is to hire the best people and to promote those who show potential for growth. The professionalism of warehousing people is enhanced by the use of the information sources described here. Training is a process with no beginning and no end.

Upgrading the tools

The most important component of warehousing is people, but even the best people need good tools. Those tools are the plant, the equipment, and the information system.

Is your warehousing plant in the right location, and does its design meet today's state-of-the-art? If the answers are no, fixing it may be beyond your control. However, eventually a new plant will be needed, and you should look for the opportunity to replace your warehouse with a new one.

The best thing about warehouse equipment is that it is portable and depreciable on a much shorter life than the building. Obsolete equipment should be replaced with new and better machinery.

The information system is the most important tool of all and the one that will become obsolete most rapidly. The search for a better information system should never end. Improving your warehouse management system may not require replacing it, and you should look for ways to modify the system to meet tomorrow's needs.

Putting it all together

In this chapter, we have considered the major forces of change, as well as the information sources and tools which would allow every good manager to stay current.

This book was designed to help you understand why warehousing is important and what it can do to improve the profitability of your organization. Perhaps the most important message is that no warehouse is ever perfect.

Warehousing is always more complex than those outside the field think it is. A broken warehouse can take months to fix, and one that seems to be running well can disintegrate quickly. Warehousing is a profession, not just an art or craft. As such, it requires dedicated professionals who are constantly absorbing the newest information about the business.

Every living thing either grows or dies. Be sure that you and your people are always growing.

Questions that solve problems

Q Does anyone in our group belong to a professional society, and which ones?
C If you draw a blank on this, find out why.

Q Which trade magazines come to our warehouse?
C Get feedback on quality as well as quantity.

Q Who has been to a warehousing seminar, and what was the "take-home" value?
C If feedback is negative, find out why.

INDEX

A

ABC report	56, 122
access roads	337-338
account performance	144-145
advanced shipping notice (ASN)	9, 91, 132, 245, 246, 319
air freight	9, 336-337
aisles	56, 57, 248, 289, 303
American Warehouse Association	3
Andersen Consulting	308
Apple, James M.	290
assets	7, 11-13, 66, 348
fixed	66
productivity	7, 11, 12, 13
automatic storage/retrieval system (AS/RS)	325, 326
automation	326, 333, 332-333
cost of	326, 332

B

bar coding	9-10, 20, 28, 47, 49, 131-132, 142, 245, 317-323, 326, 376
cost	319
2-D	322
Bartholdi, J.J., III	257
benchmarking	15, 22-24, 25, 55, 137
bill-of-lading	120, 214
billing	71-72
Bohm, John A.	55, 87
Bolger, Daniel	132, 153, 155, 206
bottlenecks	58, 316, 320

Brandman, Barry · · · · · · · · · · · 210
Brooksher, Dane · · · · · · · · · · · 348

C

Carlson, Roger · · · · · · · · · · · · 98, 102
carousel · · · · · · · · · · · · · · · · 297-299
Carter, Jimmy · · · · · · · · · · · · · 3
Champee, James · · · · · · · · · · · 392
checking · · · · · · · · · · · · · · · 142, 245-246, 322
Clark, William W. · · · · · · · · · · 119
Cleveland Consulting Associates · · 270
Cohan, Leon "Bud" · · · · · · · · · 83
common carriers · · · · · · · · · · · 64, 400
Commonwealth Handling and
    Equipment Pool · · · · · · · · · 266
computers · · · · · · · · · · · · · · 11-12, 27, 31, 48, 143, 198, 246, 307, 313, 327, 350
    simulations · · · · · · · · · · · · 143
contracts · · · · · · · · · · · · · · · 64, 76, 80, 121, 330
Coolidge, Calvin · · · · · · · · · · · 3
Copacino, William · · · · · · · · · · 54
Council of Chemical Logistics
    Providers · · · · · · · · · · · · · 281
Council of Logistics Management
    (CLM) · · · · · · · · · · · · · · · 4, 308, 391, 401
credit cards · · · · · · · · · · · · · · 71, 283, 283
cross-docking · · · · · · · · · · · · · 9, 18, 121, 244, 253, 258-259, 261, 263, 264
cube utilization · · · · · · · · · · · · 57-58
cumulative trauma disorder (CTD) 221
customer service · · · · · · · · · · · 1, 52, 166-167, 307, 316, 369-373, 386-388, 391, 399
cycle counting · · · · · · · · · · · · 200-203, 204
cycle time · · · · · · · · · · · · · · · 5, 6, 7-9, 10, 315
    order · · · · · · · · · · · · · · · · 7-8, 12, 13, 35

D

damaged product	245, 376
Deming, W.E.	192, 195
Deming Process	84-85
Deming's 14 points	192-194, 195
deregulation	1-3, 5, 16, 37
diagnostic operations review	31-32
docks	361-362, 367
Docter, Jim	282
Drucker, Peter	4-5, 65

E

Effective Motivation and Retention Programs in the Warehouse	181
efficiency	138-140, 393
Efficient consumer response (ECR)	21, 65
Einstein, D.D.	257
electronic commerce	30, 400
electronic data interchange (EDI)	20, 28-31, 319
emergency plans	239, 241
Environmental Protection Agency (EPA)	46, 280
environmental returns	44
equipment	23, 53, 289-296, 299-303, 305-306, 378
downtime	53
purchasing	292-296, 299-303, 305-306, 378
errors	33, 35, 52, 129-136, 197, 199, 202, 251, 329, 330-331
expenses	27, 40, 54, 57-58, 76-79, 100, 105-118, 133, 250, 264, 270
calculating	100, 105-118

F

Federal Drug Agency (FDA)	53, 271, 278, 379
Federal Express (FedEx)	5, 9
first in first out FIFO	28, 247, 321

first-in, still here (FISH)	141
Financial Accounting Standards Board (FASB)	349
fire prevention	231-235, 238, 239-240, 241, 249, 279, 281, 330, 343-344, 364, 367
Fisher, Gary	279
Food Marketing Institute	270
Ford, Henry	289
fourth-generation management	164-166, 172
Fourth-Generation Management	164-165
Freese, Thomas L.	67
fulfillment	275, 282-284, 282-284

G

Gagnon, Eugene	220
Genco Distribution System	47
General Foods	266
Ginter, James	400
globalization	63, 391-392, 394-395, 397
Grocery Manufacturers of America	266, 270
Grocery Pallet Council	267
guided vehicles	299-300, 326

H

Hale, Bernard J.	94
Hall, Craig T.	30
Hammer, Michael	392
handling	102, 141-142, 147, 265
productivity	141-142
standards	102
unitized	265
hazardous materials (hazmat)	33, 46, 275, 279, 288, 379
history	2-5, 7, 15, 37, 40, 44, 51, 59, 64, 257, 265-267, 276, 392, 395
honeycomb factor	99, 125
housekeeping	52-53, 146, 190, 199, 217-218, 278, 379

human resources · · · · · · · · · · 150, 329

I

improvement targets · · · · · · · · 54, 144, 193
information systems · · · · · · · · 35, 403-404
information technology · · · · · · · 1, 27-28, 35, 316
Injuries to Warehouse Workers · · · · 218
inspections · · · · · · · · · · · · · · 138, 192, 243-244
    freight · · · · · · · · · · · · · · 243-244
insurance · · · · · · · · · · · · · · · 121, 184-185, 237-238, 240, 241, 364
    costs · · · · · · · · · · · · · · · 184
    health · · · · · · · · · · · · · · 185
International Association of Refrigerated
    Warehouses (IARW) · · · · · · · 401
International Brotherhood of
    Teamsters · · · · · · · · · · · · 37
International Standards Organization
    (ISO), certification · · · · · · · · 10, 51
International Warehouse Logistics
    Association (IWLA) · · · · · · · 281, 308, 400, 401
Internet & security · · · · · · · · · · 30-31, 400
Interstate Commerce Act · · · · · · 2-3, 16
inventory
    control · · · · · · · · · · · · · · 52, 329-330
    management · · · · · · · · · · · 1, 69, 140-141
    physical · · · · · · · · · · · · · · 197-200, 203
    tickets · · · · · · · · · · · · · · · 199
    turns · · · · · · · · · · · · · · · · 101-102
    vendor-managed · · · · · · · · 18, 227, 400
Inventory Reduction Report · · · · · · 202

J

Jenkins, Mike · · · · · · · · · · · · · 400
Joiner, Brian · · · · · · · · · · · · · 164-165, 172
Joint Industry Shipping Container
    Committee · · · · · · · · · · · · 270
Jurczek, Edward · · · · · · · · · · · 135

just-in-time (JIT) · · · · · · · · · · · · 1, 15, 19-20, 21-22, 25, 65, 227, 286

K

Krause, A. Sam · · · · · · · · · · · · · 76

L

LaLonde, Bernard J. · · · · · · · · · · 7, 54, 400
labor · · · · · · · · · · · · · · · · · · 11-13, 133-134, 149, 179, 283-284, 283-284, 344
    assigning · · · · · · · · · · · · 12, 88-91, 96, 137, 162, 176-177, 180, 221-222, 229, 328
    cost · · · · · · · · · · · · · · · 97-98, 102, 150
    disciplining · · · · · · · · · · · 190-191
    employee evaluations · · · · · 186-187, 222
    incentives · · · · · · · · · · · · 38, 134, 181, 182, 184, 186
    interviewing/screening · · · · 150-159, 162, 185-186, 206-207, 370
    productivity · · · · · · · · · · 24, 28, 40, 54, 59-61
    recruiters · · · · · · · · · · · · 149, 150
    relations · · · · · · · · · · · · · 36-42, 233
    scheduling · · · · · · · · · · · 39, 86, 94, 96, 137-138, 142, 149, 150, 182-184, 195
    shortages · · · · · · · · · · · · 12, 13
    turnover · · · · · · · · · · · · · 172, 173, 195
Ledesma, Sergio · · · · · · · · · · · · 236
less-than-truckload shipments (LTL) 269, 283, 283
liability · · · · · · · · · · · · · · · · · 119-121, 128, 280
lift trucks · · · · · · · · · · · · · · · · 126-127, 128, 140, 143, 161, 178, 219, 244, 246, 269-270, 277, 289, 302, 304-305, 329, 363, 378
    cost · · · · · · · · · · · · · · · · 305
loading tally · · · · · · · · · · · · · · 260-261
locator system · · · · · · · · · · · · · 130, 146
lot numbers · · · · · · · · · · · · · · 28, 321
Lynch, Clifford F. · · · · · · · · · · · 64

M

management by walking around (MBWA)	227
manifest systems	73
manufacturing	138, 194
Maynard, Phil	348
mentoring	176
Menzies, John T.	145
Methods Time Management	102-104
Metzger, Steven	354
morale	38, 40, 42, 146, 159, 173-174, 181-182, 185, 191, 193, 217-218, 229, 338
Mulder, Dallas	149

N

Napolitano, Maida	143, 329
narrow-aisles vehicles	303-304
National American Wholesale Grocers Association	270
National Association of Wholesale-Distributors (NAW)	331
National Council of Physical Distribution Management	4, 16
National Distribution Services	5
National Fire Protection Agency	281
Ness, Robert E.	186

O

O'Donohoe, Tom	348
Obal, Philip	32
Occupational Safety and Health Administration (OSHA)	53, 219-220, 279, 304
order picking	55-56, 142, 143, 146, 221, 247, 250, 253-258, 260-262, 264, 292, 296-297, 321, 327-329
reverse	261-262

order processing	69-70, 133, 243
orientation	174-175, 180
outbound shipments	132-133, 258-259, 264, 377, 379
outsourcing	11, 40, 42, 48-49, 50, 63-81, 84, 97, 356
overnight delivery	1, 5
Ozburn, Perry	348

P

packaging	59, 97, 141, 219, 238, 249, 394
pallets	261, 265-274, 293
costs	269
record	261
standardization	266-267, 270, 274
substitutes	268-269, 274
Pareto analysis	85, 121-122
Pareto's Law	55-56, 122, 135
peer reviews	190-191, 195
performance records	187-189
physical distribution	4, 16, 43
picking documents	131, 134, 260-261
planning	
contingency	94-95
long-range	96
managerial	83
operational	83
strategic	83
point-of-sale registers	20
Porter, John, Jr.	348
postponement	8, 19-20, 393-394, 397
power failure	229
presorting	72
Price, Richard J.	166
procedures writing	375
product velocity	122, 123, 253, 264
Professional Air Controllers Association (PATCO)	3, 37
proficiency exams	156-159

Q

quality awareness	51
quality metrics	52-55, 59-61
quick response (QR)	20

R

racks	293-295
gravity flow	47, 295-296, 378
railroads	2-3, 337
Ransom, William J.	243, 254
re-warehousing	91-92
Reagan, Ronald	3, 37
real estate	65-66, 347-341
brokers	341-342
developing	357-367
investing in	347-355, 400
leasing	349
Reardon, F. Douglas	358
receiving	56, 132, 243-248, 251, 258-259, 261, 313, 376-377
recalls	44, 50, 247
reclamation centers	48
record keeping	197, 199
recycling	11, 44, 46, 272
costs	272
repackaging	258
request-for-information (RFI)	33-34
request for proposal (RFP)	67
retail	20-21, 65, 269-270
returned-goods authorization	49
returns handling	73-74, 92
reusable packaging	44-45, 50
reverse logistics	43-50, 286
Richards, Mark E.	67
Rogala, Richard E.	161
rule of performance	187

S

safety	217-219, 220-222, 224, 229, 279, 281, 373, 378, 379
scanners	8-9, 20, 27, 28, 132, 133, 142, 245, 319, 320
Searl, Hal	100
seasonal production	17
security	30-31, 159, 204, 205-215, 298, 343, 379, 388
Semco, W.B.	295
service expectations	166-167
Shear, Herb	43
Sheehan, W.G.	197
shipment processing	8
Sidor, David S.	119
site selection	335-346
Smith, Fred	5
Society for Human Resources Management	209
software	
logistics	308-309
warehouse management software (WMS)	31, 307-308, 309-316, 314
space utilization	23, 98-99, 122, 140-141, 146, 293, 373-374, 378
Speh, Thomas W.	181
staging	142
statement of requirements	32, 309-311
Stinnett, A.J.	186
stock-balancing programs	45
stock locator systems	246-248, 251
stock rotation	46
storage	31, 97-99, 100, 121, 122, 124, 137, 244, 246, 285, 291, 378
capacity measurement	124, 125-126, 128, 246
equipment	289
household goods (HHG)	284-287
layout	46, 101

productivity · · · · · · · · · · · 140, 141
    reserve · · · · · · · · · · · · · · 327
strategic missions · · · · · · · · · · 74
substance abuse · · · · · · · · · · · 224-226, 229
supply chain management · · · · · 1, 15-19, 25, 119, 253, 399

T

Tatalias, Marilee · · · · · · · · · · · 369
telecommuting · · · · · · · · · · · · 184
Tetz, John A. · · · · · · · · · · · · · 84
theft · · · · · · · · · · · · · · · · · · 206-207, 209-215, 236-237, 249, 284, 379-380
third-party logistics · · · · · · · · · 47, 63-64
Thomas, Bill · · · · · · · · · · · · · 297
Tierney, Theodore J. · · · · · · · · · 190
Tompkins, James A. · · · · · · · · · 200
total quality management (TQM) · 51-55
trailer-on-flat-car (TOFC) · · · · · · 337
training · · · · · · · · · · · · · · · · 35, 42, 50, 161, 173-179, 180, 192, 198, 219-220, 222-223, 239, 373, 378, 401-402
    hazardous materials · · · · · · 288
    management · · · · · · · · · · 161-171
    safety · · · · · · · · · · · · · · · 280-282
    WMS · · · · · · · · · · · · · · · 314
transportation · · · · · · · · · · · · 1, 16, 21, 37, 41, 48-49, 57, 64, 336, 343, 346
travel time · · · · · · · · · · · · · · 262
Turnover analysis · · · · · · · · · · 85-86

U

Uniform Commercial Code (UCC) · 119, 121, 205
uniforms · · · · · · · · · · · · · · · 217-218
    protective · · · · · · · · · · · · 278
unions · · · · · · · · · · · · · · · · · 1, 3, 37-38, 42, 65-66, 388
unloading · · · · · · · · · · · · · · · 102, 244

V

value-added services	92
van line service	286
Vigneau, Brian	31
Von Thunen, J.H.	340

W

warehousing	17, 21, 23-24, 37, 48, 65, 169
contract	121
dry	277, 278
hazardous materials	279, 288
hub warehousing	8, 9
performance evaluation	145-148
providers	67
public	11, 63, 349, 400
temperature-controlled	276-279, 401
third-party	3, 10, 18, 37, 41, 45, 66-81, 72, 141, 192, 205, 227-228, 280, 315, 341, 349, 356, 383, 391
time standards	104, 106-118
Warehousing Education and Research Council (WERC)	181, 401
Warehousing and Physical Distribution Productivity Report	197, 295
Warehousing Forum	7, 30, 31, 32, 43, 54, 55, 64, 67, 76, 84, 87, 98, 100, 102, 119, 121, 143, 145, 149, 153, 155, 161, 165, 166, 186, 190, 206, 210, 220, 236, 243, 257, 259, 261, 290, 297, 309, 312, 329, 348, 369
waste disposal	44, 46-47
water damage	231, 235, 236, 241
Westburgh, Jesse	259, 261, 276
Williams, John	325

Y

Yeomans, Morton T. · · · · · · · · · 31, 121, 309